THE ANTIETAM

AND

FREDERICKSBURG

CAMPAIGNS OF THE CIVIL WAR.—V.

THE ANTIETAM

AND

FREDERICKSBURG

BY

FRANCIS WINTHROP PALFREY,

BREVET BRIGADIER GENERAL, U. S. V., AND FORMERLY COLONEL TWENTIETH
MASSACHUSETTS INFANTRY; MEMBER OF THE MASSACHUSETTS
HISTORICAL SOCIETY, AND OF THE MILITARY HIS-
TORICAL SOCIETY OF MASSACHUSETTS.

NEW YORK
CHARLES SCRIBNER'S SONS

Facsimile Reprint Edition from
the original edition of 1881-1883
by The Archive Society, 1992.
Address all inquiries to:

The Archive Society
130 Locust Street
Harrisburg, PA 17101

PREFACE.

IN preparing this book, I have made free use of the material furnished by my own recollection, memoranda, and correspondence. I have also consulted many volumes by different hands. As I think that most readers are impatient, and with reason, of quotation-marks and foot-notes, I have been sparing of both. By far the largest assistance I have had, has been derived from advance sheets of the Government publication of the Reports of Military Operations During the Rebellion, placed at my disposal by Colonel Robert N. Scott, the officer in charge of the War Records Office of the War Department of the United States.

F. W. P.

CONTENTS.

	PAGE
LIST OF MAPS,	xi

CHAPTER I.
THE COMMENCEMENT OF THE CAMPAIGN, ... 1

CHAPTER II.
SOUTH MOUNTAIN, ... 27

CHAPTER III.
THE ANTIETAM, ... 42

CHAPTER IV.
FREDERICKSBURG, ... 136

APPENDIX A.
COMMANDERS IN THE ARMY OF THE POTOMAC UNDER MAJOR-GENERAL GEORGE B. MCCLELLAN ON SEPTEMBER 14, 1862, ... 191

APPENDIX B.

ORGANIZATION OF THE ARMY OF NORTHERN VIRGINIA, FROM AUGUST 13 TO NOVEMBER 15, 1862, FROM REPORTS OF MILITARY OPERATIONS DURING THE REBELLION, 1860–65, WASHINGTON, ADJUTANT-GENERAL'S PRINTING OFFICE, ... 194

APPENDIX C.

ORGANIZATION OF THE ARMY OF THE POTOMAC, DECEMBER, 1862, MAJOR-GENERAL A. E. BURNSIDE COMMANDING, ... 199

INDEX 211

LIST OF MAPS.

	PAGE
MARYLAND,	1
FIELD OF OPERATIONS IN VIRGINIA,	12
THE FIELD OF THE ANTIETAM,	49
THE FIELD OF FREDERICKSBURG,	142

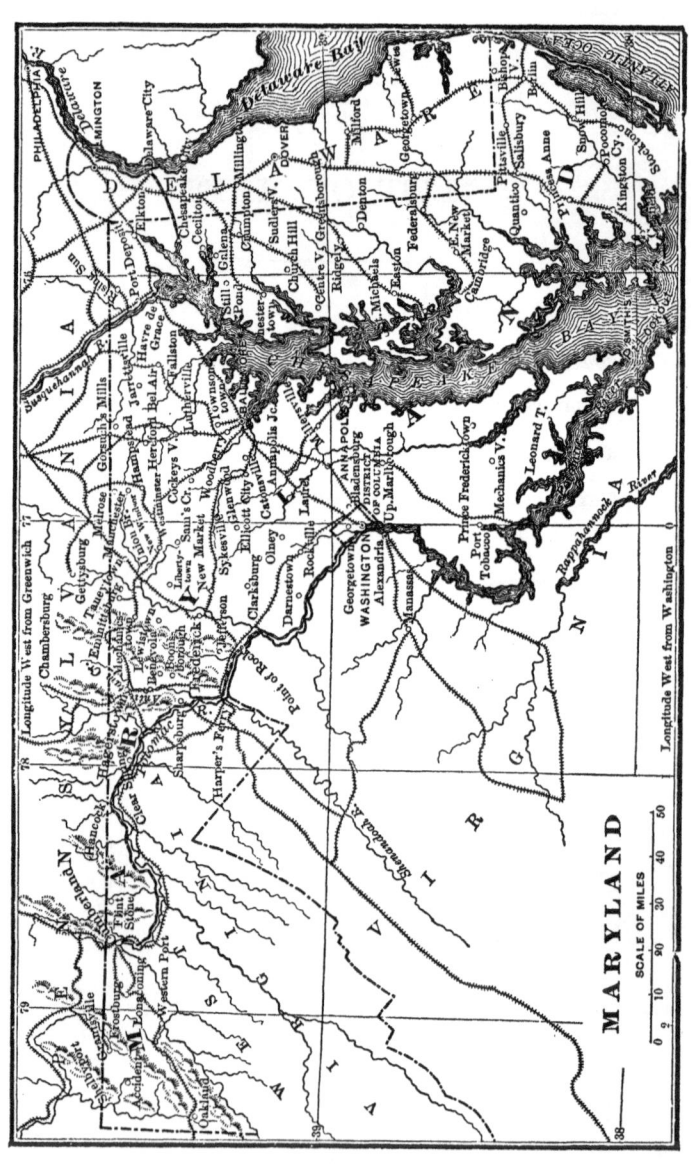

THE
ANTIETAM AND FREDERICKSBURG.

CHAPTER I.

THE COMMENCEMENT OF THE CAMPAIGN.

THE campaigns in the East in the summer of 1862 were a disappointment to the North. McClellan and the Army of the Potomac not only did not capture Richmond or disable the Confederate Army of Northern Virginia, but were forced back from the furthest point of their advance. Though they inflicted heavy loss upon the enemy, they suffered heavy losses themselves, in men, guns, and property of all kinds. The last serious fighting they did in the Peninsular campaign was at Malvern Hill, on July 1st, and no further events of importance took place in that region. The army was withdrawn from the Peninsula, under the orders of the Government, in the following month of August. Whether McClellan himself had failed, and whether he was not in a better position for offensive operations when he was withdrawn than he had ever occupied elsewhere, is an interesting question, but one which does not fall within the scheme of this volume to discuss.

While McClellan and the main Eastern army were in the Peninsula, various bodies of troops were held by the Government in positions nearer Washington, to ensure the safety of the Capital. The most important of these were the armies of McDowell, Fremont, and Banks. By an order dated June 26, 1862, these forces were consolidated into the Army of Virginia,[1] and placed under the command of General Pope. Its career under Pope was unfortunate. The Southern generals found it easier to deal with Banks and Pope than with McClellan, and at Cedar Mountain and at the second battle of Manassas they inflicted upon them disastrous defeats. The guns that they took were counted by tens, the prisoners by thousands, while the lists of our killed and wounded were long and ghastly. It is at this time, when the Army of Virginia and the Army of the Potomac were united within the lines constructed for the defence of Washington, that our story begins, on September 2, 1862.

It is not to be imagined that the Union forces thus collected in front of Washington were a rabble. It is true that even successful battle produces much disorganization, and that defeat, and still more, a series of defeats, produces much more. Officers are killed and wounded, men stray from their colors, arms and equipments are lost, and much confusion is caused, and the effective force of an army is sometimes very seriously impaired; but with even tolerable troops it is very rarely destroyed altogether, even for a day.

---

[1] It is important for the reader to bear in mind the fact that the principal Confederate Army in Virginia was known for the whole time that Lee commanded it, that is to say, from the evening of May 31st, 1862, to the end of the war, as the Army of Northern Virginia, while the name "Army of Virginia" was never applied, so far as we know, to any body of troops except Pope's army, which was under his command for only about two months. When he was relieved of command, at the beginning of September, 1862, the Army of Virginia passed out of existence, and the troops composing it became part of the Army of the Potomac.

It hardly ever happens that all the troops on either side are engaged. Some are held as reserves, and not brought into action; some are detached, guarding trains or roads or bridges, or posted to meet an attack which is not made; others are in the order of battle, but by some one or more of the singular accidents of the field, they remain practically untouched while death is busy around them. These bodies of troops, except in extreme cases, preserve their organization and their efficiency, and may be made of infinite service in forming lines under cover of which the regiments which have been more roughly handled may reform. Then, in war, it is the universal principle that there is never a vacancy. The instant a superior falls, the man next him takes his place, without an order, without an assignment. The colonel replaces the general, the line officer the field officer, the non-commissioned officer the commissioned officer. However vacancies may be filled by orders from headquarters, whatever form promotion may take, this is the universal rule in action—as soon as a vacancy occurs, the man next in rank fills it the moment he knows that it exists, and he continues to fill it till orders from superior authority make a different arrangement. Thus, except in those very rare cases in which an army becomes a mob, even defeat works no destruction of the framework of the great machine, and when the men are fairly intelligent, brave, and disciplined, order and efficiency are restored with great rapidity. Thus, after the severe defeats which Lee inflicted upon Pope, the rear guard of infantry, artillery, and cavalry was orderly and calm, and formed a strong line between the Federal and Confederate forces. Lee sent Jackson to the Little River Turnpike, to attempt to turn our right and intercept our retreat to Washington, and a sharp engagement, in which the Federal General Kearny was killed, took place on September 1, near Germantown, not far from Fairfax Court House. Lee admits that "the conflict was obstinately maintained by the enemy till dark," and that the attempt was abandoned. His army rested on the 2d, near the ground where this last engagement was fought, and marched on the 3d toward Leesburg.

It is not necessary to attempt in this place to state in detail the very peculiar position which General McClellan occupied during the last days of August.[1] It may be sufficient to say that he was practically a commander without a command. General Halleck was General-in-Chief, and he appears to have been both confused and scared, and to have been hostile to McClellan. On the 1st of September, when Pope was at and in rear of Centreville, and Jackson was moving to assail his right flank and rear, and all or nearly all of the army of the Potomac had been sent out to join Pope, McClellan left his camp near Alexandria, where he had only his staff and a small camp-guard, and went into Washington. There General Halleck instructed him, verbally, to take command of the defences of Washington, but expressly limited his jurisdiction to the works and their garrisons, and prohibited him from exercising any control over the troops actively engaged in front under General Pope.

On the morning of the 2d, McClellan says: "The President and General Halleck came to my house, when the President informed me that Colonel Kelton[2] had returned from the front; that our affairs were in a bad condition; that the

---

[1] There is some reason for believing that Pope was called from the West to command Banks and Fremont, and perhaps McDowell, and eventually to supersede McClellan; that while the belief prevailed at Washington that Pope had been successful on the 29th of August, and because of that belief, McClellan was deprived of his troops.

[2] An aide of the General-in-Chief, sent the day before to the army under General Pope, for the purpose of ascertaining the exact condition of affairs.

COMMENCEMENT OF THE CAMPAIGN.

army was in full retreat upon the defences of Washington; the roads filled with stragglers, etc. He instructed me to take steps at once to stop and collect the stragglers; to place the works in a proper state of defence, and to go out to meet and take command of the army, when it approached the vicinity of the works, then to place the troops in the best position—committing everything to my hands."

So far as appears, this verbal order of the President was the only one by which McClellan was reinstated in command, and there does not seem to have been any order issued by virtue of which the Army of Virginia ceased to exist. McClellan's first official act was to send a letter of suggestion, rather than command, to Pope, and he addressed it to "Major-General John Pope, Commanding Army of Virginia," and signed it "Geo. B. McClellan, Major-General United States Army." Eleven days later we find him dating a letter "Headquarters Army of the Potomac," and adding to his signature the words "Major-General Commanding."

McClellan's talents as an organizer are generally admitted, and there is no doubt that at the date of which we are writing he was extremely popular with his men. As all pressure of the enemy was removed, as we have seen, on the day after the President directed him to take command of the army, he had a breathing-space in which to provide for the defences of Washington and to reorganize his army, but as the information which he received on the 3d led him to believe that the enemy intended to cross the upper Potomac into Maryland, it was necessary that the process of reorganization should go on while the troops were moving.

The necessary arrangements for the defence of the Capital were made, and General Banks was placed in command. He received his instructions from McClellan, and he had under his command the Third Corps, General Heintzelman, the Fifth Corps, General Porter, and the Eleventh Corps, General Sigel. These troops, with other troops in and about Washington, which may or may not have been included in these three corps, were reported to amount in all to 72,500 men.

The army which McClellan led from Washington was made up of the First Corps, to the command of which General Hooker was assigned; of the Second Corps, under Sumner; of one division of the Fourth Corps, under Couch; of the Sixth Corps, under Franklin; of the Ninth Corps, under Reno, and the Twelfth Corps, under Mansfield. General Couch's division was attached to the Sixth Corps. The First and Ninth Corps formed the right, under General Burnside; the Second and Twelfth the centre, under General Sumner; and the Sixth Corps, reinforced by the division of Couch, the left, under Franklin. Porter's Fifth Corps was, on the 11th of September, ordered forward to join McClellan. The aggregate present for duty of these forces, as reported by McClellan, September 20th, including the cavalry under General Pleasonton, was 89,452. He reported his losses in the two battles of South Mountain and the Antietam, both fought before the latter date, as 14,794. The aggregate of these two totals is 104,246. Swinton, in his "Campaigns of the Army of the Potomac," states that the army with which McClellan set out on the Maryland Campaign made an aggregate of 87,164 men of all arms. McClellan, in his Report, states that the total of his own forces in action at the battle of the Antietam was 87,164. The coincidence is suspicious, and leads one to believe that Swinton is in error. McClellan's statement of his numbers present for duty September 20, 1862, is officially certified as accurately compiled from his morning report of that day.

The total of 89,452 therein given, not including the forces in the defences of Washington and certain detachments in Maryland, is partly made up of Porter's Corps, set down at 19,477. Deducting the latter number from the former, the remainder is 69,975. Adding the losses at South Mountain and the Antietam, 14,794, we have a total of 84,769 as the force with which he left Washington. Of course, the effective force of an army varies from day to day, from illness, death, discharge, and desertion on the one hand, and the arrival of convalescents and recruits on the other. It seems, therefore, fair to assume that McClellan left Washington with about 85,000 men, and that the arrival of Porter increased his force by an amount about equal to the losses which he sustained in the battles of the 14th and 17th of September.

General Lee's army was made up of Longstreet's command, of five divisions, containing twenty brigades; of Jackson's command, of three divisions, containing fourteen brigades; of D. H. Hill's division, of five brigades; the unattached brigade of Evans, and a very considerable force of cavalry and artillery, and probably numbered between forty and fifty thousand men, present for duty, but this question of the numbers actually engaged on each side in the Maryland campaign will receive more particular attention hereafter.

Washington and its environs presented singular sights in the early days of September, 1862. The luxury and refinements of peace contrasted sharply with the privations and squalor of war. There are few prettier suburban drives than those in the neighborhood of Washington, and no weather is more delightful than that of late summer there, when a cooler air comes with the shortening days. As the shadows lengthened in the golden afternoon, well-appointed carriages rolled along those charming drives, bearing fair women in cool and fresh costumes, and by their side the ragged, dusty, sunburnt regiments from the Peninsula trudged along. Rest, cleanliness, ice, food, drink, every indulgence of civilized life were within reach, but our hands could not be stretched out to grasp them. Military discipline was the dragon that guarded the golden apples of the Hesperides. They were so near and yet so far. The mythic Tantalus must have been present to the minds of many of those who then marched by the road which leads from Washington to the Chain Bridge. The carriages returned to their stables, the fair ladies returned to the enjoyment of every pleasure that Washington could confer, but the Army of the Potomac moved steadily northward, to bivouac under the stars or the clouds, and to march again in its tatters through the dust and the sunshine, through the rain and the mud. Fortunately we had by this time become soldiers in something more than the name; we had learned to make much out of little, we were cheered by the more wholesome air and the more variegated country, we were glad to get out of the wilderness of the Peninsula. It was pleasant, too, to be once more in a country that was at least nominally friendly. Whatever the real feelings of the Marylanders might be, the stars and stripes might often be seen in other places than above the heads of the color-guards. Whether the natives sold to us gladly or not, they had much to sell, and that in itself was a most agreeable novelty to us. In the Peninsula, the country afforded us nothing, and the change from the land where our meat was fat pork, or odious beef served quivering from an animal heated by the long day's march and killed as soon as the day's march was ended, to a land where fresh vegetables and poultry were not rare, was very cheering. Money was not scarce. The pay of the army was liberal, and we had

had no chance to spend money in the Peninsula. So our march was pleasant. Wood and water were easy to find, instead of requiring weary searches at the end of a weary day. We no longer had to send the pioneers to search for stakes, and then to fix them toilsomely in the hard, bare earth with their picks, before we could unsaddle and let our horses' bridles go. The foragers found forage for the poor beasts in abundance, and the little tins in which we had learned to cook so cleverly had often something in them better than hard bread, water, salt, pepper, and ration meat.

We knew nothing of the enemy's movements, and though we all expected to fight again, yet the general impression seemed to be that it would be, as Dickens says, at that somewhat indefinite period which is commonly known as one of these days. But it was a time of sharp surprises. No leaves to enter Washington were granted, but when the army was at Tenallytown, kind-hearted " Uncle John " Sedgwick, then commanding the Second Division of the Second Corps, ordered one of his officers into Washington for two days, " on regimental business." About noon of the second day following, the officer heard that his command had moved, and so hastened to overtake it. Nothing could have been more peaceful than the appearance of Washington as he left it on a lovely afternoon. The signs of war were always plenty there, of course, but there was absolutely nothing to indicate the neighborhood of an enemy. Every one seemed to be as absorbed in the pursuits of peaceful business and secure pleasure as if the blast of war had not been heard in the land. On foot, on horseback, in carriages, every one seemed to be out of doors, and enjoying, whether working or playing, the perfect close of a perfect day. The officer had not ridden many miles when he met a squad of prisoners, and learned that they had been taken that morning in a skirmish on the

1*

Maryland side of the Potomac. So Lee, or some of Lee's men, had invaded a loyal State, and there was every prospect that there would soon be wigs on the green. Proceeding a few miles further, the officer found his regiment, part of a line sleeping on its arms in the order of battle, and supporting some batteries, of which the guns were unlimbered, with the gunners lying at the trails of the pieces. The report was that Jackson, with a largely superior force, was close at hand, and apparently proposing to attack in the morning. It was a dramatic changing of the scene, from the comfort and careless gayety of Washington to a starlit bivouac, with every preparation made for meeting an impending attack.

Thus did the Army of the Potomac move out in the Maryland campaign. It remains to tell in what order and by what roads. As Lee had by September 3d disappeared from the front of Washington, and as McClellan had received information which induced him to believe that he intended to cross the upper Potomac into Maryland, he thought it likely that he might be obliged not only to protect Washington, but to cover Baltimore, and to prevent the invasion of Pennsylvania. He therefore, on the 3d, sent his cavalry to the fords near Poolesville, to watch the enemy and impede a crossing in that vicinity, while he sent the Second and Twelfth Corps to Tenallytown, and the Ninth to a point on the Seventh Street road, near Washington; and in these positions, and on the Virginia side of the Potomac, near Washington, the whole of the army seems to have remained on the 4th and part of the 5th, but by the 6th Couch's division of the Fourth Corps and Franklin's Sixth Corps were at Tenallytown and Offut's Cross Roads, the Second and Twelfth Corps were at Rockville, and the First and Ninth at Leesboro'. On the 7th McClellan left Washington, and headquarters and the Sixth Corps were moved to Rockville. By this time,

COMMENCEMENT OF THE CAMPAIGN. 11

McClellan knew that the mass of the rebel army had passed up the south side of the Potomac in the direction of Leesburg, and that a portion of their army had crossed into Maryland, but he had no means of determining whether Lee proposed to cross his whole force with a view to turn Washington by a flank movement down the north bank of the Potomac, to move on Baltimore, or to invade Pennsylvania. This uncertainty made it appear to him necessary " to march cautiously, and to advance the army in such order as to keep Washington and Baltimore continually covered, and at the same time to hold the troops well in hand, so as to be able to concentrate and follow rapidly if the enemy took the direction of Pennsylvania, or to return to the defence of Washington, if, as was greatly feared by the authorities, the enemy should be merely making a feint with a small force to draw off our army, while with their main forces they stood ready to seize the first favorable opportunity to attack the Capital."

The general course of the Potomac above Washington is from northwest to southeast. Harper's Ferry, at the junction of the Shenandoah with the Potomac, is nearly fifty miles northwest of Washington, in a straight line. Leesburg, on the Virginia side of the Potomac, is about thirty miles northwest of Washington. Loudoun Heights, the hills at the northern end of the Blue Ridge, and the Shenandoah River, are between Leesburg and Harper's Ferry. Maryland Heights, the hills at the southern end of Elk Ridge, the ridge next west of the South Mountain range, are on the Maryland side of the Potomac, and that river flows between them and Harper's Ferry. Frederick City is in Maryland, forty miles from Washington, and a little west of north of it. Baltimore is about thirty-five miles northeast of Washington, measuring in a straight line, and Philadelphia, measuring in the same way, is about ninety miles northeast of Baltimore. Thus McClellan's field of possible operations was, or was likely to be, the quadrant of a circle, of which the radius must be thirty miles, and might be four times

Field of Operations in Virginia.

that. Experience had shown that his adversary and one of his first lieutenants were enterprising, and that their army was extremely mobile. His left was tied to the Potomac, if

COMMENCEMENT OF THE CAMPAIGN. 13

not by the necessities of the case, at least by the fears of the authorities at Washington, and he could only reach out to the right so far as was consistent with the preservation of a line of prudent strength, and with the possibility of rapid concentration.

The army moved slowly, but the process of reorganization proceeded rapidly, the more rapidly, no doubt, by reason of the slowness of the march. On the 9th, Couch's division, the extreme left of the army, touched the Potomac, at the mouth of Seneca Creek. Franklin's corps was at Darnestown. The Second and Twelfth Corps, constituting the centre, were at Middleburg (or Middlebrook), and the First and Ninth Corps, forming the right, were at Brookville, while the division of Sykes, of Porter's Fifth Corps, was in the rear at Tenallytown. Thus the army, Sykes's division excepted, was on the 9th on the circumference of a circle described from the centre of Washington, with a radius of twenty miles, and with an extension from left to right of about twenty-five miles.[1] Couch's division moved by the river road, watching the fords of the Potomac, and ultimately following and supporting the Sixth Corps. Moving through Poolesville and Barnesville, it reached Licksville by the 13th. Franklin moved by Dawsonville and Barnesville to Buckeystown, "covering the road (to the rear) from the mouth of the Monocacy to Rockville, and being in a position to connect with and support the centre should it have been necessary (as McClellan supposed) to force the line of the Monocacy." It reached Buckeystown on the 13th. Sykes's division moved by Rockville, Middleburg, and Urbanna to

---

[1] "It seems as if our left rested on the river, and advanced slowly, while our line stretched far inland, the right advancing more rapidly, as if we were executing a vast left wheel, one end of the spoke, the hub end, being on the river."
—Extract from army letter, dated September 11, 1862.

Frederick, which place it reached on the 13th. The Second Corps moved from Middleburg through Clarksburg and Urbanna, and the Twelfth through Damascus and thence between Urbanna and New Market, to Frederick, which place both corps reached on the 13th. The First and the Ninth Corps, constituting the right wing as before, moved on Frederick, the latter by Damascus and New Market, and the former, holding the extreme right, by Cooksville and Ridgeville. All of the right wing was at Frederick on the 13th, except that by night of that day all of the Ninth Corps except Rodman's division was advanced to Middletown. Thus by night of the 13th of September, the Army of the Potomac was disposed as follows: The bulk of the army was near Frederick, with a part of the Ninth Corps advanced some eight miles to Middletown, Franklin was at Buckeystown, some five miles to the left and rear, and Couch was at Licksville, a place in the northern angle formed by the junction of the Monocacy with the Potomac. The average distance of the army from Washington may be set down at forty miles. By this time, McClellan had come into possession of some very important information, but what it was may better be left untold till some account has been given of what Lee had been doing in the last ten days, and of the state of things existing at Harper's Ferry, which place was separated by probably ten miles from the nearest troops of McClellan, as well as by a river and some very mountainous country.

The views entertained by General Lee when he entered upon the Maryland campaign are here given in his own words, taken from his official Report, dated March 6, 1863, and printed in the first volume of the "Reports of the Operations of the Army of Northern Virginia, Richmond, 1864."

COMMENCEMENT OF THE CAMPAIGN. 15

The armies of General McClellan and Pope had now been brought back to the point from which they set out on the campaigns of the spring and summer. The objects of those campaigns had been frustrated, and the designs of the enemy on the coast of North Carolina and in Western Virginia thwarted by the withdrawal of the main body of his forces from those regions. Northeastern Virginia was freed from the presence of Federal soldiers up to the intrenchments of Washington, and soon after the arrival of the army at Leesburg information was received that the troops which had occupied Winchester had retired to Harper's Ferry and Martinsburg. The war was thus transferred from the interior to the frontier, and the supplies of rich and productive districts made accessible to our army. To prolong a state of affairs in every way desirable, and not to permit the season for active operations to pass without endeavoring to inflict further injury upon the enemy, the best course appeared to be the transfer of the army into Maryland. Although not properly equipped for invasion, lacking much of the material of war, and feeble in transportation, the troops poorly provided with clothing, and thousands of them destitute of shoes, it was yet believed to be strong enough to detain the enemy upon the northern frontier until the approach of winter should render his advance into Virginia difficult, if not impracticable. The condition of Maryland encouraged the belief that the presence of our army, however inferior to that of the enemy, would induce the Washington Government to retain all its available force to provide against contingencies which its course toward the people of that State gave it reason to apprehend. At the same time it was hoped that military success might afford us an opportunity to aid the citizens of Maryland in any efforts they might be disposed to make to recover their liberties. The difficulties that surrounded them were fully appreciated, and we expected to derive more assistance in the attainment of our object from the just fears of the Washington Government, than from active demonstration on the part of the people, unless success should enable us to give them assurance of continued protection.

Influenced by these considerations, the army was put in motion, D. H. Hill's division, which had joined us on the 2d, being in advance, and between September 4th and 7th crossed the Potomac at the fords near Leesburg, and encamped in the vicinity of Fredericktown.

It was decided to cross the Potomac east of the Blue Ridge, in order, by threatening Washington and Baltimore, to cause the enemy to withdraw from the south bank, where his presence endangered our communications and the safety of those engaged in the removal of our wounded and the captured property from the late battle-fields. Having accomplished this result, it was proposed to move the army into Western Maryland, establish our communications with Richmond through the Valley of the Shenandoah, and by threatening Pennsylvania induce the enemy to follow, and thus draw him from his base of supplies.

It may be remarked, in relation to this allegation of incomplete equipment, that it seems like an excuse for failure, made after the failure had occurred, and antedated, for Lee asserts in the same Report that in the series of engagements on the plains of Manassas, which had taken place just before, there had been captured more than nine thousand prisoners, wounded and unwounded, thirty pieces of artillery, upwards of twenty thousand stand of small arms, and a large amount of stores, besides those taken by General Jackson at Manassas Junction. Jackson says[1] that he captured there eight guns, with seventy-two horses, equipments and ammunition complete, "immense supplies" of commissary and quartermaster stores, etc. With these additions to his supplies, it would seem as if the little army with which Lee says he fought the battles of the Maryland Campaign, might have been fairly well equipped, especially when we remember how far from scrupulous the Confederates were in exchanging their shoes and clothing for the better shoes and clothing of their prisoners.

Lee's plan was a good one. It is not probable that he promised himself the capture of Philadelphia, or Baltimore, or Washington, but he might fairly believe that the chances of war might change the improbable into the possible, and the possible into the actual. He had a right to expect to

---

[1] A. N. Va., ii., 93.

get more recruits from Maryland when his army was there, than when it was on the other side of the Potomac, without anticipating that "my Maryland" would breathe or burn in any exceptional fashion, or "be the battle-queen of yore." Without indulging in the illusions of audacious hope, he might fairly count upon great and certain gains from transferring his army to the soil of Maryland. By so doing he shifted the burden of military occupation from Confederate to Federal soil. He secured to the Virginians the precious crops of the Shenandoah Valley and their other Northeastern counties. He had two or three months of fine weather before him. He had for his opponent McClellan, and experience had shown him that McClellan never attacked, and always let him choose his own time and place for fighting. His army had learned to march with great rapidity and to fight with great gallantry and tenacity, and he had several lieutenants upon whom he knew he could place very great reliance. Under all the circumstances, he might well think that at the head of his army, with its habit of victory, and with the Shenandoah Valley open behind him, he had everything to gain and nothing to lose from an autumn campaign in Maryland, against the Army of the Potomac with its habit of defeat, and against McClellan with his want of initiative. Whether he knew or even suspected how heavily the brave and loyal and long-suffering Army of the Potomac was handicapped by the miserable jealousies, civil and military, that prevailed at the time, cannot be told. If he did, the knowledge must have greatly raised his hopes and increased his confidence. If Lee had been in McClellan's place on the 17th of September, and had sent Jackson to conduct the right attack and Longstreet to force the passage of the lower bridge and turn the Confederate right, the Army of Northern Virginia, though commanded by a second Lee, a second

Jackson, and a second Longstreet, would have ceased to exist that day.

In the northward movement of Lee's army, D. H. Hill had the advance. The crossing of the Potomac was effected at the ford near Leesburg, between the 4th and the 7th of September, and the army encamped in the vicinity of Frederick. The march was unopposed. The concentration was effected while McClellan's army was still twenty miles or more away.

Lee had expected that the advance upon Frederick would lead to the evacuation of Martinsburg and Harper's Ferry, and thus open his line of communication through the Valley of Virginia. Troops had been placed there, 2,500 men at Martinsburg under General White, and 9,000 men at Harper's Ferry, under Colonel Miles, of the Second United States Infantry, to command the débouché of the Shenandoah Valley. Whatever the propriety of placing such forces in such positions in ordinary times may have been, it is plain that the presence of Lee's army in Maryland put a new face upon the matter, and that these troops must then either be able to hold their position till relieved, in other words, be able to stand a siege, or ought at once to decamp and join themselves to the nearest substantial Union force. Lee thought they or their superiors would see this, and that they would be ordered to go. He says [1] "it had been supposed that the advance upon Frederick would lead to the evacuation of Martinsburg and Harper's Ferry, thus opening the line of communication through the Valley. This not having occurred, it became necessary to dislodge the enemy from those positions before concentrating the army west of the mountains." McClellan perceived that

---

[1] A. N. Va., i., 28.

these troops were of little or no use where they were, in the altered position of affairs, and he probably knew that they could not hold Harper's Ferry against Lee if Lee turned against them. At any rate he telegraphed General Halleck, the General-in-Chief, on the 11th, "Colonel Miles . . . can do nothing where he is, but could be of great service if ordered to join me. I suggest that he be ordered at once to join me by the most practicable route." General Halleck replied by telegraph the same day : "There is no way for Colonel Miles to join you at present. The only chance is to defend his works until you can open a communication with him. When you do so, he will be subject to your orders." General Halleck seems to have been mistaken in the facts, as Loudoun Heights were not reached by the enemy till the 13th, and there seems to be no reason why Miles might not have retreated by the south bank of the Potomac long before the toils were drawn around him. Halleck seems to have been in error, as a matter of military principle, but the error probably resulted favorably for the Union arms, as will be seen.

The position, then, was this : Lee, with his army concentrated at Frederick, knew that there was a comparatively small force of the enemy in his rear, and on his main line of communication, and thought that it must be dislodged before he concentrated his army west of the mountains. He also knew that the Federal army was advancing slowly, and giving him a chance to operate against Harper's Ferry. McClellan knew by the 10th that it was "quite probable" that Lee's army was in the vicinity of Frederick, and on the next day that the General-in-Chief declined to move Miles from Harper's Ferry, and left him to open communications with him. Here, then, was the best possible opportunity for a race. It should be said, in justice to McClellan, that before he left Washington, and when the movement was not only possible but easy, he had recommended that the garrison of Harper's Ferry should be withdrawn by the way of Hagerstown, to aid in covering the Cumberland Valley, or that, taking up the pontoon bridge across the Potomac, and obstructing the railroad bridge, it should fall back to Maryland Heights, and there hold out to the last. Neither of these suggestions was adopted, and there was nothing left for McClellan to do but to endeavor to relieve the garrison. It was plainly a case for great activity on McClellan's part. His uncertainty, up to the 13th of September, as to the intentions of the enemy, and the telegraphic messages from Halleck, the General-in-Chief, cautioning him against exposing his left and rear and uncovering Washington, may be accepted as valid excuses for the slowness of his movements, and his unwillingness to advance his left more rapidly than his other columns, but on the 13th the position of things changed, and all uncertainty as to the intentions of the enemy were dispelled. On that day, at an hour which we have no means of fixing, further than that it was before 6.20 P.M., an order of such importance fell into his hands that we copy it in full.

SPECIAL ORDERS No. 191.

HEADQUARTERS ARMY OF NORTHERN VIRGINIA,
September 9, 1862.

The army will resume its march to-morrow, taking the Hagerstown road. General Jackson's command will form the advance, and, after passing Middletown, with such portion as he may select, take the route toward Sharpsburg, cross the Potomac at the most convenient point, and by Friday night take possession of the Baltimore and Ohio Railroad, and capture such of the enemy as may be at Martinsburg, and intercept such as may attempt to escape from Harper's Ferry.

General Longstreet's command will pursue the same road as far as

COMMENCEMENT OF THE CAMPAIGN. 21

Boonsboro', where it will halt with the reserve, supply, and baggage trains of the army.

General McLaws, with his own division and that of General R. H. Anderson, will follow General Longstreet; on reaching Middletown, he will take the route to Harper's Ferry, and by Friday morning possess himself of the Maryland Heights, and endeavor to capture the enemy at Harper's Ferry and vicinity.

General Walker, with his division, after accomplishing the object in which he is now engaged, will cross the Potomac at Cheek's Ford, ascend its right bank to Lovettsville, take possession of Loudoun heights, if practicable, by Friday morning, Keys' ford on his left and the road between the end of the mountain and the Potomac on his right. He will, as far as practicable, co-operate with General McLaws and General Jackson in intercepting the retreat of the enemy.

General D. H. Hill's division will form the rear guard of the army, pursuing the road taken by the main body. The reserve artillery, ordnance and supply trains, etc., will precede General Hill.

General Stuart will detach a squadron of cavalry to accompany the commands of Generals Longstreet, Jackson, and McLaws, and with the main body of the cavalry will cover the route of the army and bring up all stragglers that may have been left behind.

The commands of Generals Jackson, McLaws, and Walker, after accomplishing the objects for which they have been detached, will join the main body of the army at Boonsboro' or Hagerstown.

Each regiment on the march will habitually carry its axes in the regimental ordnance wagons, for use of the men at their encampments, to procure wood, etc.

By command of GENERAL R. E. LEE.

R. H. CHILTON,
Assistant Adjutant General.

MAJOR-GENERAL D. H. HILL,
Commanding Division.

It appears from the statement of Colonel Taylor, Adjutant-General of the Army of Northern Virginia, that at this time General D. H. Hill was in command of a division which had not been attached to nor incorporated with either of the two wings of that army, and that one copy of Special Orders No. 191, was sent to him directly from headquarters, and that General Jackson also sent him a copy, as he regarded Hill in his command, and that the order sent from general headquarters was carelessly left by some one in Hill's camp; while the other, which was in Jackson's own hand, was preserved by Hill.

This order told McClellan two things, both of great importance.

First.—That Lee, by orders issued four days before, had divided his army, sending Jackson and his command, and Walker's division, across the Potomac.

Second.—That the object of this division was the capture of the garrison at Harper's Ferry, and the large outpost at Martinsburg. It also gave him the additional and scarcely less important information, where the rest of the army, trains, rear guard, cavalry, and all, were to march and to halt, and where the detached commands were to join the main body.

The finding of this paper was a piece of rare good fortune. It placed the Army of Northern Virginia at the mercy of McClellan, provided only that he came up with it and struck while its separation continued. If he hurried his left column by Burkittsville, through Crampton's Gap, it would come directly upon the rear of McLaws's force on Maryland Heights. If he pressed his right by Middletown, through Turner's Gap, he would interpose between Hill and Longstreet on the one hand, and all the troops beyond the Potomac on the other. The case called for the utmost exertion, and the utmost speed. He could afford to let one of the three great divisions of his army move less rapidly, but not a moment should have been lost in pushing his columns detailed for the left and right advance through the South Mountain passes. Twenty miles is a liberal estimate of the distance which each column had to march. It was a case for straining every nerve, and, though it is not certain at just what times the Confederate troops sent back to hold these passes actually occupied them, yet it is certain that they were very feebly held as late as the morning of the 14th, and that Harper's Ferry was not surrendered till 8 A.M. on the 15th, thirty-eight hours certainly, probably considerably more, after the lost order came to the hands of McClellan. It cannot be said that he did not act with considerable energy, but he did not act with sufficient. The opportunity came within his reach, such an opportunity as hardly ever presented itself to a commander of the Army of the Potomac, and he almost grasped it, but not quite. As Lee's movements were earlier in point of time, we will describe them first, and it will be seen that nothing could have been neater or completer than the way in which his lieutenants carried out his orders.

Jackson's command left the vicinity of Frederick on the 10th, and passing rapidly through Middletown, Boonsboro' and Williamsport, twenty-five miles or more from Frederick, crossed the Potomac into Virginia on the 11th. From Williamsport, one division moved on the turnpike from that town to Martinsburg. The two other divisions moved further to the west, to prevent the Federal forces at Martinsburg from escaping westward unobserved. General White, in command of the outpost at Martinsburg, becoming advised of the Confederate approach, left that town on the night of the 11th, and retreated to Harper's Ferry. Early on the 12th, the head of the Confederate column came in view of the Federal troops, drawn up on Bolivar Heights, above Harper's Ferry. The three divisions went into camp at and near Halltown, about two miles from the Federal position. There they waited for news from the co-operating columns.

General McLaws, with his own and General Anderson's divisions, moved on the 10th by Burkittsville, into Pleasant Valley. This valley runs north and south, between the South Mountains on the east and Elk Ridge on the west. The southern extremity of Elk Ridge, where it is cut by the Potomac, is called Maryland Heights, and these heights completely command Harper's Ferry with a plunging fire. While Maryland Heights were held by the Federals, Harper's Ferry could not be occupied by the Confederates. If the Confederates gained possession of those heights, the town was no longer tenable by the Federals. After meeting and overcoming some opposition, McLaws gained full possession of Maryland Heights by 4.30 P.M. of the 13th. He promptly made such dispositions of his troops as prevented all possibility of escape from the town to the east, and then waited to hear from Jackson and Walker. He employed his time in getting artillery into position on the heights, and by 2 P.M of the 14th he opened fire from four guns.

General Walker crossed the Potomac at Point of Rocks, during the night of the 10th and by daylight of the 11th, and proceeded the next day toward Harper's Ferry, encamping at Hillsborough. On the morning of the 13th, he reached the foot of the Loudoun Heights, and presently occupied them with two regiments. In the afternoon, he learned that McLaws had possession of Maryland Heights, which commanded the Loudoun Heights as well as Harper's Ferry, and he proceeded to place all of his division which was not on the heights in position to prevent the escape of the garrison of Harper's Ferry down the right bank of the Potomac.

By these movements of Jackson, McLaws, and Walker, the Federal force at Harper's Ferry was surrounded, and at the mercy of the enemy. Colonel Miles, its commander, was killed in the operations which led to the reduction of the place, and it is not known upon what grounds he could have expected to hold the place, if attacked with energy and intelligence, without retaining possession of Maryland Heights. It is stated by McClellan, however, that on the morning of the 14th, a messenger reached him from Colonel Miles, and told him that Maryland Heights had been abandoned by his troops, and that they as well as the Loudoun and Bolivar Heights had been occupied by the enemy. The messenger also said that Colonel Miles instructed him to say that he could hold out with certainty two days longer. If Colonel Miles really sent this message, it is difficult to understand how he could have entertained such a belief.

A man may travel far and wide in America without coming upon a lovelier spot than the heights above Harper's Ferry. The town itself is low and possesses no particular attractions, but one who stands above it may see the beautiful Valley of Virginia extending far to the folded hills of the southwest. As he looks to the town, the Loudoun Heights rise boldly on his right, and between him and them the Shenandoah, a stream that deserves the epithet of arrowy as well as the Rhone, rushes to its union with the broad and yellow and sluggish Potomac. In the hollow before him is the town, with Maryland Heights rising like the Trossachs beyond the river, and, that nothing may be wanting to the picture, there is the canal, with its "margin willow veiled," and its barges, to give the contrast of utter, dreamy repose to the vehemence of the Shenandoah and the rugged grandeur of the hills.

On September 14th Jackson made his final dispositions, causing A. P. Hill to advance on his right till he reached the Shenandoah, and from there to move forward till his guns and troops were above, to the right, and in rear of the

V.—2

left of the Federal line of defence. Ewell's division, under Lawton, moved along the turnpike, to support Hill and aid in the general movement. Jackson's own division, under J. R. Jones, secured with one brigade a commanding hill to the left, near the Potomac, the rest moving along the turnpike as a reserve. During the night, seven batteries were placed in advanced positions, and ten guns were taken across the Shenandoah, and established on its right bank, in a position which gave them an enfilade fire on the Federal line on Bolivar Heights, while the remaining batteries of Jackson's command were placed in position on School House Hill. Early on the 15th every Confederate gun opened fire—the numerous batteries of Jackson's command, Walker's guns from Loudoun Heights, the guns sent across the Shenandoah during the night, McLaws's guns from Maryland Heights. In an hour the Federal fire seemed to be silenced, the signal for storming the works was given, and the advance was begun, when the Federal fire reopened. The Confederate guns replied, and at once the white flag was displayed by the Federals, and presently General White, who had succeeded to the command when Colonel Miles received a mortal wound, surrendered himself and 11,000 men, with 73 pieces of artillery, many small arms and other stores.

The first part of the Confederate programme had been carried out with complete success, but with greater expenditure of time than Lee had anticipated, and it will be seen that the delay almost proved fatal to him, and that McClellan ought to have made it absolutely fatal to him.

CHAPTER II.

SOUTH MOUNTAIN.

JACKSON left Hill to receive the surrender of the Federal troops and property, and moved at once with his remaining divisions to rejoin Lee in Maryland. By what he calls a severe night march,[1] he reached the vicinity of Sharpsburg on the morning of the 16th. Walker's division followed closely, and also reported to General Lee near Sharpsburg early on the 16th.

We left McClellan at Frederick, on the 13th, with the copy of Lee's order in his hands. For military reasons, which seem sufficient as he states them, he determined not to attempt to move by the most direct road, through Jefferson to Knoxville, and thence up the river to Harper's Ferry, but to move his left by Burkittsville to and through Crampton's Pass, while his centre and right marched by Middletown to Turner's Pass. These passes are gaps or gorges through which the roads across the South Mountains run. It must be remembered that the South Mountains are a continuous range of hills, and not detached heights. By moving through Crampton's Pass, the Union left would debouch in rear of Maryland Heights and of the forces under McLaws which Lee had ordered there, while the route chosen for the rest

---

[1] Seventeen miles. A. N. Va., ii., 128.

of the army would place it between Longstreet and D. H. Hill on the right, and Jackson's forces beyond the Potomac on the left, and also between Lee and McLaws.

It has been said that it does not appear at what hour on the 13th McClellan came into possession of Lee's order. A somewhat long letter written by him to General Franklin on the 13th, is dated 6.20 P.M. In that letter he gave Franklin the substance of the information which he had obtained from Lee's order, and also told him that his signal officers reported that McLaws was in Pleasant Valley, and that the firing showed that Miles still held out. He also informed him that his right advance had occupied Middletown in the Catoctin Valley, and that the four corps of his centre and right, with Sykes's division, would move that night and early the next morning upon Boonsboro', to carry that position; that Couch[1] had been ordered to concentrate his division and join him as rapidly as possible; that, without waiting for the whole of that division to join, he was to "move at daybreak in the morning by Jefferson and Burkittsville upon the road to Rohrersville." The letter proceeded thus: "I have reliable information that the mountain pass by this road is practicable for artillery and wagons. If this pass is not occupied by the enemy in force, seize it as soon as practicable, and debouch upon Rohrersville in order to cut off the retreat of, or destroy McLaws's command. If you find this pass held by the enemy in large force, make all your dispositions for the attack, and commence it about half an hour after you hear severe firing at the pass on the Hagerstown pike, where the main body will attack. Having gained the pass, your duty will be first to cut off, destroy, or capture McLaws's command, and relieve Colonel Miles.

---

[1] Who was at Licksville.

If you effect this, you will order him to join you at once with all his disposable troops, first destroying the bridges over the Potomac, if not already done, and, leaving a sufficient garrison to prevent the enemy from passing the ford, you will then return by Rohrersville on the direct road to Boonsboro', if the main column has not succeeded in its attack. If it has succeeded, take the road to Rohrersville, to Sharpsburg and Williamsport, in order either to cut off the retreat of Hill and Longstreet to the Potomac, or prevent the repassage of Jackson. My general idea is to cut the enemy in two and beat him in detail. I believe I have sufficiently explained my intentions. I ask of you, at this important moment, all your intellect and the utmost activity that a general can exercise."

It is proper to dwell upon this letter of McClellan's, because it seems to be the first order that he issued after he came into possession of Lee's lost order, and it seems to be indisputable that in issuing it he made a mistake, which made his Maryland campaign a moderate success, bought at a great price, instead of a cheap and overwhelming victory. His "general idea" was excellent, but time was of the essence of the enterprise, and he let time go by, and so failed to relieve Miles, and failed to interpose his masses between the wings of Lee's separated army. "Move at daybreak in the morning." Let us see what this means. Franklin was at Buckeystown. The orders were issued from "Camp near Frederick," at 6.20 P.M. Buckeystown is about twelve miles by road from the top of Crampton's Gap. Franklin's troops, like all the troops of a force marching to meet and fight an invading army, were, or should have been, in condition to move at a moment's notice. The weather on the 13th was extremely fine, and the roads in good condition. There was no reason why Franklin's corps should not have moved that night, instead of at daybreak the next morning. There was every reason for believing that there were no Confederate troops to interfere with him in his march to the Gap, for McClellan knew that they were all fully employed elsewhere, and, if there were, the advance guard would give him timely notice of it, and if he stopped then he would be just so much nearer his goal. We know now that if he had marched no farther than to the foot of the range that night, a distance which he ought to have accomplished by or before midnight, he could have passed through it the next morning substantially unopposed, and that advantage gained, the Federal army ought to have relieved Harper's Ferry or fatally separated the wings of Lee's army, or both. And what we know now, McClellan had strong reasons for believing then, and strong belief is more than sufficient reason for action, especially where, as in this case, he could not lose and might win by speed, and gained nothing and might lose almost everything by delay. He was playing for a great stake, and fortune had given him a wonderfully good chance of winning, and he should have used every card to the very utmost, and left nothing to chance that he could compass by skill and energy. But there are some soldiers who are much more ingenious in finding reasons for not doing the very best thing in the very best way, than they are vigorous and irresistible in clearing away the obstacles to doing the very best thing in the very best way.

As McClellan respected the night's sleep of Franklin and his men, so did he that of the rest of his army. No portion of it was ordered to move that night, with the possible exception of Couch, who was ordered to join Franklin "as rapidly as possible," and no portion of it other than Franklin's was ordered to move so early as daybreak the next morning. The earliest hour for marching that was prescribed to any other command was "daylight," on the 14th, at which hour Hooker was to set out from the Monocacy and go to Middletown.

As the distance between Crampton's Gap and Turner's Gap is about six miles in a straight line, and as the country between is a practically unbroken range of rugged hills, the attack and defence of each pass was quite isolated from the other, though the fighting was going on at each place on the same day, all day at Turner's Gap, and all the afternoon at Crampton's. As the most immediate object, in point of time, was the relief of Harper's Ferry, and as the Union left carried its pass much earlier than the Union right, the action at Crampton's Gap may as well be described first.

General McLaws does not seem to have apprehended any very prompt action on the part of McClellan by the way of the South Mountain passes, but he was too good a soldier to leave his rear quite unprotected. So, while he was busy in taking Maryland Heights, at the southern end of Pleasant Valley, and aiding in the capture of Harper's Ferry, he not only drew a thin line of troops across the valley in his rear, but sent some troops and guns to the lower passes of the South Mountain range. On the 13th, cannonading to the east and northeast, and the reports of his cavalry scouts, indicated the advance of the enemy from various directions; but he did not attach much importance to these indications, as the lookout from the mountains saw nothing to confirm them. On the following day, news of an advance of the enemy toward the Brownsville Gap (the one next south of Crampton's Gap, and about a mile from it) led him to call up two more brigades, and he sent word to General Cobb, who commanded one of them, to take command of Crampton's Gap so soon as he should arrive in that vicinity. The Gap was over five miles from the position of his main force, and he himself was directing the fire of his guns on Maryland Heights, when he heard cannonading from the direction of Crampton's. Still he did not feel any solicitude at first, and simply sent orders to Cobb to hold the Gap to the last man, but presently he set out for the Gap himself. On his way there, he met one of his messengers returning, who told him that the Federals had forced the Gap, and that Cobb needed reinforcements. The news was true, and the comparative ease and rapidity with which the Federals had achieved this success, showed how possible it would have been to gain it earlier, and so save several priceless hours. Franklin's superiority of force was such that he gained the crest after a spirited action of three hours, beginning at about noon on the 14th. He lost about five hundred and thirty men, and estimated the enemy's loss in killed and wounded at about the same; but he took from him four hundred prisoners, a gun, and three colors. His advance moved into Pleasant Valley that night, and the remnant of the brigades he had beaten, those of Cobb, Semmes, and Mahone, helped to form McLaws's defensive line of battle across Pleasant Valley.

The action at Turner's Gap was on a larger scale, took longer to decide, and was more costly. By the afternoon of the 13th, Lee heard that McClellan was approaching by that road, and D. H. Hill was ordered to guard the pass, and Longstreet to march from Hagerstown to his support. Lee's information seems to have come from Stuart, who commanded his cavalry, and it was undoubtedly Pleasonton's cavalry advance which Stuart encountered and reported. Hill sent back the brigades of Garland and Colquitt to hold the pass, but subsequently ordered up the rest of his division from the neighborhood of Boonsboro'. This, however, he did not do till the next day, after an examination of the pass, made by him very early on the morning of the 14th, had satisfied him that it could only be held by a large force.[1]

So much of the battle of South Mountain as was fought at Turner's Gap hardly admits of a precise description. It lasted a long time, from about seven in the morning till well into the evening, and a good many troops were used first and last, but the ground was so peculiar and so little known to our commanders, that much precious time and many gallant efforts were almost wasted, and it was not till the day was near its end that the Federal advance was conducted with *ensemble*. There was plenty of hard fighting, but much of it was sharp skirmishing, and the whole affair, till near the end, was rather many little battles than one connected battle. There were frequent charges and counter-charges, and many attempts, more or less successful, to turn the flanks of the opposing forces.

The main road from Frederick, by Middletown to Hagerstown, crosses the South Mountain at Turner's Gap. The mountain is at this point about one thousand feet high, but the depression of the Gap is some four hundred feet. The mountain on the north side of the main road is divided into two crests by a narrow valley, which is deep where it touches the road, but much less so a mile to the north. At Bolivar, a small village between Middletown and the Gap, roads branch to the right and left. The one on the right, called the "Old Hagerstown Road," passes up a ravine and leads to the left over and along the first of the two crests above mentioned, and enters the turnpike at the Mountain House, near the summit of the pass. The left-hand road, called the "Old Sharpsburg Road," follows a somewhat cir-

---

[1] The map of South Mountain, prepared in 1872, in the Bureau of Topographical Engineers, gives an excellent idea of this peculiar position.

cuitous route to Fox's Gap, at the top of the Mountain, and about a mile south of the Mountain House, and thence descends to the westward. Two or three wood roads lead northward from this road to, and to the westward of, the Mountain House. The mountains are steep, rugged, and thickly wooded, and rendered peculiarly hard to climb by reason of the presence of many ledges and loose rocks. A good many stone fences also were found there, and they afforded much protection to the troops defending the position.

At 6 A.M., on Sunday the 14th, General Cox, commanding the Kanawha division of Reno's (Ninth) Corps, marched from Middletown under an order received by him from Reno, directing him to support with his division the advance of Pleasonton's command, which was composed of cavalry and artillery. He took the road to the left of the main road, and ordered his leading brigade, Colonel Scammon commanding, to feel the enemy, and to ascertain whether the crest of South Mountain on that side was held by any considerable force. As the brigade moved out, he accompanied it, and presently met a paroled officer returning. An involuntary exclamation of this officer, when he told him where he was going, made him suspect that the enemy was in force at the Gap, and he thereupon ordered his second brigade, Colonel Crook commanding, to follow in support, and sent word back to Reno that he was moving his whole division, and notified Pleasonton that if the command got into an engagement, he should command as senior till Reno should come up. Reno sent word that Burnside and he approved, and that he would bring up the rest of the corps. As the first brigade advanced, Colonel Hayes (our late President) was sent with his regiment to the left, to gain, if possible, the enemy's right. He succeeded in gaining the crest on the left, and established himself there, in spite of vigorous resistance on the part of the Confederates. The rest of the command, with some aid from the artillery of the division, carried the entire crest by about 9 A.M. The enemy made several attempts to retake it, but though the fortunes of the fight were for some time uncertain, the Federals were solidly established by noon upon the ground they had won. The Confederate troops opposed to the Federals on this part of the field, were Garland's brigade, which lost its commander and was badly demoralized by his fall and the rough treatment it received, Anderson's brigade, Ripley's brigade, and part of Colquitt's, all of D. H. Hill's division, and Colonel Rosser, who had some cavalry, artillery, and sharpshooters.

At about 2 P.M., Federal reinforcements began to appear in masses, and something like a continuous line was formed. Willcox's division of the Ninth Corps was the first to arrive upon the ground, and it took position on the right of Cox, sending one regiment, however, to the extreme left, where a turning movement was threatened. Sturgis's division of the same corps supported Willcox, and of Rodman's division Fairchild's brigade was sent to the extreme left and Harlan's was placed on the right; but all these troops were on the south of the turnpike, that is to say, to the left of it, as seen from the Federal headquarters. Of Hooker's corps, Gibbon's brigade was placed on the turnpike, to make a demonstration on the centre so soon as the movements on the right and left had sufficiently progressed. The next troops to the right were Hatch's division, and beyond him was Meade, who moved up the "Old Hagerstown Road" to Mount Tabor Church, and deployed a short distance in advance of it. General Ricketts's division came up considerably later, and was deployed in the rear. Artillery was placed in position wherever it was thought it could be of service to the Federal attack, cavalry was thrown out to watch suspicious roads, and skirmishers were used freely to cover the front of the advancing brigades. At about 4 P.M. the general advance of the Federals began. The general scheme of it was that Reno's men should close in upon the Gap from the ground which they had won to the south, while Hooker's men were to reach the same point by circling round through the valley which formed the approach from the north to the Mountain House. In executing this movement, it was intended that Gallagher's and Magilton's brigades of Meade's division should pass through the ravine. Seymour's brigade of the same division was to move along the summit on the right, parallel to the ravine, and Hatch's division was to take the crest on the left; Ricketts's division was to follow in reserve; Gibbon's employment has already been indicated. Thus, including the reserves, eighteen Federal brigades, with artillery and cavalry, were used in this final operation.

To meet this general attack, there were present on the Confederate side the five brigades of D. H. Hill, viz.: Garland's, Colquitt's, Ripley's, Rodes's, and G. B. Anderson's. To these were added, about 3 P.M., from Longstreet's command, the brigades of Drayton and D. R. Jones (under Colonel G. T. Anderson), and at about 4 P.M. the brigades of Evans, Pickett (under Garnett), Kemper, and Jenkins (under Walker), and Hood's division of two brigades, commanded respectively by Wofford and by Law. If we call Rosser's command a brigade, it will appear that the Confederates at Turner's Gap met with fourteen brigades the assault of the Federal right, made with eighteen brigades.

In the afternoon fighting, Colquitt's brigade was in the centre, astride of the turnpike. The right was formed of the brigades of Drayton, G. T. Anderson, Ripley, and G. B.

SOUTH MOUNTAIN.

Anderson, in the order named from left to right, supported by Hood's two brigades, and with Rosser's men and what was left of Garland's brigade at and in rear of the right; on the left were the brigades of Rodes, who did most of the fighting there, and of Evans, Kemper, Pickett, and Jenkins. The Confederates had plenty of artillery, and they placed guns wherever they could find ground for them.

The Confederate reports of this action are not characterized by that fine tone of superiority with which all students of their reports are familiar. They claim to check and repulse and drive back the Federals, but the general result is an admission of defeat. It is refreshing to find that farcical overestimates of the strength of the enemy were not confined to the Federal side. General Garnett's report contains these words: "It has been subsequently ascertained that General McClellan's army, consisting of at least eighty thousand men, assailed our position, only defended by General D. H. Hill's division, and a part of General Longstreet's corps." The burden of all their reports, indeed, is that they were overwhelmed by numbers, and by them forced to yield, and were "withdrawn," one of their division commanders says, "in comparatively good order to the foot of the hill." D. H. Hill does not write like a soldier, and permits himself strange assertions. After describing his formation of a line of four brigades, with Drayton on one flank, he says: "Three Yankee brigades moved up in beautiful order against Drayton, and his men were soon beaten and went streaming to the rear. Rosser, Anderson, and Ripley still held their ground, and the Yankees could not gain our rear." If Rosser, Ripley, and Anderson could hold their ground, when three Yankee brigades had uncovered their flank, they were heroes indeed.

The truth is that this engagement was far from being

creditable to the Confederates. Some of them undoubtedly fought extremely well, notably Rodes's brigade, which lost very heavily. They were not well handled. The position was not one of a

> Straight pass in which a thousand,
> Might well be stopped by three,

because of the lateral roads which led into it and partially by it; but it was one which gave great advantage to the defenders. It is probable that the Federals outnumbered the Confederates to some extent, but probably not to a very great extent. If Ricketts's three brigades, which were hardly, if at all, used, be subtracted from the Federal total of eighteen, it will leave them fifteen brigades against fourteen Confederate brigades, and there is no reason for supposing that these Federal brigades went into action very much stronger than their opponents. It is true that Longstreet's men went into action after a toilsome march, but the Union troops had done some marching, too, and they had to fight up hill. Moreover the Confederates were familiar with the *terrain*, and the Federals were not. It is altogether probable that D. H. Hill's assertion is true, that if Longstreet's troops, as they came on the ground, had reported to him, who had become familiar with the ground and knew all the vital points, the result might have been different. "As it was, they took wrong positions, and in their exhausted condition, after a long march, they were broken and scattered." [1]

General McClellan's estimate of the numbers on each side is about as oriental as usual. He calls the Confederate force "probably some thirty thousand in all," and says, "we went

---

[1] A. N. Va., ii., 113.

into action with about thirty thousand men." This is an extract from his report dated August 4, 1863, when he had had plenty of time to think, and must be accepted as deliberate. It deserves attentive consideration. In the first place, let us consider his own numbers. It is impossible, from his own figures, to place the aggregate of the First and Ninth Corps present for duty September 14, 1862, higher than 35,155. If he went into action with 30,000, he took in more than five-sixths of his aggregate present for duty, and no soldier who served in the second year of our war will believe that he even approximated that. In the second place, did he believe in August, 1863—did he believe in September, 1862—that he had driven from a very strong position 30,000 of Lee's army—a force sufficient to occupy the whole position—with 30,000 of his own? Bunker Hill, if he had read no further in the history of war, might have taught him the absolute folly of such an idea. And Lee's men were not embattled farmers, or raw levies, or discontented conscripts. They were men passionately in earnest, men who had developed a natural aptitude for fighting by fourteen months of sharp and usually successful campaigning. They had shown that they could fight hard and march hard—that their audacity and tenacity were alike remarkable—that they were far more likely to carry difficult positions than to be driven from them. For McClellan, a year after the event, to profess to believe that he drove Longstreet and Hill with 30,000 men from the heights of South Mountain with 30,000 of his own men, is one of those extraordinary, inconceivable, aggravating things that stirs everything that is acrid in the nature of those who follow his career.

General McClellan reported a loss in this engagement of 1,568 men, of whom all but 22 were killed or wounded. Of this loss a large part fell upon Cox's Kanawha division, which had 442 men killed and wounded. Willcox's division also suffered heavily. The Federal General Reno [1] was killed almost as soon as he came up to the line occupied by his men, at about dark. About fifteen hundred Confederate prisoners were taken. Many of them were taken from Rodes's brigade, which also had 218 men killed and wounded. Five Confederate colonels and lieutenant-colonels were killed or dangerously wounded, besides one brigadier-general killed.

The untrustworthy character of military reports is illustrated by what we read in print from Federal and Confederate sources as to the advance up the turnpike made late in the engagement by Gibbon's brigade. McClellan says: " The brigade advanced steadily, driving the enemy from his positions in the woods and behind stone walls until . . . The fight continued until nine o'clock, the enemy being entirely repulsed, and the brigade . . . continued to hold the ground it had so gallantly won until twelve o'clock, when it was relieved." Colonel Meredith, commanding a regiment in this brigade, says: " It was a glorious victory on the part of General Gibbon's brigade, driving the enemy from their strong position in the mountain gorge." On the other hand, General Hill reports that this advance was " heroically met and bloodily repulsed " by two regiments of Colquitt's brigade, and that the fight " gradually subsided as the Yankees retired." Colquitt himself says: " Not an inch of ground was yielded." It is of little consequence which is nearer the truth. The great fact remains that the two battles of South Mountain were tactical defeats to the Confederates, but strategical victories won by them. General Hill was right in saying, "We retreated that night to Sharpsburg, having

---

[1] General D. H. Hill sweetly says (A. N. Va., ii., 111), " a renegade Virginian, who was killed by a happy shot from the Twenty-third North Carolina."

accomplished all that was required, the delay of the Yankee army until Harper's Ferry could not be relieved." This of itself was bad enough for McClellan, but it was not all. He had lost his opportunity not only to save the garrison of Harper's Ferry, but to interpose between the wings of Lee's army. A night march of his left and right wing on the evening of the 13th—a far easier march than Jackson made on the night of the 15th, from Harper's Ferry to Sharpsburg—would have given him possession of both passes early in the morning of the 14th, and if he had been there it is hard to see how he could have failed to do such things as fairly startle one to think of. To crush McLaws, relieve Harper's Ferry, turn every gun he could get on to Maryland Heights upon Jackson and Walker, and hurl forty or fifty thousand men on to D. H. Hill and Longstreet while he interposed between them and Jackson, seem things not only within the range of possibility, but of easy possibility. But he was not equal to the occasion. He threw away his chance, and a precious opportunity for making a great name passed away. It is no wonder that Lee and Jackson were audacious at Chancellorsville. After their experiences with Pope and McClellan, they had some right to believe that a division of their forces in the immediate presence of the enemy might be ventured upon. It may be said that McClellan did better than Pope, and this is true, but such faint praise is the most that can be said of his action on this important occasion, and as for his tactical victory, it is curious to read, as we shall presently, that he did not learn till daylight the following morning, that the enemy had abandoned his positions.

CHAPTER III.

THE ANTIETAM.

LEE and his generals were not slow to act in presence of the danger which still impended. General McLaws made haste, during the night of the 14th, to form his command in line of battle across Pleasant Valley, about a mile and a half below Crampton's, leaving one regiment to support the artillery on Maryland Heights, and two brigades on each of the roads from Harper's Ferry, *i.e.*, the road which ran from there over the Brownsville Pass, and that by the Weverton Pass. The object of this was to prevent the escape of the garrison of Harper's Ferry by either road, as well as to protect his own right flank. The commands of Longstreet and D. H. Hill reached Sharpsburg on the morning of the 15th, and were placed in position along the range of hills between the town and the Antietam, nearly parallel to the course of the stream, Longstreet on the right of the road to Boonsboro', and Hill on the left.

Lee moved to Sharpsburg, because he would there be upon the flank and rear of any force moving against McLaws, and because the army could unite there to advantage. Longstreet says that this position was a strong defensive one, besides possessing the advantage just mentioned. As no other Confederate troops came up to this position till the following day, it is convenient to return to the Federal headquarters, and tell what McClellan and his troops did after the fighting at South Mountain ended.

It has already been said that Franklin's advance moved into Pleasant Valley on the night of the 14th. An hour after midnight of that day, McClellan sent Franklin orders to occupy the road from Rohrersville to Harper's Ferry, placing a sufficient force at Rohrersville to hold the position against an attack from the Boonsboro' direction, that is to say, from the forces of Longstreet and Hill. He also directed him to attack and destroy such of the enemy as he might find in Pleasant Valley, and, if possible, to withdraw Miles's command. The letter ends : " You will then proceed to Boonsboro', which place the Commanding General intends to attack to-morrow, and join the main body of the army at that place. Should you find, however, that the enemy have retreated from Boonsboro' towards Sharpsburg, you will endeavor to fall upon him and cut off his retreat." These orders made Franklin's duty perfectly clear, and it is not easy to see why he did not obey them, except that he seems to have had a fatal tendency to see lions in his path. Couch joined him at 10 P.M. of the night of the 14th, thus raising his forces to a nominal aggregate of upward of eighteen thousand men present for duty, which must have much more than equalled the strength of the twelve brigades which McLaws had to oppose to him. He was fully informed of McClellan's plans and wishes before these orders reached him, and he knew from the tenor of McClellan's letter, if he did not know it directly and in terms, that he had forced the passage of Turner's Gap. Under these circumstances the duty was pressing to put forth, as McClellan had begged him to, "the utmost activity that a general can exercise." Unfortunately for the success of the Union arms, Franklin was not the man for the place. At ten minutes before 9 A.M. of the

15th, he was two miles from the line of the enemy, which was drawn between him and the place he was ordered to relieve, and waiting (which McClellan had not told him to do) to be sure that Rohrersville was occupied before moving forward to attack the enemy, and reporting that this might require two hours' further delay. He also reported that the cessation of firing at Harper's Ferry made him fear that it had fallen, and his opinion that, if that proved to be true, he would need to be strongly reinforced. By eleven o'clock he had satisfied himself that the enemy in his front outnumbered him two to one.

Harper's Ferry was surrendered at 8 A.M. of this day. It was lost because Miles did not make his main defence on Maryland Heights, because McClellan's orders were not equal to the emergency, and because Franklin's action was not equal to the orders he received. After what has been said, it is hardly necessary to say that Franklin did not make himself disagreeable in any way to McLaws. McClellan seems to have thought that the "gigantic rebel army"[1] before him was so gigantic that, with Longstreet and D. H. Hill and Walker and Jackson's entire command away, McLaws could still outnumber three Federal divisions two to one, for he ordered General Franklin to remain where he was "to watch the large force in front of him," and protect his left and rear till the night of the 16th, when he was to send Couch's division to Maryland Heights, and himself join the main army at Keedysville. How he could have expected to beat the whole of Lee's army, when he attributed such

---

[1] McClellan's letter of September 11, 1862 (Com. C. W., i., 39). The army estimate of the relative strength of the two armies was not, at least in the Second Corps, the same as McClellan's. "We outnumber the enemy" (extract from army letter, dated Frederick, September 13, 1862).

strength to a fraction of it, is a riddle which it passes human powers to solve.

General Franklin watched the large force in front of him to so much and so little purpose, that they sent their trains back across the river, and gradually withdrew themselves, marched through Harper's Ferry, camped at Halltown, and joined the main army at Sharpsburg on the morning of September 17th. The scheme of interposing the Federal army between the wings of Lee's army was rapidly coming to naught.

On the night of the 14th September, the centre, under General Sumner, came up in rear of the right wing, shortly after dark. Richardson's division of the Second Corps was placed at Mount Tabor Church on the "Old Hagerstown Road," about a mile north of Bolivar, and the rest of the Second Corps, and all the Twelfth Corps around Bolivar. Sykes's division and the artillery reserve halted for the night at Middletown. Orders were given to the Federal commanders to press forward the pickets at early dawn. Their advance revealed the fact that the Confederates had retreated during the night.[1] An immediate pursuit was ordered. Pleasonton's cavalry, the First Corps under Hooker, the Second under Sumner, and the Twelfth, now under Mansfield, were to follow the turnpike to and through Boonsboro', while Burnside and Porter, with the Ninth Corps and Sykes's division, were to take the "Old Sharpsburg Road" on the left. Burnside and Porter were to be governed by circumstances on reaching the road from Boonsboro' to Rohrersville, whether to reinforce Franklin or to move on Sharpsburg. The Federal advance made its appearance

---

[1] Meade says in his report: "Morning opened with a heavy mist, which prevented any view being obtained, so that it was not till 7 A.M. that it was ascertained the enemy had retired entirely from the Mountain."

on the west side of the Boonsboro' Pass at 8 A.M. of the
15th. This was the hour at which Harper's Ferry was surrendered. The fact of the surrender, and the hour at which
it took place, were speedily made known to McClellan. It
was reasonably certain that the troops assigned by Lee's
special order No. 191 to the duty of capturing the garrison
at Harper's Ferry, were then around that place, and most of
them far from Lee, and all of them separated from him
either by distance and the Potomac, or by Union troops, or
both. Whatever his estimate may have been of the amount
of the force so employed, he knew that it comprised all or
part of Jackson's command, and the divisions of McLaws,
R. H. Anderson, and Walker. If he looked for no aggressive action on the part of Franklin and Couch, he could at
least look to them to hold in check and neutralize the
forces of McLaws and R. H. Anderson, and this left him free
to use his First, Second, Ninth, and Twelfth Corps, with all
of the Fifth Corps that was with him, and Pleasonton's cavalry command, against Longstreet and D. H. Hill. In other
words, in fine country and in fine weather, he had thirty-five
brigades of infantry to use against Longstreet's nine brigades, and D. H. Hill's five brigades. Pleasonton's cavalry
and the reserve artillery were probably as numerous as
Stuart's and Rosser's cavalry and their artillery. We assume
this, in the absence of figures. At any rate, McClellan
claims that his cavalry on the 15th overtook the enemy's
cavalry, made a daring charge, and captured 250 prisoners
and two guns. Here again was a great opportunity. With
a long day before him, a force that outnumbered his opponent as five to two, and probably as six to two,[1] and the

---

[1] It will be observed that here and elsewhere numbers are treated in accordance with the facts, and not in accordance with McClellan's statements of his estimate of them. It is true that a commander must shape his action with ref-

knowledge that the large detachments his opponent had
made could not join him for twenty-four hours, and might
not join him for forty-eight or more, it was a time for rapid
action. It would seem that he ought to have pressed his
troops forward unrestingly till they reached cannon-shot distance from the enemy, and made his reconnoissances as his
columns were advancing. He would speedily have learned
the length of the enemy's line, and as the distance from the
summit of Turner's Gap to Sharpsburg is only seven or eight
miles, it is not easy to see why he might not have attacked
in force early in the afternoon. He had every reason for
believing that delay would strengthen the enemy much
more proportionately than it would strengthen him, and he
might be sure that delay would be at least as serviceable to
the enemy as to him in acquiring knowledge of the ground,
and much more so in putting that knowledge to account.
But it was not to be. With all his amiable and estimable
and admirable qualities, there was something wanting in
McClellan. If he had used the priceless hours of the 15th
September, and the still precious, though less precious
hours of the 16th as he might have, his name would have
stood high in the roll of great commanders; but he let those
hours go by, and, as will presently be told in detail, it took
him forty-eight hours to get ready to deliver his main attack, and then he had to deal not only with Lee and Longstreet and Hood and D. H. Hill, but with all of them, with
Stonewall Jackson added, with two of his divisions, and

---

erence to his estimate of his own and his opponent's force, but it must be said
without reservation that it is impossible to believe that McClellan believed that
on the Peninsula or in Maryland the Confederates had the forces he attributed
to them. If he did believe it, he ought, with his knowledge of their fighting
qualities, to have abandoned offensive operations and thrown his army behind
fortifications constructed to protect Washington, Baltimore, and Philadelphia,
and waited for more troops.

McLaws and Walker. It has already been suggested that Halleck's error in insisting on retaining Miles at Harper's Ferry came near being very damaging to Lee. In the sequel it proved damaging only to the extent of the weakening of his force by straggling upon the march, and the somewhat enfeebled condition of some of his troops at Sharpsburg; but if the most had been made of the opportunity by the Federal commander, Halleck's error would have proved more useful than the wisest piece of strategy has often been.

Richardson's division of the Second Corps moved rapidly through Boonsboro' and Keedysville, and found the Confederates occupying the position they had chosen beyond the Antietam. In obedience to orders, it halted and deployed on the east of the stream, on the right of the Sharpsburg road. Sykes's division came up and deployed on the left of Richardson, and on the left of the Sharpsburg road. The Confederate artillery opened on the Federal columns as they came in sight, from positions on the high ground on the west side of the stream.

Between Mercersville on the north and the confluence of the Antietam with the Potomac on the south, a distance of about six miles in a straight line, the Potomac follows a series of remarkable curves, but its general course is such that a line of battle something less than six miles long may be drawn, from a point a little below Mercersville to a point a little above the mouth of the Antietam, so as to rest both its flanks upon the Potomac, to cover the Shepherdstown Ford and the town of Sharpsburg, and to have its front covered by Antietam Creek. The Antietam is crossed by four bridges, of which that nearest its confluence with the Potomac was not used during the battle, except by the troops of A. P. Hill, coming from Harper's Ferry to reinforce Lee. The

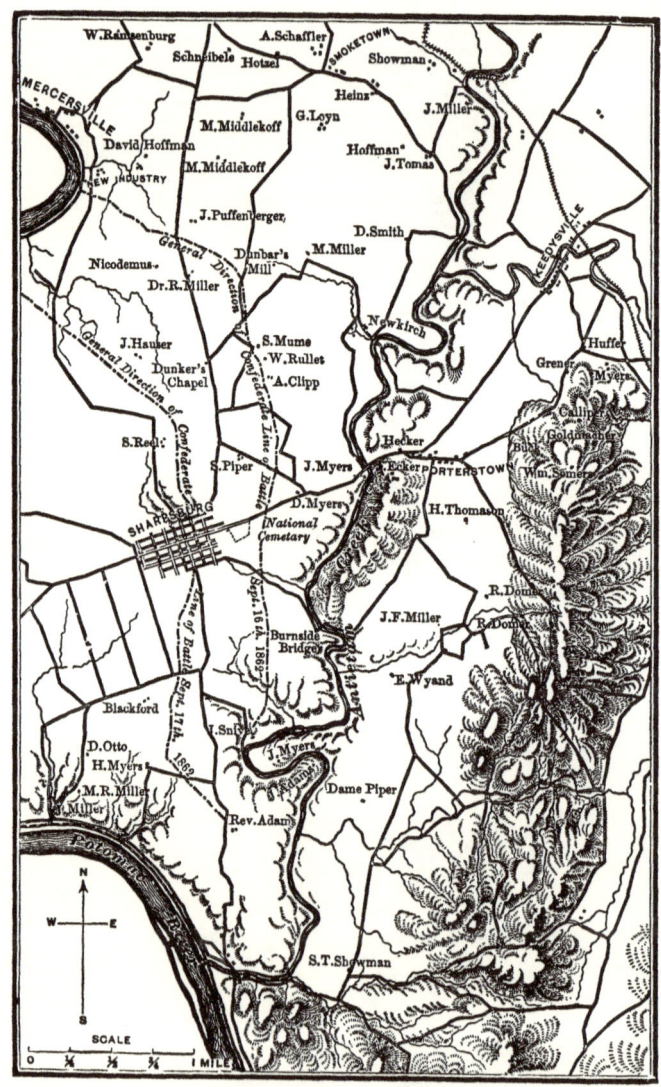

The Field of the Antietam.

next, known as the "Burnside Bridge," is that by which the road from Sharpsburg to Rohrersville crosses the stream. The next above is the bridge of the Sharpsburg, Keedysville, and Boonsboro' turnpike, and another, two miles and a half higher up, is the bridge of the road from Keedysville to Williamsport. The stream is sluggish and winding, and though it possesses several fords, they are difficult. In the rear of Sharpsburg a good road leads to the Shepherdstown Ford of the Potomac. Besides the roads already mentioned, an important turnpike leads northward from Sharpsburg to Hagerstown. On the western side of the Antietam, the ground rises in a slope of woods and fields to a somewhat bold crest, and then falls away to the Potomac.

In this "strong defensive position," Lee proceeded to form his men for the action which events had so forced upon him that he could not avoid it without loss of prestige. His front was covered by the Antietam, his line of retreat was convenient and open, and the way was clear for all his detachments to join him. He was in a position from which he could not hope to escape without serious fighting and serious loss, but he had not to fear destruction unless his opponent struck at once and struck hard. His position was very different from what he appears to have expected, and it must have been with a strong sense of disappointment as well as of anxiety that he formed his thin lines in front of Sharpsburg. The dream of raiding northward to the Susquehanna, and of drawing McClellan so far away as to permit him to make a point on Washington, had to be abandoned, and instead of that he had to prepare for a tough struggle to be made with a small army at best, and with only half of that if his opponent was prompt.

The National Cemetery at Sharpsburg is situated upon the crest of a hill to the eastward of the town, and just outside

the houses. It fronts upon the main road from the town to
Keedysville, and lies on the southerly side of that road. It
commands a view of remarkable beauty and extent. Within
its enclosure is a small mass of limestone upon which it is
said Lee stood to direct the battle. If one enters the cemetery and takes his position at the base of the flag-staff, which
stands on the highest ground, he will be within the concave
of the Confederate line as it stood at the commencement of
the battle. On his left, as he looks northward, is the town
of Sharpsburg, lying in a hollow between the ridge which
rises to the west of the Antietam, and the Potomac, which is
not in sight. The Hagerstown pike may be partially seen,
extending northerly from the town, and with a slightly ob-
lique direction to the right. At the distance of about a
mile, upon the western edge, and in plain view, stands the
famous Dunker Church, in the border of a patch of woods.
To the right of it, and to the east of the turnpike, is open
ground, and this is bordered on the right by another patch
of woods. These two patches of timber, with the fields between, were the scene of the most sanguinary fighting of the
17th of September. Looking further to the right, to the
northeast of the position of the observer, and at a distance
of something less than two miles, a large brick building
may be seen. This is Fry's house, round which the tents
of McClellan's headquarters were pitched before and during
the battle. The Antietam cannot be seen, because of
the depth of the ravine which forms its bed, but its course
may easily be traced by the abundant growth of the
trees which fringe its banks. Yet further to the right, and
at a distance of about a mile, one sees the upper part of a
basin formed by some hills. At the base of these hills the
"Burnside Bridge" crosses the stream. In the further distance to the right, the spurs of Maryland Heights and the

stately South Mountain range frame the picture, which is as full of beauty as it is of interest. Practically the whole of the battle-field may be seen from this single point. To complete the description of it, it is to be added that the woods in which the Dunker Church stands, fringe the western side of the Hagerstown pike for about a quarter of a mile. Then they turn to the westward for about one hundred and fifty yards, and, turning again at right angles, the edge of the woods is parallel to the turnpike for another quarter of a mile. Further to the north, the ground is open immediately to the west of the pike, and there are two sizable woods, detached from each other, further to the west.[1] For convenience of description, the woods to the west, north and northwest of the Dunker Church will be called the West Woods, and the woods opposite and to the east of the pike, and separated from it by open ground, will be called the East Woods. At the Dunker Church two roads meet the turnpike, almost forming a right angle with each other. The course of the easterly of these two roads is southwesterly to the pike, while the other, which is little more than a wood road, runs a little north of west from the church. The West Woods are full of outcropping ledges of limestone, which afford excellent cover for troops. To the west of the northern portion of the West Woods is a height, far enough to the west to enable the force holding it to take not

---

[1] Some of the reports speak of a stone house, with straw stacks near it. It is probable, but not certain, that the stone house was Nicodemus's, west of the Hagerstown pike, and in the angle between it and the road to Williamsport. The "burning buildings" were, almost certainly, one Mume's, east of the Hagerstown Pike, and not very far from D. R. Miller's house. They are not shown on the plan. I saw them in flames, on the right of Sedgwick's division, as I went into action, and when I next visited the ground, some few years after, I was assured that they were Mume's. The Dutch or German settlers of the neighborhood seem to have been family connections. I found three separate families of Poffenbergers, for instance.—F. W. P.

only in flank but in reverse the whole of the Confederate position.

As we have now reached the point at which the nucleus of Lee's army has taken position in front of Sharpsburg, while two divisions of McClellan's army have formed up for the attack, the time seems to have come for some remarks upon the character of the two armies. There is no occasion for saying much about the rank and file of either side, for the soldierly qualities of both are too well known. After eighty years of peace, the surface of which had been scarcely ruffled by the war of 1812 and the Mexican war, the men of the North and of the South had shown that they still possessed the soldierly qualities of the Anglo-Saxon race. For fourteen months they had been opposed to each other, and from the first to the second Bull Run, at Williamsburg and Fair Oaks, and Gaines's Mill, and Malvern Hill, and in all the campaigning which came between the first clash of arms and the last struggle at South Mountain, they had displayed intelligence, courage, endurance, tenacity, and patriotism. The qualities that had enabled the South to win the first battle of Bull Run, and had made Massachusetts men "stand in the evil hour" at Ball's Bluff, had been developed and disciplined by the experience of war, and Lee and McClellan now had each an instrument to work with, which had been not perfected, but much bettered by the tempering processes of the field.

When we pass from the men to the commanders, there is more to be said. Lee had Longstreet and D. H. Hill and Hood and Stuart with him, while Jackson and A. P. Hill and McLaws and Walker were hastening to join him. McClellan had for corps commanders, Hooker and Sumner, and Porter and Franklin, and Burnside and Mansfield, while his division commanders were Cox, Couch, Doubleday,

THE ANTIETAM. 53

French, Greene, Hatch, Meade, Morell, Richardson, Ricketts, Rodman, Sedgwick, Slocum, W. F. Smith, Sturgis, Willcox, and Williams. If a student of military history, familiar with the characters who figured in the war of secession, but happening to be ignorant of the story of the battle of the Antietam, should be told that the men we have named held the high commands there, he would say that with anything like an equality of forces, the Confederates must have won, for their leaders were men who made great names in the war, while the Federal leaders were, with few exceptions, men who never became conspicuous, or became conspicuous only through failure. Their names are for the most part unknown to the public, and few can say who among them are alive or dead.

In September, 1862, McClellan had been for fifteen years a graduate of the Military Academy, and for all but about four of these years he had been in the military service of the United States. He had resigned in January, 1857, giving up the commission of a captain of cavalry, and he had been raised at one step from civil life, in May, 1861, to the position of major-general in the army. He was a man of short and solid figure, good carriage, and singularly pleasing manners. He was never in a hurry, and always seemed to have plenty of time at his command. He had shown marked ability as an organizer, and his men generally felt an almost idolatrous enthusiasm for him. He had been so slow to commence operations against the army that had beaten McDowell in 1861, that many people had come to entertain grave doubts of his capacity, and the doubters had grown more numerous and positive since the failure of his Peninsular campaign, though his shortcomings there did not then incur all the censure they deserved, because of the very generally entertained belief that the failure was owing to interference at Washington with his plans. After

Pope's defeat the army turned to him passionately, and the people hopefully, and the time was now coming that was to test the question of his talents.

McClellan's lieutenants were Sumner, Burnside, and Franklin. Sumner was quite an old man, though still vigorous and active. He was not a graduate of West Point, but he had been a soldier all his life, and he was rapidly promoted from a colonelcy of cavalry to the grade of major-general of volunteers. He was a most excellent and every way respectable man, and he had in the highest degree the courage of a soldier, but he was wanting in the courage of a general. He was apt to be demoralized by hard fighting, and to overestimate the losses of his own side and the strength of the enemy, and he seems to have possessed no judgment as a tactician. It is probable that his training as a cavalry officer had done him positive harm as a leader of infantry. Franklin had been a soldier all his life—that is to say, he had been first in his class at West Point, and from 1843, when he graduated, he had been serving in the Topographical Engineers, till May, 1861, when he was commissioned brigadier-general of volunteers. Something has been said of him already, and more will be said of him, when his part in the battle of Fredericksburg is discussed. For the present it is sufficient to say that whatever his merits may have been, he distinctly did not belong to the class of fortunate and successful soldiers. Burnside, also, was a West Point graduate, but he had been out of the service more than seven years when the war broke out. Few men, probably, have risen so high upon so slight a foundation as he. He is dead, and what must be said of him is therefore to be said with forbearance. His personal appearance was striking and fine, and his manner was frank and captivating. Nobody could encounter his smile and receive the grasp of his hand with-

THE ANTIETAM. 55

out being for some time under a potent influence. It is probably true that that man's manners made his fortune, for he remained long in the service in high places, and yet his presence was an element of weakness where he was a subordinate, and was disastrous when he held a great command. Hooker, too, is dead. Brave, handsome, vain, insubordinate, plausible, untrustworthy, he had many of the merits of a lieutenant, but not all, and he too failed dismally when he was made commander-in-chief. As an inferior, he planned badly and fought well; as chief, he planned well and fought badly. He was so unfortunate in his bearing as a corps commander that his great chief Sherman was glad to be rid of him, and he left the army in front of Atlanta, and never was set to work against troops again. Of the unfortunate Porter it is unnecessary to speak. His vindication at the hands of the Military Commission is magnificent, but he had little to do at the battle of the Antietam, and nothing to do afterward. The excellent Sedgwick never climbed high on the hill of fame, and Grant's presence so overshadowed Meade from the spring of 1864, that one is left to saying with some diffidence that he seems to have been rather a meritorious than a brilliant commander. The names which afterward became more or less splendid, such names as Hancock, Humphreys, Griffin, Warren, Barlow, and Miles, belonged to men who, in September, 1862, were brigade commanders or not so high. The only other division commander who went into action on the Federal side at the Antietam who calls for special mention, was Cox, a useful citizen of the Garfield type, a good soldier, and an admirable man. As a corps commander in Sherman's army, and afterward as Governor of Ohio, he came to be widely and favorably known in the West, but he was almost a stranger to the army of the Potomac, with which he only served for about two months.

On the afternoon of the hot fifteenth of September, while the long columns of the Federal army were resting along the Boonsboro' road, General McClellan passed through them to the front, and had from them such a magnificent reception as was worth living for. Far from the rear the cheers were heard, faintly at first, and gradually the sound increased and grew to a roar as he approached. The weary men sprang to their feet and cheered and cheered, and as he went the cheers went before him and with him and after him, till the sound receding with the distance at last died away. The troops moved on later, slowly and wearily, and some of them were not in position till the next morning.

General McClellan says that after a rapid examination of the position, he found it was too late to attack on Monday. He does not say at what hour he reached the front, but, as has been said, it was well into the afternoon. Neither does he tell us why he arrived so late. Besides making the rapid examination of which he speaks, he seems to have done nothing beyond directing the placing of the batteries in the centre, and indicating the bivouacs for the different corps. This last was a simple matter, as he merely massed them near and on both sides of the road from Keedysville to Sharpsburg. So all this day, the fifteenth of September, Lee stood in front of Sharpsburg with the troops of Longstreet and D. H. Hill alone, while the whole army of the Potomac, excepting Franklin's command and Morell's division of the Fifth Corps, was near him.

Tuesday the sixteenth was a terribly hot day in its early hours, with a burning sun and no breeze, but at about eleven the sun became overcast, and a little air stirred from time to time. It was a day of mere idleness throughout, for a large part of the army,[1] and no one but the gunners had anything

---

[1] The Second Corps, at any rate, did not move that day, but remained massed near Fry's house.

THE ANTIETAM. 57

to do in the forenoon. We lay about on the eastern slope of the ridge which interposed between us and the valley of the Antietam, and occasionally we would go to the crest of the ridge to see what we could see. There was plenty to see, but unfortunately that was not all of it. The Confederate batteries were wide awake, and their practice was extremely good, and projectiles flew over the crest so thickly that mere curiosity was not sufficient to keep any one there long.

On the morning of this day Jackson arrived at Sharpsburg with his own division, under J. R. Jones, and Ewell's division, under Lawton. His troops were allowed some rest, and then his own division was placed on the left of Hood, who, being himself on the left of D. H. Hill, prolonged the Confederate line northward and westward to the Hagerstown pike. Jackson's right rested on the pike. Winder's and Jones's brigades formed his front line, and Taliaferro's and Starke's his second. Early's brigade of Ewell's division was formed on his left, to guard his flank, and Hays's brigade was formed in his rear. Stuart, with the cavalry, was still further to the left, near the Potomac. Lawton's and Trimble's brigades, of Ewell's division, were left to rest near the Dunker Church. Walker, also, early this day, crossed the Potomac on his return from Harper's Ferry, but he also seems to have rested till daylight the next morning, when he placed his two brigades on the extreme right of the Confederate position, about a mile and a half south of Sharpsburg, and in support to General Toombs, whose brigade was guarding the approach by the "Burnside Bridge." These were all the troops which Lee had with him all day on the 16th, for McLaws did not come on the ground till sunrise the next morning, Anderson's division followed him, and A. P. Hill did not arrive till half-past two P.M. Artillery seems to have been singularly plenty among the Confederates, for

3*

58   ANTIETAM AND FREDERICKSBURG.

D. H. Hill, after stating that on the morning of the 17th he had but 3,000 infantry, proceeds as follows: "I had, however, twenty-six pieces of artillery of my own, and near sixty pieces of Cutts's battalion temporarily under my command."[1] As twenty-six pieces is a liberal allowance for 9,000 infantry, this statement excites some surprise.

The ground occupied by the Confederates near the "Burnside Bridge" was favorable for their defence. It consisted of undulating hills, their crests commanded in turn by others in their rear. The bridge itself is a stone structure of three arches, with a stone parapet above. This parapet to some extent flanks the approach to the bridge at each end. The stream runs through a narrow valley. On the right bank (held by the Confederates), a steep slope comes very near the edge. In this slope the roadway is scarped, running both ways from the bridge, and passing to the higher land above by ascending through ravines. On the hill-side immediately above the bridge was a strong stone fence, running nearly parallel to the stream. The turns of the roadway were covered by rifle-pits and breastworks made of rails and stone. The slope was wooded to a considerable extent.

For some reason which has never been made public, the right division of the army, Burnside's command, was divided at Sharpsburg. Hooker's corps was made the extreme right of the army, and the other corps, the Ninth, now under Cox, with whom Burnside went, was made the extreme left. It was the understanding of the time at Burnside's headquarters that Hooker had in some way procured this separate duty, with a view to giving himself more importance. Burnside declined to assume personal command of the Ninth

---

[1] A. N. Va., ii., 114.

Corps when this separation took place, intimating that if he should so assume command, it would look like acquiescence on his part with the arrangement, and might tend to make it permanent. Thus Burnside's position became somewhat anomalous. It is possible that this division of his command may have been the commencement of the estrangement between him and McClellan, of the existence of which at a later date there is strong evidence.

General McClellan went to the left of his line himself, to see that the Ninth Corps was properly posted, his idea being that that force must be prepared both to resist an attack by the left bank of the stream, and to carry the bridge at the proper time. It is believed in some quarters [1] that Burnside was very slow in moving to the position assigned him, but McClellan simply says that he found it necessary to make considerable changes in his position, and that he directed him to advance to a strong position in the immediate vicinity of the bridge, and to carefully reconnoitre the approaches to the bridge.

By this time McClellan's plan for the battle seems to have taken definite shape in his mind. It was extremely simple, and ought to have been successful. It was in brief to attack the Confederate left with the corps of Hooker and Mansfield, supported by Sumner's, and if necessary by Franklin's, and, as soon as matters looked favorably there, to move the Ninth Corps against their extreme right, and whenever either of these movements should be successful, to advance

---

[1] It is even asserted that on coming up to the line formed at the Antietam, on the 15th, Burnside placed his command behind some of the troops already in position, instead of moving at once to the ground assigned to him on the left, and that he stayed there till a late hour, in spite of repeated orders to move; that again on the 16th he did not move to his assigned position till after the receipt of repeated urgent orders from McClellan. This is given for what it is worth. The success of our army was undoubtedly greatly lessened by jealousy, distrust, and general want of the *entente cordiale*.

his centre with all the force disposable. With what McClellan knew then, with all we know now, nearly twenty years after the battle, the plan seems to have been well suited to the position of affairs. There is no censure too strong for his delay, but, having determined or permitted himself to delay, he shaped his programme well enough.

But for the success of this as well as every other military enterprise, two things were important, if not indispensable—first, that he should not tell his opponent what he was going to do; and second, that he should do well the thing he proposed to do. Able commanders seek to delude their opponents. They use all the craft which they possess to induce the enemy to believe that the blow is to fall at some place other than the place which they have chosen. If possible, they lead the enemy to strengthen the point where the feigned attack is to be made, and to weaken the point where the real attack is to be made. Thus Marlborough carried the line of the Mehaigne at Ramillies. Thus Thomas deluded Hood at Nashville. Military history is full of such examples. But McClellan resorted to no such artifices; on the contrary, he informed Lee that he proposed to make his main attack with his right, and not only that, but almost certainly told him that he had greatly strengthened it for the purpose. With Maryland so full of Confederate sympathizers as it was, we cannot doubt that Lee knew by this time the general division of McClellan's army, and we can hardly doubt that he knew that he had departed from it to fight this battle. However this may have been, it seems undeniable that McClellan's dispositions on the 16th were exactly appropriate to a plan of battle which contemplated a main attack to be made by his left, strengthened by troops to be moved there under cover of the night, and that they were extremely inappropriate to the plan which he had formed and to which he adhered.

On the high ground in the centre of his position, between the Keedysville road on the left and Fry's house on the right, McClellan placed several batteries of long range guns. Standing among those guns, one could look down upon nearly the whole field of the coming battle, while the view was perhaps more complete from the high ground on the left of the road, where some of the Fifth Corps batteries were placed. From this point one could look to the right through the open space between the "East and West Woods." From the further bank of the stream in front, the land rose gently toward the ridge occupied by the Confederates, checkered with cleared fields and corn-fields, and traversed by many fences. The famous "sunken road" was almost in front of the spectator looking west. It branched off from the northern side of the Keedysville pike, about half way from the river to Sharpsburg, and ran in broken lines to the Hagerstown pike, which it entered about half-way between Sharpsburg and the Dunker Church, but nearer the latter.

The conformation of the ground was such that these central Federal batteries could sweep almost the whole extent of the hostile front. Some of them had a direct fire through the space between the East and West Woods, and others of them could enfilade the refused left wing of the Confederate army.

About 2 P.M. McClellan ordered Hooker to cross the Antietam at the upper bridge and a ford near by, to attack and, if possible, turn the enemy's left. He also ordered Sumner to cross Mansfield's Twelfth Corps during the night, and to hold the Second in readiness to cross early the next morning. He seems to have devoted the rest of the day to examinations of the ground, finding fords, clearing approaches, and hastening the arrival of the ammunition and supply trains.

It is an ungrateful task to be always finding fault, but an important battle is to be described, and the reasons why its results were what they were, and only what they were, must be fully given. The perniciousness of the mistake which McClellan made in delaying his attack cannot be too strongly insisted upon. The reasons which he gives for his delay are entirely inadequate, and part of the use which he made of the time thus placed at his command was positively damaging. But having delayed his attack till the enemy was largely or completely concentrated, and having informed him, by the language of acts which it was difficult to misinterpret, where he meant to strike, it yet remained possible to strike with vigor and with concert. Instead of doing so, he issued such orders to his corps commanders on the right as made it impossible that they should act with concert early on the 17th, and improbable that they would act with concert at all. Under such orders, the attacks were far more likely to be successive than to be simultaneous.

On Tuesday the 16th, at 4 P.M., Hooker moved. He crossed the Antietam without opposition, at the points indicated. Circling around until he faced southward, he presently came upon the Confederate pickets. His troops were deployed at once, with Meade in the centre, Doubleday on his right, and Ricketts on the left. The attack, such as it was, fell upon Hood's two brigades, Meade's division of Federals being principally engaged. The advantage seems to have been slightly upon the side of the Federals, though each side claims to have forced back the other. Longstreet says "Hood drove him back, but not without severe loss," and Hood admits that he was relieved by Lawton, with two brigades, at the close of the fighting, though he claims that this was to enable his half-starved men to cook. The relieving brigades were those of Trimble, which formed up next to the division of D. H. Hill, and Lawton's, which took position on its left.

During the night Mansfield crossed the Twelfth Corps, following in the track of Hooker, and passed what was left of the night about a mile in rear of Hooker. The Federal and Confederate pickets on Hooker's front were exceedingly close together. Sumner's Second Corps, Burnside's Ninth Corps, and all of Porter's Fifth Corps that had arrived, remained in bivouac. Morell's division of the Fifth Corps arrived in the evening of the 16th.[1] Franklin's Sixth Corps and Couch's division of the Fourth Corps were still at a distance, in the neighborhood of Crampton's Gap. Of the Confederate army, all the divisions were now in position excepting those of McLaws and Anderson, which, as has been said, arrived very early on the morning of the 17th, and A. P. Hill's, which arrived after noon of that day.

As the Federal and Confederate armies have now been brought face to face, it may be well to say what there is to be said about the strength of each army. The Confederates have always claimed that they fought this battle with such vastly inferior numbers that it deserved to be considered a glorious victory for them. Jackson's soldierly report of this battle contains no boastful assertions upon this point, and Early, contrary to his later habit, is equally temperate, but A. P. Hill declares that three brigades of his division, not numbering over two thousand men, with the help of his "splendid batteries," drove back Burnside's corps of 15,000 men. D. H. Hill, whose writing in his report is especially offensive, declares that he opened upon an "imposing force of Yankees" with five guns at twelve hundred yards distance,

---

[1] Statement of a colonel. But Porter's Report says, at about noon. Morell relieved Richardson on the 17th, when he went into action with the other divisions of the Second Corps.

and routed them by artillery fire alone, unaided by musketry. He also declares that the battle was fought with less than thirty thousand men, and that if all their stragglers had been up, McClellan's army would have been completely crushed or annihilated. It is but fair to him to say that his compliments are not paid to his opponents alone. He declares that "thousands of thieving poltroons" had kept away from the battle on his side "from sheer cowardice." Hood declares that his "two little giant brigades" became engaged with "not less than two corps" of the Federal army, "wrestled with this mighty force," and drove it from its position and forced it to abandon its guns. McLaws considered the battle of Sharpsburg a very great success, regard being had to the "enormous disparity" between the opposing forces. D. R. Jones uses the same phrase of enormous disparity. Longstreet says that the Confederate forces seemed but a handful when compared with the hosts thrown against them, and permits himself the following assertion: "Before it was entirely dark, the hundred thousand men that had been threatening our destruction for twelve hours, had melted away into a few stragglers."[1] Lee declares that this great battle was fought by less than forty thousand men on his side. Finally, Colonel Taylor, in his "Four Years with General Lee," makes Lee's entire strength at Sharpsburg 35,255.[2]

Apropos of Southern statements as to the forces present on their side in the battles of the War of Secession, a New England man who had served in the Army of the Potomac said: "A few more years, a few more books, and it will

---

[1] A. N. Va., ii., 86.
[2] The Richmond Enquirer account, dated September 23, gives Lee about sixty thousand, and McClellan from a hundred to a hundred and fifty thousand. V. Reb. Rec., 476.

THE ANTIETAM. 65

appear that Lee and Longstreet, and a one-armed orderly, and a casual with a shot-gun, fought all the battles of the rebellion, and killed all the Union soldiers except those who ran away." The wit of this speech will be most enjoyed, and its point most clearly seen, by those who are familiar with Southern military writings, but it is no more than simple justice to Colonel Taylor to say, that in estimating the force of the Federal and Confederate troops present at Sharpsburg, he has gone to sources which he had a right to consider original, and that he has used his material fairly. His total of 35,255 Confederates was arrived at by using the official reports of the Maryland Campaign, published by authority of the Confederate Congress, and as these reports are for the most part dated within a very short time after the battle, they are entitled to the credit which attaches to evidence which is substantially contemporaneous. He next asserts that McClellan states in his official report that he had in action, at the battle of the Antietam, 87,164 of all arms, and this is true, though it was undoubtedly a careless utterance of McClellan. His comments, however, are unfair, and this must be put in a clear light. He says, for instance: "As a wall of adamant the 14,000 received the shock of the 40,000, and the latter, staggered by the blow, reeled and recoiled in great disorder." This he says in speaking of the fighting on the Confederate left, and then he says: "The disproportion in the centre and on our right was as great as, or even more decided than, on our left." And in summing up he says: "These 35,000 Confederates were the very flower of the Army of Northern Virginia, who, with indomitable courage and inflexible tenacity, wrestled for the mastery in the ratio of one to three of their adversaries." This is calculated to give not only an erroneous but a false impression. The battle was very creditable to the Confederates, but in no just sense, nor in any sense at all, could they be said to wrestle for the mastery in the ratio of one to three. So far is this from being true, that it is highly probable that all the wrestling that was done was done by nearly equal forces, and reasonably certain that there was not an hour, nor a quarter of an hour, when Lee's lines were simultaneously pressed by 15,000 Union soldiers. If this be shown, it will detract from the credit of the Federal commander, but it will dispose of the extravagant claims made for the Confederate soldiers.[1]

Colonel Taylor says explicitly: "Every man was engaged. We had no reserve." The first thing to be done, therefore, is to test the accuracy of his estimate of the Confederate strength. Without undertaking to reject the statements of other Confederate commanders as to their strength, we cannot accept D. R. Jones's statement, which Colonel Taylor adopts, that "on that morning (September 17th), my entire command of six brigades comprised only two thousand four hundred and thirty men." There were twenty-seven regiments in these brigades, they had been on the ground since the morning of the 15th, and so their stragglers had had plenty of time to come up, and were sure to have done so, as the Federal army had been following them all the way from Turner's Gap. General Jones himself says that two of his regiments, the Second and Twentieth Georgia, numbered 403 men. Therefore he must be understood as asserting that twenty-five regiments numbered only 2,027, or about 81 men each. The summer had been a hard one for the Army of Northern Virginia, it is true, but the Confederate

---

[1] One does not look for humor in a stern story like this, but the Charleston Courier account of the battle contains the following statement: "They fought until they were cut to pieces, and then retreated only because they had fired their last round." V. Reb. Rec., 474.

brigades, which General Johnston said averaged 2,500 before Seven Pines, could not have been so nearly annihilated as this would indicate, especially when it is remembered that a very large part of the men who were wounded at Seven Pines on the 31st of May and 1st of June, and in the Seven Days at the end of June, had had time to recover and to rejoin their colors. Moreover, the other Confederate brigades, thirty-three in number, present on the 17th September, averaged over 700 men, without counting their artillery. We conclude, therefore, that D. R. Jones's estimate of his force is at least 2,000 too low.

It is further to be remarked that it is highly probable that Colonel Taylor's figures do not include all the officers present. Thus D. H. Hill speaks of having, by reason of straggling, but 3,000 infantry. As officers are not wont to straggle, infantry probably means muskets. Rodes speaks of having less than eight hundred effective men. This language, again, is more appropriate to musket-bearers than to a total of officers and men. McLaws reports the number of men in his four brigades, and of the officers in three, but says that the number of officers in Cobb's brigade was not known. D. R. Jones says that his entire command of six brigades comprised only 2,430 *men*. McLaws's report shows that in three of his brigades the officers numbered over eleven per cent. of the men. If we suppose that not all, but half of the Confederate officers, in reporting their totals, gave the number of muskets only, and add eleven per cent. for officers to half their infantry as given by Colonel Taylor, it will add 1,500 to their total present in the battle. Moreover, the report of the officer commanding the Hampton Legion of Wofford's brigade, at the Antietam, shows that he does not include in his total present, "skirmishers, scouts, cooks, and men barefooted, unfit for duty." If skir-

68   ANTIETAM AND FREDERICKSBURG.

mishers and scouts alone were habitually omitted, this would make a great difference, as the Confederates were accustomed to use skirmishers very freely.

Finally, many of the reports contain such phrases as so many "at the beginning of the fight," "on the morning of the 17th," "when we went into action." It is probable that this means that their numbers were increased during the action by the arrival of gallant men who had been delayed by fatigue or by being footsore, but who got into the fight as soon as they could. This would be likely to be the case with many of the commands, but particularly with those which arrived on the very day of the battle. Taking all these things into consideration, it seems to be fair to conclude that Lee's total at the battle of the Antietam was not less than forty thousand men, which is certainly not a large total for thirty-nine brigades of infantry and 8,000 cavalry and artillery. It gives a little over eight hundred officers and men to an infantry brigade, and the infantry brigades seem to have averaged something over four regiments to a brigade. One or two had only three, but many had five. Those who believe that the Confederate officers habitually and designedly understated their forces, will think 40,000 a low estimate,[1] but it is offered for the acceptance of those who are contented to accept the result of the best evidence accessible, with entire confidence that it is not too high.[2]

---

[1] Estimate of chief clerk in office of the Adjutant-General of the Army of Northern Virginia, made from recollection, in 1865: Sharpsburg, total effective of all arms, 41,500. Taylor's Four Years, etc., p. 158. Field Return of Army of Northern Virginia, September 22, 1862. Present for duty, 36,187. Ib., p. 165. This return seems to include no cavalry or artillery, and of course excluded the loss at Sharpsburg, and included such stragglers as may have come up.

[2] At about 10 A.M. of the 17th, the writer, having just received a severe wound from a canister shot fired by one of Stuart's batteries, fell into the hands of Colonel (now Senator) Ransom, then commanding the Thirty-fifth North Carolina Regiment of R. Ransom's brigade. As he was taken to the Confederate rear, he

THE ANTIETAM. 69

The next thing to be considered is the number of the Federal troops which the Confederates encountered. It must be carefully borne in mind that this is the precise question. No matter how many men McClellan had, we are to determine how many men he *used*. The credit of Lee may be increased, and the credit of McClellan diminished, by proving that there were on either side of the Antietam, on September 17th, two Federal soldiers to one Confederate, but the question under discussion is different. It is whether "the Army of Northern Virginia . . . . wrestled for the mastery in the ratio of one to three." Fortunately for the patience of those who are intolerant of statistics, the answer is simple and the proof is easy. The answer is that the Army of Northern Virginia did nothing of the kind. It wrestled gallantly, but it did not wrestle in the ratio of one to three, or anything like it. The proof is taken from McClellan's Report.[1] He says:

Our own forces at the battle of Antietam were as follows:

		Men.
First	Corps...................................	14,856
Second	"	18,813
Fifth	" (one division not arrived)............	12,930
Sixth	"	12,300
Ninth	"	13,819
Twelfth	"	10,126
Cavalry Division		4,320
Total in action		87,164

saw a small body of men marching by the flank, and carrying four battle flags. He inquired whether it was the custom in the Confederate army for a regiment to carry more than one set of colors, and was informed that the body of men was a brigade. It is to be remarked, however, that most of the sharp fighting on that part of the ground had then been done, and that the brigade he then saw may well have been two or three times as large three or four hours before.

[1] P. 214. Washington: Government Printing Office. 1864.

This assertion of McClellan's was most unfortunate in form, and most untrue in spirit. It only meant that the morning reports of the several corps showed so many men present for duty, and left entirely untouched the vital questions :

First.—How many officers and men were *with the colors* that day?

Second.—How many officers and men really engaged the enemy?

It is probable that no one who did not actually see service with the Army of the Potomac in 1862 can be brought to believe how enormous was the difference between the "present for duty" of the morning report and the number of actual effectives, whether for drill, dress parade, or battle. The conduct of military affairs was incredibly extravagant in the matter of the use of men who were supposed to be bearing arms. The details for the Quartermaster and Commissary departments were lavish in the extreme, and also for field hospital duty, and what with the added details for headquarter guards and orderlies, for wagoners and company cooks, for officers' servants and pioneers, the number of men which a colonel could take into action was vastly below what his morning report would indicate. Different officers will estimate the proportion differently, no doubt, and probably the varying character of superior officers made the evil greater or less in the various commands; but in well-disciplined regiments in good divisions, commanders were fortunate who could take into action fourfifths of the "present for duty" of the morning report. It is probable that this statement will be considered quite within the truth by most officers who served in the Army of the Potomac in 1862. It was discreditable. It showed poor discipline to some extent, and poor management to a greater, but the fact existed. If one-fifth and no more be taken from McClellan's total, it will reduce it below seventy thousand men. But as it is not probable that assertions of this character will be accepted by the Southern men who are supporters of the one-to-three thesis, it is sufficient to make them and to leave them. They will be accepted by those who know.

Colonel Taylor says: "Every man was engaged. We had no reserve." Again he says: "With consummate skill were they manœuvred and shifted from point to point, as different parts of the line of battle were in turn assailed with greatest impetuosity."[1] This is all true, and there is but one word for the Confederate losses—they were awful. But the question for discussion is, how many Federal soldiers were engaged against them? No matter how many men were looking on, nor even how many were in the fringes of the engagement, the question is how many Federals were *wrestling* with these thirty-five or forty thousand Confederates?

The Federal troops which really fought at the battle of the Antietam were the First, Second, Ninth, and Twelfth Corps. This is proved by the statement of losses. These corps lost over twenty per cent. of their numbers, as given by McClellan, while the Fifth and Sixth Corps and the cavalry division, numbering, according to McClellan, 29,550 men, lost only 596, or almost precisely two per cent.; in other words, they were hardly used at all. If due allowance be made for the almost total absence from the actual fighting of nearly all these commands, and any allowance be made for the notorious difference in McClellan's army between morning report totals and effectives in action, it will appear that the Federals engaged cannot have outnumbered the Confederates in more

---

[1] Four Years with General Lee, pp. 69, 73.

than the proportion of three to two, and probably did not outnumber them so much. This is by no means large odds, when the attacking force has to deal with a force occupying a strong defensive position, as the Confederates confessedly did, and one where the ground was admirably adapted for the safe and secret and rapid transfer of their troops from a less pressed to a more pressed portion of their line. Whatever difference there may be about details, however severe may be the condemnation of McClellan for not fighting his army more thoroughly as well as more simultaneously, no candid person can examine the figures without coming to the conclusion that the one-to-three theory is purely visionary, and that the disproportion fell below two to three.[1]

The night before the battle passed quietly, except for some alarms on Hooker's front, and most of the men in both armies probably got a good sleep. The morning broke gray and misty, but the mists disappeared early, and the weather for the rest of the day was perfect. As a great battle cannot be described in detail except at immense length, and even then must be described imperfectly, there seems to be no better plan than to state the parts into which a particular action is divisible, and then to give reasonable development to the description of those parts. Of the battle of the Antietam it may be said that it began with the attack made by the First Corps under Hooker upon the Confederate left. The next stage was the advance of the Twelfth Corps under Mansfield to the support of Hooker. The next was the advance of the Second Corps, under Sumner, and this again must be divided into three parts, as Sumner's three divisions went into action successively, both in time and place. The division that first became engaged was furthest to the Federal right, the next was to the left, and the last still farther to the left. The fourth stage was the slight

---

[1] See note p. 210.

THE ANTIETAM.   73

use of a few troops from the centre, mostly Franklin's, made as late as one o'clock or thereabouts, and the fifth and last was the fighting of the Ninth Corps on the extreme right of the Confederate position.

It will be remembered that McClellan had virtually told Lee where he proposed to attack. That the notice given by him was comprehended by the enemy is shown by the language of Colonel Wofford, commanding a brigade in Hood's division, who says: "It was now evident that the enemy had effected a crossing entirely to our left, and that he would make the attack on that wing early in the morning, moving his forces over and placing them in position during the night." Colonel Wofford's judgment was correct in the main, although he gave McClellan credit in advance for carrying out his own plan more thoroughly than he did.[1] At a very early hour the skirmishers of the Pennsylvania Reserves, Meade's division of the First Corps, advanced, and their advance was followed by that of the whole corps—Meade's division in the centre, Doubleday's on its right, and Ricketts's on its left. The advance was impetuous, and the Confederate resistance was obstinate. The Federal advance was aided by the fire of the batteries posted by McClellan on the east side of the Antietam, which, Jackson says, enfiladed his line, and proved severe and damaging, and it received some assistance from the batteries of the corps, but they do not seem to have been used with remarkable skill or dash. Some of the guns were very roughly handled by Confederates who crept around through the corn and behind rises of ground, and the chief of artillery of one of the Federal divisions

---

[1] See also the Report of Colonel S. D. Lee, commanding artillery battalion, who says: "It was now certain that the enemy would attack us in force on our left at daylight, compelling us to change our line, and give him an opportunity to use his long range batteries across the Antietam, enfilading our new position."

seems to have wanted judgment as well as audacity. The batteries most mentioned were I, of the First New York Artillery; B, of the Fourth Artillery; D, of the Rhode Island Artillery; a battery of the First New Hampshire Artillery; F, of the First Pennsylvania, and the Independent Pennsylvania Battery. It was upon Jackson that the blow fell, and he met it with his front line, composed of the brigades of Jones and Winder, of the Stonewall division, and those of Lawton and Trimble, and probably Hays, of Ewell's division. He had also not less than six batteries in action, and more or less aid from Stuart, whose command consisted of cavalry and horse artillery,[1] from S. D. Lee's guns, from Hood and D. H. Hill, and from "a brigade of fresh troops," which Early says came up to the support of Lawton and Hays, but soon fell back. It is impossible to tell what number of troops on each side was engaged in this opening struggle, the more so that Jackson himself says that "fresh troops from time to time relieved the enemy's ranks," which seems to indicate that Hooker's men were not all used at once. As far as can be made out from the various reports, which are singularly wanting on both sides in clear topographical indications, the fighting began not far from the western edge of the East Woods, and resulted, after very severe losses on both sides, in the gradual withdrawal of the Confederates to the West Woods. The story might be told with far greater fulness and completeness, but for the defective character of the reports in the particular to which allusion has been made. They are very numerous, and many of them are not short, but they hardly ever tell to what point of the compass the faces of the troops were turned,

---

[1] Colonel Hoffman, commanding the second brigade of the first division of the First Corps, saw a large force of cavalry evidently attempting to attack in flank. Lieutenant Woodruff, commanding Battery I, First Artillery, also speaks of the enemy's using cavalry near his position.

and the indefinite article is constantly used. A lane, a road, a fence, a wall, a house, a corn-field, a piece of woods, such are the constantly recurring phrases which constantly baffle and disappoint the curious student.

To go a little more into detail. Hooker's command seems to have passed the night of the 16th about a mile and a half north of Sharpsburg, and in the neighborhood of the point on the Hagerstown pike where the Williamsport road branches off. A signal station was established that night, close to the Hagerstown pike, and near Hooker's headquarters. Hooker's forces seem to have been vastly less than the 14,856 accorded to him in McClellan's Report. He had ten brigades. Ricketts, who commanded his Second Division, comprising three of them, says he took into action 3,158 men. Phelps, who commanded the First Brigade of the First Division, says he had 425 men. If we take the average strength of these four brigades, and compute the strength of the corps from it, Hooker's infantry will fall below nine thousand men. Doubleday's division was formed astride of the turnpike; Gibbon's brigade, supported by Patrick's, advanced along the west side of the Hagerstown pike, while Hoffman's right just reached the pike. Gibbon's front line contained the Second and Sixth Wisconsin; but the resistance he encountered as he advanced caused him to bring forward around his right the Seventh Wisconsin and the Nineteenth Indiana, which obtained to some extent a flank fire along his front. Patrick supported him, and Phelps formed up on his left, and the line was continued to the left by Hoffman. Meade formed Hooker's centre, and Ricketts his left. The Federal troops gained some ground, and as they advanced Hooker's line seems to have gradually advanced its left, until it came nearer to being parallel to the pike than at right angles to it. His right gained ground but little, but gradually his left and centre drove the Confederates into the West Woods, of which Ricketts even claims to have gained the edge. Ricketts advanced with his Third brigade in the centre, and the First and Second in echelon to the rear, to the right and left respectively. The advance had been stubbornly contested throughout, but when the command approached the West Woods, a more terrible struggle took place. The Confederates appear to have then brought into action the whole of Jackson's two divisions, with the exception of Early's brigade, and to have used Stuart's cavalry and artillery both. The two lines almost tore each other to pieces. Ricketts lost a third of his division, having 153 killed and 898 wounded. Phelps's brigade lost about forty-four per cent. Gibbon's brigade lost 380 men. On the Confederate side the carnage was even more awful. General Starke, commanding the Stonewall division, and Colonel Douglas, commanding Lawton's brigade, were killed. General Lawton, commanding Ewell's division, and Colonel Walker, commanding a brigade, were severely wounded. More than half of the brigades of Lawton and Hays were either killed or wounded, and more than a third of Trimble's, and all the regimental commanders in these brigades, except two, were killed or wounded.[1] No better evidence of the exhaustion of both sides need be given than Jackson's own statement: "Jackson's division and the brigades of Lawton, Hays, and Trimble retired to the rear, and Hood, of Longstreet's command, again took the position from which he had before been relieved."[2] Hood had but two brigades, and Jackson's two divisions and Hooker's three must have been nearly annihilated, if Hood could take the place of the one and make

---

[1] A. N. Va., ii., 103.   [2] Ibid.

head against the other. If Jackson's and Hooker's had been the only forces present, there would have been a lull from necessity, and probably an end of the battle, but D. H. Hill, with five brigades, was close to Jackson's right, McLaws, with four, was coming up in his rear, and several other Confederate brigades were near or hastening toward his part of the field, while Mansfield's Twelfth Corps was near Hooker. If troops moved as chessmen are moved, if corps and divisions went into action as complete wholes, the story of a battle could be told with more precision, but it is not only not so, but as far as possible from being so. The combinations of a battle-field are almost as varying, and far less distinctly visible and separable than those of a kaleidoscope. A supporting force sends forward a regiment, or a battery, or a brigade, or a division, or sends detachments to various points to fill gaps and strengthen parts of the line which are especially threatened, or it advances as a whole, but even in the last case the accidents of the ground, the superior discipline or enthusiasm or handling of the men, or the more or less controlling fire of the enemy, make the advance of a large body irregular. General Patrick, commanding the Third Brigade of the First Division of Hooker's corps, says that the Twelfth Corps came in in succession and at considerable intervals. It is probably not known, and not knowable, at what hour or at what point the First Corps received its first assistance from the Twelfth.

It has already been stated that Mansfield's Twelfth Corps passed the latter part of the night of the 16th September about a mile in rear of Hooker. There are various statements as to the time when Mansfield was ordered forward, but it is quite clear that his whole corps was engaged by, if not before, 7.30 A.M. Before he reached Hooker's position he received information that Hooker's reserves were all engaged, and that he was hard pressed. He himself was killed during the deployment of his corps, while examining the ground in front. General Williams succeeded to the command. There were in the Twelfth Corps two divisions. Of the first, Crawford now took command. He had the brigades of Knipe and Gordon. Greene commanded the second division, composed of the brigades of Tyndale, Stainrook, and Goodrich. The reports of the Twelfth Corps division and brigade commanders make it plain that it went into action with only about seven thousand men, instead of the ten thousand odd with which McClellan credits it.[1] Very early in the advance, one brigade of Greene's division was sent to the right to Doubleday. In the deployment, the First Division was to the right and front, with Knipe's brigade on the right and Gordon's on the left. Greene's division was on the left of the First Division. The attack was opened by Knapp's, Cothran's, and Hampton's batteries. The divisions moved together, but the First Division was somewhat earlier in getting into action. As the First Division advanced, it found Hooker's men badly cut up and slowly retreating from the historic cornfield, which lay between the pike and the East Woods, and the Confederates occupying almost all the cornfield. There are good grounds for believing that the Twelfth Corps received no assistance,

---

[1] Greene says his three brigades numbered 2,504. Gordon had 2,210. Williams says his loss of 1,744 was twenty-five per cent. of his total. This would leave 2,262 for Crawford's brigade, commanded by Knipe. The regiments of this corps varied much in size, as appears from the Reports. The Sixty-sixth Ohio took in 120; Third Maryland, 148; One Hundred and Eleventh Pennsylvania, Sixtieth New York, and Seventy-eighth New York, each less than 250; Third Delaware, 126; while the Twenty-seventh Indiana took in 443 rank and file. Knipe's and Gordon's brigades were made very large by the presence in them of five perfectly new regiments, the Thirteenth New Jersey, the One Hundred and Seventh New York, and the One Hundred and Twenty-fourth, One Hundred and Twenty-fifth, and One Hundred and Twenty-eighth Pennsylvania.

or next to none, from the First Corps. The admirable troops of Gordon's brigade, which contained the Second Massachusetts, Third Wisconsin, and Twenty-seventh Indiana, succeeded in clearing the cornfield, apparently with some aid from Greene's men, who would seem to have obtained an enfilading fire along their front. Knipe's brigade was less successful, but Greene did well on the left. He seems to have found some of the enemy so far to the east as the East Woods, though this is not easy to believe, but whatever force he encountered he succeeded in driving back, and entering open ground, partly covered with corn, and moving to his left and front, he overcame all opposition and entered the woods near the Dunker Church at about eight o'clock. There is no doubt that the fighting of this second stage of the battle was between the Federal Twelfth Corps and the remains of the First Corps, and Hood's Confederate division and such other troops as could then be got together on their left and right. The Federal pressure had caused all of the Confederate line which was to the left of D. H. Hill to fight nearly or quite at right angles to his line. It may have been at this time and place that the disparity of numbers was greatest. The usual difficulty of determining just what troops are engaged at a particular time is illustrated by the contradiction between Hood and Jackson. Jackson, as has been stated, speaks of Hood's going to the front when his own division and the three brigades of Ewell's division retired to the rear. Hood, on the other hand, says:[1] "At six o'clock I received notice from Lawton that he would require all the assistance I could give him. A few minutes after, a member of his staff reported to me that he was wounded, and wished me to come forward as soon as possi-

---

[1] A. N. Va., ii., 212.

ble. Being in readiness, I at once marched out on the field, in line of battle, and soon became engaged with an immense force of the enemy, consisting of not less than two corps of their army." If Hood is right—and he is corroborated by his brigade commander, Wofford, who says: "Our brigade was moved forward at sunrise to the support of General Lawton,"—Jackson met Hooker with over two thousand men more than he has been credited with, and the fifteen brigades of the First and Twelfth Corps encountered the divisions of Jackson, Ewell,[1] and Hood, with such aid as Stuart from their left and D. H. Hill[2] from their right could give them. It also appears that G. T. Anderson's brigade of D. R. Jones's division was there.[3]

The general result of the second stage of the battle seems to have been that by nine A.M. the Federals held parts of a line extending from the woods near Miller's house on their right to the Dunker Church on the left, though Knipe on the extreme right does not seem to have had a firm hold on his ground. The Federals had gained a good deal of ground, but they were about fought out, and if they could hold what they had gained, it was probably the utmost they could do, especially as their leaders had failed to see and appreciate the importance of seizing and holding a height to the west of where Hooker's right had rested, the possession of which would have enabled them to take in flank and partly in reverse the whole of the wooded and rocky ground which they had thus far failed to carry, and which was to remain in possession of the enemy till the close of the battle.

We have said that the Twelfth Corps held parts of a line extending from the neighborhood of Miller's house to the Dunker Church. The statement requires development. The

---

[1] Early's brigade was absent, but another unnamed brigade was present.
[2] A. N. Va., ii., 115. [3] Ibid., 318.

THE ANTIETAM.   81

truth is that the position of the Twelfth Corps when Sumner began to arrive was very peculiar. The First Division was established well to the north of the Dunker Church, perhaps half a mile from it, and it, or much of it, was facing south. The Second Division had effected a lodgment in the woods about the Dunker Church, and it, or much of it, was facing north or northwest. There were practically no troops at all on the ground over which Sedgwick presently advanced with the front of a deployed brigade, or still further to the north, for the statements are positive that there was a stiff post and rail fence on both sides of the pike in the part of the field where Crawford's men were, and it is certain that all or most of Sedgwick's men encountered no such obstacle. At somewhere about nine o'clock, the Twelfth Corps seems to have about lost all aggressive force. Knipe's brigade on the extreme right was retiring, part of Gordon's brigade was preparing to advance, and Greene's division, with a mere handful left from Ricketts's, was hanging on to the corner of the woods about the Dunker Church, and pouring a heavy fire upon the right and rear of Hood's right brigade. At this time the advance of the Second Corps was announced.

On September 17th, Sumner's Corps, the Second, comprised three divisions. The First, under Richardson, contained three brigades, commanded by Meagher, Caldwell, and J. R. Brooke; the Second, under Sedgwick, contained three brigades, commanded by Gorman, Howard, and Dana; the Third, under French, contained three brigades, commanded by Kimball, Morris, and Weber. The corps contained some poor but many very excellent soldiers. The hard fate which its Second Division met in this battle may be an excuse for stating that up to May 10, 1864, the Second Corps never lost a gun nor a color, and that it was then and had long been the only corps in the army which could make that proud claim. General Sumner received orders on the 16th to hold his corps in readiness to march an hour before daylight, to support Hooker, but his orders to march were not received till 7.20 A. M. on the 17th. He put Sedgwick in motion immediately, and French followed Sedgwick, but Richardson was not moved till an hour later, when the General commanding ordered him to move in the same direction. It is probable that this delay was caused by the need of having Morell occupy the ground which he was about to vacate. It would seem that this simple operation should have been attended to earlier, but, whatever the cause may have been, Richardson was delayed. The marching and fighting of the three divisions of the Second Corps were so distinct that they must be described separately.

The three brigades of Sedgwick's division crossed the stream at the same ford at which the First and Twelfth Corps had crossed it, and, moving by the flank in three columns, entered the East Woods. These were a grove of noble trees, almost entirely clear of underbrush. There were sorry sights to be seen in them, but the worst sight of all was the liberal supply of unwounded men helping wounded men to the rear. When good Samaritans so abound, it is a strong indication that the discipline of the troops in front is not good, and that the battle is not going so as to encourage the half-hearted. The brigades entered these woods from the south, and marched northward, and then were faced to the left, and thus formed a column of three deployed brigades, Gorman's leading, next Dana's, next Burns's, commanded that day by Howard. The column was now facing west, parallel to the Hagerstown pike, and separated from it by the famous cornfield. The corn was very high and very strong. There was a short halt while a fence which formed

THE ANTIETAM. 83

the eastern boundary of the cornfield was thrown down. Then the column marched straight forward, through the corn, and into the open ground beyond. Few troops were in sight. So far as the men of Sedgwick's division could see, they were to have the fighting all to themselves. As they advanced, Crawford's division retired, so Crawford says, but Knipe, of his division, claims to have advanced with Sedgwick. If he did, Sedgwick's men did not know it. Accidents of the ground hid from their view such of Greene's and Ricketts's men as remained at the left front. So far as they could see, their advance, at least from the pike, was made all alone. Williams himself reports that soon after news of Sumner's advance was received, the firing on both sides wholly ceased.

General Sumner rode forward gallantly with his advance. He found Hooker wounded, and his corps not only repulsed, but gone,—routed, and dispersed. He says himself:[1] "I saw nothing of his corps at all as I was advancing with my command on the field. There were some troops lying down on the left, which I took to belong to Mansfield's command. . . . General Hooker's corps was dispersed. There is no question about that. I sent one of my own staff officers to find where they were, and General Ricketts, the only officer we could find, said that he could not raise three hundred men of the corps."

Sedgwick's division emerged from the cornfield into the open ground near the pike, and swept steadily forward. There were no fences at the part of the pike where they crossed it to delay them. Their march was rapid, and nearly directly west. There was very little distance between the lines. The recollections of the survivors range from fifty

---

[1] C. C. W., i., 368.

feet to thirty paces. Not a regiment was in column—there was absolutely no preparation for facing to the right or left in case either of their exposed flanks should be attacked. The total disregard of all ordinary military precaution in their swift and solitary advance was so manifest that it was observed and criticised as the devoted band moved on. A single regiment in column on both flanks of the rear brigade might have been worth hundreds of men a few minutes later, might indeed have changed the results of the battle. As the column pressed forward into the space between the pike and the West Woods, its left just reaching the Dunker Church, it came under sharp artillery fire, and met with some loss. The lines were so near together that the projectile that went over the heads of the first line was likely to find its billet in the second or third. The swift shot were plainly seen as they came flying toward us. They came from Stuart's unseen guns, planted beyond the woods on or near the high ground which the Federal troops ought to have occupied. As the division entered the West Woods, it passed out of fire, and it moved safely through them to their western edge. There there was a fence, and, bordering it on the outside, a common wood road. The brigade of Gorman, followed by that of Dana, climbed this fence, and then their lines were halted. For some cause unknown, the left of the two brigades almost touched, while the line of Gorman's brigade diverged from the line of Dana's, so that there was a long interval from the right of the former to the right of the latter. It is doubtful whether the third line even entered the West Woods. If they did, they did not stay there long. There was a little, and only a little, musketry firing while the troops were in this position, but the Confederate guns to the right front of Sedgwick's position were active and efficient, firing now canister.

As Sedgwick's troops have now been led to the furthest point of their advance, which was also the furthest point reached by any Federal troops in the right attack, it is time to say a word about the ground, and about the Confederate troops which were collected to oppose them, but it is to be remembered that Sedgwick was quite alone. No Federal troops were on his right or left, nor near his rear. Hooker's corps was non-existent. The Twelfth Corps was all of it weary, and much of it withdrawn to a considerable distance, and French had not come up.

There runs through the West Woods to the Dunker Church a little wood road, which leaves the open ground to the west of the West Woods, not far from where Sedgwick's left rested. In these woods, and especially to the left of the ground over which Sedgwick passed, there were many inequalities of surface, and many ledges of limestone which cropped out, and thus excellent cover was afforded to troops on the left of the Federals, and such of their opponents as might be in the little road were so concealed that nothing but their bayonets revealed their presence. Why French was so far from Sedgwick is not explained, but, as will presently appear, he first engaged the enemy in the vicinity of Rullet's house, about half a mile east of the Dunker Church, and considerably more than that from the ground where Sedgwick's three brigades were halted.

It seems to be certain that Law's and Wofford's brigades had been "almost annihilated," as Wofford says, by their fight with the First and Twelfth Corps, and that they were withdrawn by General Hood just before Sedgwick reached them. This must have been at or shortly after nine o'clock, and accounts, in part at least, for the cessation of firing which Williams observed, and the comparative silence which accompanied Sedgwick's advance. General Jackson was the ranking officer on the Confederate left. He had sent word to Early, who had been sent with his brigade to support Stuart, to return and take command of Ewell's division, in place of Lawton, disabled. Early returned, with all of his brigade but one very small regiment, at just this time, and found near the Dunker Church a portion of Jackson's division, which formed on his left. Presently Confederate reinforcements began to arrive from their right, as "another heavy column of Federal troops (*i.e.*, Sedgwick's division) was seen moving across the plateau on his left flank." The reinforcements consisted of Semmes's, Anderson's, Barksdale's, Armistead's, Kershaw's, Manning's, Cobb's, and Ransom's brigades, some of which had been hurried across from the Confederate right.

Early's line was formed perpendicular to the Hagerstown road, and his troops were concealed and protected by the rise in the ground. It is altogether probable that many of them were in the little wood road which has been mentioned. The approach of a Federal battery, which might, if Early's line had been seen, have raked his flank and rear, caused him to throw back his right flank quietly under cover of the woods, so as not to have his rear exposed in the event of his presence being discovered, and threatening movements of the Federal infantry caused him to move his own brigade by the right flank, while he directed Colonel Grigsby, who commanded what was left of Jackson's division, to move his command back in line so as to present front to the enemy. The reinforcements, as they came up, formed line facing the west face of the West Woods, and filled the wood road on Sedgwick's left. Sumner had marched his second division into an ambush. There were some ten Confederate brigades on his front and flank and working rapidly round the rear of his three brigades. The result was not doubtful. His fine division, containing such sterling regiments as the First Minnesota and the Fifteenth, Nineteenth, and Twentieth Massachusetts, was at the mercy of their enemy. The fire came upon them from front and flank and presently from the rear. Change of front was impossible. The only fire delivered by the Twentieth Massachusetts regiment of the second line was delivered faced by the rear rank. In less time than it takes to tell it, the ground was strewn with the bodies of the dead and wounded, while the unwounded were moving off rapidly to the north. So completely did the enemy circle round them that a strong body of Confederates marched straight up northward through the open fields between the West Woods and the Hagerstown pike. Nearly two thousand men were disabled in a moment.

The third line, the Philadelphia brigade, so called, was the first to go. Sumner tried to face it about preparatory to a change of front, but, under the fire from its left, it moved off in a body to the right in spite of all efforts to restrain it. The first and second lines held on a little longer, but their left soon crumbled away, and then the whole of the two brigades moved off to their right, where a new line was presently formed. Federal batteries proved very serviceable in checking the Confederates at this juncture. The new line was formed, facing south, at no very great distance northward of the point where the right of the lines had rested. As disaster fell upon Sedgwick, Williams was ordered by Sumner to send forward all of his command immediately available. He sent forward Gordon. Gordon advanced, but it was too late. The troops for whom his support was intended were no longer in position. He reached the fence by the turnpike, and suffered heavy loss, but was forced to retire after a stubborn contest. Greene, at about the same time, reformed his line, refused his right, sent forward skirmishers, and sent to his corps commander for aid. None coming, he eventually retired from or was forced out of his advanced position, though this did not happen till much later in the day.

Thus, by about ten o'clock, the successes of the morning were lost. Our lines had been withdrawn almost altogether to the east of the turnpike, though we had more or less of a lodgment near the Dunker Church, and some of Sedgwick's men were west of the turnpike in the neighborhood of the Miller house, or nearly as far north. Two corps and one division of the Federal army had been so roughly handled that but small account could be made of them in estimating the available force remaining. Most of these troops had damaged the enemy in good proportion to the damage they had themselves received, but there was no such consolation for Sedgwick's men. Their cruel losses were entirely uncompensated. There is no reason for believing that they had inflicted any appreciable injury upon the enemy. The Fifteenth and the Twentieth Massachusetts had been at Ball's Bluff, but their fate at Sharpsburg was harder yet.

What General Sumner may have expected or even hoped to accomplish by his rash advance, it is difficult to conjecture. It is impossible that he can have been ignorant that French had not come up upon his left. His old cavalry training may possibly have planted in his mind some notions as to charging and cutting one's way out, and he may have had a shadowy idea that he could with infantry as well not only charge but cut his way out, should they chance to be surrounded. Indeed there is in his testimony before the Committee on the Conduct of the War, given February 18, 1863, a very significant statement: "My intention at the time was," he says, "to have proceeded entirely on by their left and moved down, bringing them right in front of Burnside, Franklin, and Porter." With French properly closed up, so as to take care of his flank and rear, and Sedgwick properly formed, such an enterprise might have had some chance of success against an army weakened by the long and hard struggle against Hooker and Williams, but with French at a distance, and Sedgwick formed as he was, the attempt was madness. There is nothing more helpless than a column of long lines with short intervals between them, if they have anything to do other than to press straight forward with no thought of anything but the enemy before them. They cannot take care of their own flanks, and if they are attacked there, disaster is certain.

The jubilant assertions of the Confederate officers in regard to their repulse of Sedgwick's division are not more than the facts warrant. They did "drive the enemy before them in magnificent style," they did "sweep the woods with perfect ease," they did "inflict great loss on the enemy," they did drive them "not only through the woods, but (some of them, at any rate) over a field in front of the woods and over two high fences beyond, and into another body of woods (i.e., the East Woods) over half a mile distant from the commencement of the fight." But it must not be forgotten that it was almost as easy to drive Sedgwick's men, in the unfortunate position in which they found themselves, as to drive sheep, and that, besides the immense advantages which Sumner's blunder gave the Confederates, they probably considerably outnumbered the forces they encountered. As well as can be made out from the Confederate reports, they must have used nearly ten thousand men against Sedgwick's division and what was left of the First and Twelfth Corps, in this vigorous onset.[1] Sedgwick's division may be said, from the

---

[1] Early's brigade, about 1,000; remains of Jackson's division, under Grigsby and Stafford, 600 (conjectured); McLaws's four brigades, Semmes, Barksdale,

best information accessible, to have gone into action not over five thousand strong, and it was absolutely alone from the time it crossed the Hagerstown pike, and the troops that helped to check the pursuing Confederates were not numerous, and were not engaged till the repulse was complete.

General McClellan reports the loss of Sedgwick's division as 355 killed, 1,579 wounded, and 321 missing, a ghastly total of 2,255. The Twelfth Corps lost 1,744, Greene's division losing 651, Gordon's brigade 649, and Crawford's (commanded by Knipe), 427; being one in four of all of the division who were present. The Third Wisconsin, of Gordon's brigade, lost very nearly sixty per cent.

When the Confederates fell back, after their sharp pursuit of the retreating Federals, for want of immediate support, their line was formed in the West Woods, with the brigades of Ransom, Armistead, Early, Barksdale, Kershaw, and Cobb, with Semmes in reserve. Read's and Carleton's batteries were with them, but they were so cut up by the Federal artillery that they were ordered back. The fire of the Federal artillery upon this part of the Confederate line was terrific, but almost harmless, because of the perfect shelter which the ground afforded to infantry. The Confederate force so assembled was judged to be too weak to warrant a second advance.

Under orders from McClellan, Franklin, commanding as before the Sixth Corps and Couch's division of the Fourth Corps, at half-past five on the morning of the 17th, put Couch in motion for Maryland Heights, and moved with his

---

Kershaw, Cobb, 3,000; Anderson's brigade, 600; Walker's two brigades, 3,200; co-operation from Stuart and D. H. Hill (conjectured), 1,600. This leaves out Armistead, whose brigade was one of six numbering "some" three or four thousand.

own corps from Pleasant Valley toward the battle-field. Smith's division of the Sixth Corps led the column, followed by Slocum with the other division. Smith came near the field before 10 A.M., and at first took position in a wood on the left of the stone bridge, but was presently ordered to the right, to the support of Sumner, who was then fiercely engaged and hard pressed by the enemy, that is to say, at about the time when Sedgwick's division gave way. The leading brigade, under Hancock, moved rapidly forward to support two of Sumner's batteries, which the Confederate skirmishers had approached closely. He formed a line of guns and infantry, with Cowan's battery of three-inch guns on the right, Frank's twelve-pounders in the centre, and Cothran's rifled guns on the left. He placed the Forty-ninth Pennsylvania on the right of Cowan, the Forty-third New York and a part of the One Hundred and Thirty-seventh Pennsylvania between Cowan and Frank, and the Sixth Maine and the Fifth Wisconsin between Frank and Cothran. His line was parallel to the line of woods in front, and within canister distance. The enemy placed two batteries opposite him and in front of the woods, and opened fire. He obtained from Sumner the Twentieth Massachusetts of Sedgwick's division to place in the woods on the extreme right of his line. With the fire of his guns and his infantry he drove away the threatening skirmishers, and silenced the Confederate batteries. He took possession of some buildings and fences in his front, and there his brigade remained. His loss was very slight. The enemy in his front was controlled in some measure by the presence and action on his left of the Third (Irwin's) Brigade of Smith's division.

Brooks, with Smith's Second Brigade, went first to Sumner's right, but was presently sent to French, and his experiences may better be told in connection with those of

French's division. Irwin's Brigade, the Third of Smith's division, was placed by Smith on the left of Hancock, and it was on his left that Brooks came up when he was sent to French. The clearness of the narrative will be promoted by telling first the story of French's advance, and then that of what Brooks and Irwin did when they came up to his aid.

General French commanded the Third Division of the Second Corps, composed of the brigades of Kimball, Morris, and Weber. Morris's troops were new men, and under fire for the first time. The division followed Sedgwick's division across the ford, immediately in its rear. It marched about a mile from the ford, then faced to the left, and moved in three lines toward the enemy, Weber's brigade in front, next Morris's, and then Kimball's. It advanced steadily under a fire of artillery, drove in the Confederate skirmishers, and encountered their infantry in some force at the group of houses on Rullet's farm. From their position about these houses, Weber's brigade gallantly drove the enemy. Rullet's house is about half a mile from the Dunker Church, and a glance at the map will show that troops which marched toward that house from the ford would take quite a different route from that followed by troops which marched from the same ford through the East Woods to the West Woods. Why French so separated himself from Sedgwick does not appear. Whether it was by accident or under orders, it proved a most unfortunate divergence.

D. H. Hill's five Confederate brigades formed the left centre of the Confederate line, between (and in front of) Sharpsburg on the south and the Dunker Church on the north. They had not been mere spectators of the morning fighting, as so many of the Southern reports would lead one to suppose. On the contrary, Ripley's brigade, the left brigade of D. H. Hill's command, was ordered at about 8

THE ANTIETAM.   93

A.M. to close in to its left and advance. It became engaged almost as far north as the southern edge of the East Woods, between that line and the burning buildings. Colquitt's brigade went into the same fight on the right of Ripley. He says this was at about 7 A.M., and that Ripley was engaged when his brigade entered the fight. He probably puts the hour too early. Garland's brigade, under McRae, formed on the right of Colquitt, but its severe losses at South Mountain, where its commander was killed, had demoralized it, and one of its captains in the midst of the fighting cried out, "They are flanking us," and thereupon a general panic ensued and the troops left the field in confusion. At about 9 A.M., Rodes was ordered to move to the left and front, to assist Ripley, Colquitt, and McRae. He says that he had hardly begun the movement before he saw that Colquitt and McRae had met with a reverse, and that the best thing he could do, for them and for all parties, would be to form a line in rear of them and endeavor to rally them before attacking or being attacked. General Hill entertained the same view, and a line was formed in the hollow of an old and narrow road, just beyond an orchard, and east of the Hagerstown road. Some of Colquitt's men formed on Rodes's left, bringing the line to the road,[1] and G. B. Anderson's brigade formed on his right. The men busily improved their position by piling rails along their front. While they were so employed, the Federals deployed in their front "in three beautiful lines," Rodes says, "all vastly outstretching ours, and commenced to advance steadily," "with all the precision of a parade day," Hill says.

---

[1] Rodes says that "a small portion" of Colquitt's brigade occupied about one hundred and fifty yards. Every military man knows that this would require upward of four hundred men in the usual two rank formation. If "a small portion" of a brigade exceeded four hundred after a severe repulse, the whole brigade before the repulse was probably more than one-fifth of three thousand.

Both Rodes and Hill lament their almost total want of artillery, but it does not seem to occur to Hill to explain where the eighty-six guns had gone which he says he had on the morning of the 17th.

These troops, this small force in the sunken road, were some of the troops which resisted the advance of French, when he moved forward in the three beautiful lines which Rodes and Hill saw. It is probable that they were not alone there; indeed D. H. Hill himself speaks of a certain Walker's brigade as uniting with Ripley's, and forming near the old road and to his left of it. It is not easy to identify the brigade spoken of as Walker's. It certainly was not one of Hill's, and may possibly have been the brigade of Walker's division formerly commanded by himself, and this day first by Manning and then by Hall.[1] The too common practice of Confederate generals of declaring that the fighting done by many was done by few, makes much patient study necessary to determine what troops they used at a particular time and place.

While Weber, of French's division (the Third) of the Second Corps, was hotly engaged with the enemy near Rullet's house, French received an order from Sumner to push on with vigor to make a diversion in favor of the attack on the right. A part of the troops which had turned Sedgwick's left moved forward, and brought a strong pressure to bear on Weber. Under the orders received by French from Sumner, Kimball's brigade hastened to the front, leaving Morris's new troops to act as a reserve, and formed up on the left of Weber. There is no doubt that French's division did some very severe fighting, and met and repulsed succes-

---

[1] Joseph Walker commanded Jenkins's brigade of D. R. Jones's division in the Antietam fight. He was with Kemper and Drayton, south of the town, in the afternoon. He may possibly have been with D. H. Hill for a while.

sive attacks on its left, front, and right, but it did not succeed in driving the Confederates out of the old road. The smartest push made by the Confederates was on Kimball's left, and Kimball's losses were very heavy, amounting to about seven hundred out of about fourteen hundred in three of his regiments, the Eighth Ohio, One Hundred and Thirty-second Pennsylvania, and the Fourteenth Indiana. The three new regiments of Morris' brigade lost 529. The whole division had 1,614 men killed and wounded, besides 203 missing. Their gallant fighting did not accomplish much, as Federal and Confederate accounts agree that they finally took position behind the crest of a hill which looked down upon the old road. The Confederates had great advantages of position, as the old road and the rails piled before it placed them, as it were, in a fort, and they got some guns into a place from which they were able to partially enfilade the Federal line.

It has already been said that when Smith's division (the Second) of the Sixth Corps came on the ground, the Third Brigade, under Irwin, was sent to the left of Hancock's brigade of the same corps. This was at about 10 A.M. Brooks, commanding the Second Brigade of the same division, was sent to the left of Irwin and to the right of French's division. Brooks found the enemy before him checked, and seems to have had little to do, but Irwin was instantly ordered into action by his division commander. Irwin had some success at first, but presently two of his regiments, the Thirty-third and Seventy-seventh New York, got into serious trouble, and were obliged to face by the rear rank, and suffered heavily before they got out. The advance of this brigade carried them forward so far that they came abreast of the Dunker Church. It is quite possible that, if Irwin's advance had been supported, a decisive advantage might have been gained. That it was not, appears to have been owing to the fact that its division commander, Smith, as soon as Irwin's brigade was established in its position, found, on sending back for Brooks's brigade to act as a support, that it had been, "without his knowledge or consent, ordered away." General Smith complains bitterly and with great force of this proceeding, saying: "It is not the first or the second time during a battle that my command has been dispersed by orders from an officer superior in rank to the general commanding this corps, and I must assert that I have never known any good to arise from such a method of fighting a battle, and think the contrary rule should be adopted, of keeping commands intact." It is probable that it was at about the time at which French's men and some of Smith's were withdrawn from the points of their extreme advance, and formed in the rear of crests, that the remnants of Rickett's division of the First Corps and of Greene's division of the Twelfth Corps gave up their hold of the woods about the Dunker Church, if, indeed, they were there so long. Ricketts almost certainly retired earlier, but Greene's positive assertion that he did not retire till he was driven away, at about 1.30 P.M., is entitled to respect, though it is a hard saying.

The usual difficulty of determining with what troops the Confederates met a given attack is rather greater than usual in the matter of French's attack. There is very little definite information accessible. Something has already been said on this point. D. H. Hill writes as if there were only a few men in and near the old road when French advanced, but he says, and seems to say that it was before his fight ended, that R. H. Anderson reported to him "with some three or four thousand men as reinforcements to his command." As language is commonly used, this would imply that his own command was considerably in excess of three or four thousand, and yet he declares that in the morning he had but three thousand infantry, and that in the early fighting three of his five brigades were broken and much demoralized. However this may be, Anderson's men were directed to form behind Hill's, and must have been under fire, whether engaged or not, for Anderson himself was presently wounded, and the command devolved on Pryor, one of his brigade commanders.

One of the most puzzling questions which the battle of the Antietam presents to the student is the question just where the divisions of French and Richardson fought. General McClellan and those who have followed him write so as to produce the impression that the "sunken road" where French found the enemy posted, and the cornfield in rear of it, where, he says, were also strong bodies of the enemy, were the same sunken road and cornfield where Richardson's division found the enemy posted. This is not the case, though it has a basis of truth. Richardson confessedly went in on the left of French, and it was French's left brigade which encountered the enemy in the sunken road. Richardson's men first met the enemy to the (Federal) left of Rullet's house, and it is stated that there was soon a space, near Rullet's house, between French's left and Richardson's right. Richardson's advance got possession of Piper's house, which is two-thirds of a mile south and west from Rullet's, and two-thirds of a mile south and east of the Dunker Church, and very near the Hagerstown road. It is in the angle between that road and an old sunken road which runs northwesterly to the former from the Keedysville pike, entering the latter about half way between Sharpsburg and the river, and McClellan says that the sunken road where French fought runs in a northwesterly direction. The map shows that the ground between the East Woods on the north,

V.—5

98   ANTIETAM AND FREDERICKSBURG.

the Hagerstown pike on the west, and the Keedysville pike on the south, measuring about a mile and a third from north to south, is intersected by numerous roads, the lines of which are somewhat broken, and it is probable that the assertions of the various reports could not be accurately fitted to the ground without the actual presence there of an assemblage of officers from both sides, such as Mr. Batchelder succeeding in collecting at Gettysburg.

It must be admitted that the report of the Confederate General Rodes, which is quite full, seems to be distinctly in favor of the theory of the identity of the two roads, but the general current of the testimony, and especially McClellan's assertion that Richardson's *right* brigade advanced nearly to the crest of the hill overlooking Piper's house, are so strongly the other way, that the topography of this part of the field requires particular examination. About half way between Rullet's house and Piper's house a road runs across from the Hagerstown pike to the Keedysville pike in a broken line of six parts—first a little north of east, then southeast, then southwest, then southeast again, then nearly south, and again southeast. The longest straight portion of this road, perhaps a third of a mile long, would appear to an observer in McClellan's position to run in a northwesterly direction. Troops passing Rullet's house and marching southwest would reach the portion of this road nearest the Hagerstown pike. Troops marching in the same direction, but from a point somewhat farther east, would come upon its sharpest zigzags, and then would reach the ridge overlooking Piper's house. Moreover, Piper's house is, as nearly as can be measured on the map, a little less than six hundred yards south of the part of the road next the Hagerstown pike. This agrees very well with McClellan's statement that Piper's house was several hundred yards in advance of the sunken road. It may therefore be accepted as established that the troops of the First and Third Divisions of the Second Corps, French's and Richardson's, fought for and on and across the same road, but that this road was one possessing the singular angularities which have been mentioned. It will, of course, be constantly borne in mind that Richardson's men advanced on the left of French's, that is to say, a little to the east and a good deal to the south.

Richardson's (First) division of the Second Corps comprised the brigades of Meagher, Caldwell, and Brooke. It crossed the Antietam at 9.30 on the morning of the 17th, at the same ford where the other divisions of the corps had crossed it. It moved southward on a line nearly parallel to the stream. In a ravine behind the high ground overlooking Rullet's house, the command was formed, with Meagher's brigade on the right and Caldwell's on the left, and Brooke's in support. Meagher's brigade advanced nearly to the crest of the hill overlooking Piper's house, and found the enemy in strong force in the sunken road in its front. After some sharp fighting, with considerable loss on both sides, Caldwell's brigade was marched up behind it and took its place, the two brigades breaking by company, the one to the front the other to the rear. Meagher's brigade went to the rear to replenish its cartridge-boxes, and Brooke's brigade remained as a support to Caldwell. When the smart push on Kimball's left, before referred to, was made by the Confederates, Brooke hurried into action three of his regiments, the Fifty-second New York, Second Delaware, and Fifty-third Pennsylvania, and they, with some troops from the left of French's division, the Seventh Virginia and One Hundred and Thirty-second Pennsylvania, dislodged the enemy from the cornfield on their right rear, and restored the line. At about this time Caldwell's left was threatened by a movement toward its left and rear, which the Confederates were found to be making under cover of a ridge. Colonel Cross promptly changed front to the left and rear with his regiment, the Fifth New Hampshire, and thus brought his line to be parallel with the line of the flanking force. There was a spirited race between the Federals and Confederates, the goal being some high ground on the left rear of the Federal position. Cross not only won the race and gained the coveted position, but, aided by the Eighty-first Pennsylvania, inflicted severe punishment upon his competitor. Brooke moved forward, to fill the space which Cross's detachment had vacated on the left of Caldwell, the two regiments left to him after detaching to the right, viz.: the Fifty-seventh and Sixty-sixth New York. Caldwell and Brooke, thus united, pressed forward gallantly, and gained possession of Piper's house. Colonel Barlow particularly distinguished himself in these operations of Richardson's division. He had under his charge the two right regiments of Caldwell's brigade, the Sixty-first and Sixty-fourth New York. As Caldwell's line was forcing its way forward, he saw a chance and improved it. Changing front forward, he captured some three hundred prisoners in the sunken road to his right, with two colors. He gained this advantage by obtaining an enfilading fire on the Confederates in the road, and it seems to have been owing entirely to his own quickness of perception and promptness of action, and not to the orders of any superior officer. He was also favorably mentioned for his action in helping to repel another attempt of the enemy to flank Caldwell on his right, and also for contributing largely to the success of the advance which finally gave the Federals possession of Piper's house. This was the end of the serious fighting on this part of the line. Musketry fire ceased at about 1 P.M. Richardson, still holding Piper's house, withdrew his line to the crest of a hill, and at about the same time received a mortal wound. Why he withdrew his line, and whether his wound was the cause of the cessation of operations at this part of the ground, does not appear. Hancock was placed in command of his division. A sharp artillery contest followed the withdrawal of Richardson's line, in which a section of Robertson's horse battery of the Second Artillery and Graham's battery of brass guns of the First Artillery were engaged on the Federal side. Meagher's brigade, now under Burke, returned to the front, with cartridge-boxes refilled, and took position in the centre of the line. French sent something less than two regiments to the support of Richardson's division, and they were placed between Caldwell's and Burke's (Meagher's) brigade.

It so happened that at this time Hancock's application for artillery for the division of which he had assumed command, could not be, or was not, complied with. The length of the line which he was obliged to hold prevented him from forming more than one line of troops, and, from his advanced position, that line was partially enfiladed by batteries on the Confederate left, which were hidden from the Federal batteries by the West Woods. He therefore felt himself too weak to attack. He aided in frustrating an attack toward or beyond his left, by obtaining from Franklin Hexamer's battery, and when Hexamer had expended his ammunition, the very gallant and accomplished Lieutenant Woodruff relieved him with Battery I of the First Artillery.

There is little more to be said of the operations on the Federal right. The serious fighting there ended at about 1 o'clock. In the afternoon, between 4 and 5, the Seventh Maine performed a very brilliant exploit. It belonged to Irwin's brigade of the Second Division of the Sixth Corps, which was in the centre of Smith's division, which was to the right of French's division. It was ordered out to drive away some skirmishers, and performed the task not only gallantly but brilliantly, encountering Texas, Georgia, Mississippi, and Louisiana troops of Hood's division, and losing half the men it moved out with.

The Federal account of the operations of Richardson's division is only slightly illuminated by the Confederate accounts. General Lee says in substance that the attack on the centre was met by part of Walker's division, G. B. Anderson's brigade, Rodes's brigade, and artillery, with R. H. Anderson formed in support; that, Rodes being erroneously withdrawn, the Federals pressed in, broke G. B. Anderson's brigade, mortally wounded him, and wounded General R. H. Anderson and General Wright, but did not follow up their advantage, and, after an hour and a half, retired; that another attack, made further to his right, was repulsed by artillery, *i.e.*, Miller's guns, supported by a part of R. H. Anderson's troops. It is rather a matter of ingenuity than of importance to make the Confederate and Federal accounts of the later morning fighting dovetail. The right attack spent its force when Sedgwick was repulsed. Up to that time there had been close connection of place and some connection of time between the movements of the First, Twelfth, and Second Corps, but after that the attacks were successive both in time and place; and good as were some of the troops engaged, and gallant as was some of the fighting, the movements of French's and Richardson's divisions excite but a languid interest, for such use as was made of these troops was not of a kind to drive Hill and Hood and Jackson and Longstreet and Lee from a strong position from which six divisions of the Federal army had already recoiled, and recoiled in a condition which left them for the moment almost incapable of further service.

THE ANTIETAM. 103

As is usual in Confederate reports, Barlow's success is accounted for on the ground that it was owing to a singular error on the part of an individual, and not to good generalship or good soldiership on the Federal side. It was not till Hotchkiss and Allan began to write that there was much Southern recognition of the fact that Federal merit and Confederate demerit might have something to do with a Federal success. After French's advance had lost its momentum, and after a charge attempted by Rodes and Colquitt had failed so entirely that Rodes barely prevented his men from falling back to the rear of the sunken road, Rodes noticed troops going in to the support of Anderson (G. B.), or to his right. He says that he saw that some of them, instead of passing on to the front, stopped in the hollow immediately in his rear, and that he went to them and found that they belonged to General Pryor's brigade. General Pryor was one of R. H. Anderson's brigadiers. The fire on both sides was now desultory and slack, that is to say, as above stated, French's attack had spent its force, and his men had retired behind high ground. General Rodes found General Pryor in a few moments, and told him how his men were behaving, and General Pryor immediately ordered them forward. General Rodes returned to his command in the sunken road, and met the Lieutenant-Colonel of the Sixth Alabama, looking for him. That officer reported to him that the right of his regiment was subjected to a terrible enfilading fire, which the enemy were enabled to deliver by reason of their gaining somewhat on G. B. Anderson. This undoubtedly means that the pressure of Richardson's advance was beginning to be felt. Rodes ordered his Lieutenant-Colonel to hasten back, and to throw his right wing back out of the old road. "Instead of executing the order, he moved briskly to the rear of the regiment, and gave the command, 'Sixth Alabama, about-face, forward, march.' Major Hobson, of the Fifth, asked him if the order was intended for the whole brigade. He replied, 'Yes,' and thereupon the Fifth, and immediately the other troops on their left, retreated."[1] Rodes says that a duty to a wounded comrade kept him from seeing this retrograde movement till it was too late to rally his men, and that his attention to his command was further delayed by a wound which he at first thought was serious, but presently found to be slight. When he again turned to his brigade, he discovered it "retreating in confusion," and hastened to intercept it at the Hagerstown road, and there found that, with the exception of about forty men, the brigade had completely disappeared. G. B. Anderson was killed at this time, and as the Fifth and Sixth Alabama belonged to Rodes's brigade, there can be little doubt that this disaster was the Federal success gained by Caldwell's brigade, and especially by Barlow's two regiments.

There is no doubt that the brigades of Featherston and Pryor, of R. H. Anderson's division, shared in the fighting at the sunken road. When Pryor went forward at about 10 A.M., Featherston followed him. He passed a barn (which was probably one of the outbuildings of the Piper house), and proceeded several hundred yards, and there found in a road beyond the first cornfield after passing the barn, the brigade of Pryor and a brigade of North Carolina troops. As the old road is from four hundred and fifty to six hundred yards from Piper's house, and as G. B. Anderson's brigade was all from North Carolina, while Rodes and Colquitt to the left had no North Carolina regiments, it is clear that Featherston came up in rear of the right of the line in the road. He claims that his men passed over Pryor's and the

---

[1] A. N. Va., ii., 345.

North Carolinians, and encountered the enemy three hundred yards further to the front. He was presently ordered to fall back, and found great confusion in the road, from the mingling of different brigades, and continued to fall back till he reached the barn.[1] There the command was rallied, and thence it advanced into the cornfield in front of the barn, where the enemy was met. That is to say, the Federals had nearly reached Piper's house. A desperate fight ensued,[2] and was ended by his being ordered to fall back to his original position, on account of a terrific cross fire of artillery. This, being interpreted, probably means simply that the Federals were stronger or fought better than the Confederates at this time and place, and it may well have been at this time that Cross and the Fifth New Hampshire captured the colors of the Fourth North Carolina of G. B. Anderson's brigade. It would be tedious to follow the operations of the centre into much more detail, and it would not be worth the while. It may be said briefly that Willcox, as well as Featherston and Pryor, of R. H. Anderson's division, undoubtedly took part in the fighting in the centre, and that the stories, of which the Confederate reports are so full, of Federal advances made late in the day and heroically repulsed, are only highly colored accounts of the coming up of the brigades of Slocum's division of Franklin's Corps to the places assigned them, and of the gentle pressure which Pleasonton was able to exert with the guns of his horse artillery and their infantry supports from the regular brigade.

---

[1] The report is made, not by Featherston, but by a Captain of the Sixteenth Mississippi, of Featherston's brigade.

[2] It might well be called a desperate fight, if all the regiments of Featherston's brigade suffered as much as the Sixteenth Mississippi, whose commanding officer reports for the brigade. It lost one hundred and forty-four out of two hundred and twenty-eight.

Slocum, with the First Division of the Sixth Corps, reached the field by or before noon. The brigades of Newton and Torbert were immediately formed in column of attack, to carry the woods about the Dunker Church. The brigade of Bartlett was to form the reserve for this column, but Franklin found that Sumner had ordered it to keep near his right, and he waited for it to return; but first Sumner and then McClellan interfered, and the attack was not made. Wisely or unwisely, Sumner paralyzed the action of Franklin's Corps, first detaching from Smith and then from Slocum. Slocum's fine division was so little used that its total loss was only sixty-five.

Pleasonton, in the morning of this day, after fighting had begun on his right, advanced his skirmishers on the Keedysville pike, cleared his front, and caused the batteries of Tidball, Gibson, Robertson, and Hains to open fire, having a direct fire in front, and obtaining an enfilade fire along the front of Sumner, a mile away, and giving some aid to the Ninth Corps, which was at a greater distance on his left. At a later hour, he used the batteries of Randol and Kuserow, and supported them with five small battalions of regulars under Captain Hiram Dryer. In the afternoon, between three and four, he saw a Confederate line, "fully a mile long," bearing down on Richardson, and directed the fire of eighteen guns upon it, and in twenty minutes saw the "immense line first halt, deliver a desultory fire, and then break and run to the rear in the greatest confusion and disorder." A line a mile long is not an immense line, as it would only consist of about five thousand men, but it is not easy to identify the Confederate advance to which Pleasonton refers. At 4 P.M. he asked Porter for infantry to support his guns in an advance, but the request was not granted, as Porter had no troops to spare.

The attentive reader will remember that McClellan says it was his plan to attack the enemy's left, and as soon as matters looked favorably there, to move the corps of Burnside against the enemy's extreme right, but as he states in a later paragraph of his report that the attack on the right was to have been supported by an attack on the left, and that preparatory to this attack, on the evening of the 16th, the Ninth Corps was moved forward and to the left, and took up a position nearer the bridge, he must be understood to mean rather that he intended that these attacks should be simultaneous than that they should be successive. Independent of any utterance of McClellan upon the subject, no one who credited him with a share of military ability could believe that he could have contemplated leaving a corps of four divisions idle for hours upon his left, while he attacked on the right with three corps, held the centre with a fourth corps and his cavalry and horse artillery, and had another strong corps hastening up to the rear of his line. This, however, is precisely what he did do, whatever his orders may have been, and it is one of the vexed questions of this battle whether Burnside failed McClellan and virtually lost the battle for him, or rather kept it from being a great victory, and whether McClellan was or was not satisfied with Burnside at the time. With the abundant knowledge which has long been accessible, there cannot be a shadow of a doubt that if the Ninth Corps had been thrown vigorously into action early on the 17th, Lee's army must have been shattered, if not destroyed. There is as little doubt that McClellan was dissatisfied with Burnside when he published his report, but his report is dated August 4, 1863, nine months after Burnside had taken his place as commander of the Army of the Potomac, and when McClellan was very prominent as an injured hero, and not very unlikely to be the next

President of the United States. As for McClellan's feeling at the time, there is in existence the strongest and most respectable testimony to the effect that a week after the battle, McClellan and Burnside appeared to be on terms of the most intimate friendship, and that some, at least, of those best qualified to judge, believed that Burnside's part in the battle had McClellan's unqualified approval. Those who know McClellan thoroughly are the only persons who are qualified to judge whether he may have then been acting a part, and treating Burnside as he might not have treated him if he had not felt his own position to be one of delicacy and instability; but as this volume is an account of some great campaigns, and not a study of psychology, it is sufficient to state the fact that McClellan subsequently disapproved of Burnside's action, without undertaking to settle the question just when the feeling of dissatisfaction arose in his mind—still less whether he concealed it when he first felt it. Those who believe that Burnside was a faithful, intelligent, and brave soldier, will probably retain a different opinion of his conduct at the Antietam from that of those who believe that his presence was an element of weakness, or worse, wherever and whenever he held an important command.

The Ninth Corps at the battle of the Antietam contained four divisions, those of Willcox, Sturgis, and Rodman, and the Kanawha division, temporarily attached to the Army of the Potomac, under General Cox. Willcox's First Division comprised the brigades of Christ and Welsh; Sturgis's Second, those of Nagle and Ferrero; Rodman's Third, those of Fairchild and Harland; the Kanawha division comprised the brigades of Crook and Ewing As has already been stated, Cox had the personal command of the Ninth Corps this day, and Scammon took command of his division. The position of the Ninth Corps before the battle has already been stated in general terms. On the afternoon of the 16th, the whole corps, except Willcox's division, was moved forward and to the left to the rear slope of the ridges on the left bank of the Antietam, its centre being nearly opposite the stone bridge. The following positions were assigned to the divisions: the right front of the position to be occupied by Crook's brigade, supported by Sturgis's division; a commanding knoll in the centre to be occupied by Benjamin's battery (E, Second Artillery) of 20-pounder Parrott guns; Rodman's division was to occupy the left front, supported by Ewing's brigade; Willcox's division and the rest of the artillery were to be held in reserve. Durell's battery was sent forward early the next morning to the right of the general position, and took part with Benjamin's battery in a brisk artillery fight which commenced soon after daybreak. General Toombs held the ground on the opposite side, with two Georgia regiments, the Second and Twentieth, four hundred and three muskets strong. He placed these men upon the margin of the river, in rather open order, occupying a narrow wood just above the bridge, which he calls an important and commanding position. The Twentieth Georgia was posted with its left near the Sharpsburg end of the bridge, extending down the stream, and the Second Georgia on its right, prolonging the line down to a point where a neighborhood road approaches a ford about six hundred yards to the right and rear of the position. Subsequently, the Fiftieth Georgia, numbering (Toombs says he should suppose) scarcely one hundred muskets, reported to him, and was placed on the right of the Second Georgia, to guard a blind plantation road leading to another ford. He had one more company, not named, and Ewbank's battery, and also, at a distance in his rear, Richardson's battery of his own brigade. General Toombs says that the position was not strong, the ground descending gently, and the narrow strip of woods upon it affording slight cover. This language underestimates the strength of the position, but this point need not be insisted on, for Toombs's next statement shows what a bad place it was for carrying a bridge, whatever the slope of the ground and whether the woods were thin or thick. " Its chief strength lay in the fact that, from the nature of the ground on the other (*i.e.*, Federal) side, the enemy were compelled to approach mainly by the road, which led up the river for near three hundred paces, parallel with my line of battle, and distant therefrom from fifty to one hundred and fifty feet, thus exposing his flank to a destructive fire the most of that distance."[1] General Cox says that the position afforded the most perfect natural and artificial cover. Most of D. R. Jones's division was in Toombs's rear or to his left.

Early on the morning of the 17th, McClellan ordered Burnside to hold his men in readiness to assault the bridge, and to await further orders. The order reached Burnside at about 7 A.M., and the command promptly moved forward and took the positions directed the previous evening. Besides the advance of Durell's and Benjamin's batteries, already mentioned, the batteries of McMullin, Clark, Muhlenberg, and Cook were placed on the heights to right and left, and somewhat further forward than Benjamin's battery. A section of Simmons's 20-pounders was temporarily attached to Benjamin's battery. For some two hours after the receipt of the order, Burnside and Cox stood together on the knoll where Benjamin's battery was placed. From that point they looked down between the lines of battle on their right, as if they were looking along the sides of a street. They saw the Confederates taking advantage of

---

[1] A. N. Va., ii., 323.

THE ANTIETAM. 111

walls and fences, and the Federals uncovered and in the open. They saw the Federal lines halt, open fire, and gradually melt away, or straggle to the rear. They saw that the right attack had failed before they got orders to cross.

At eight o'clock, McClellan says, an order was sent to Burnside to carry the bridge, gain possession of the heights beyond, and to advance along their crest upon Sharpsburg and its rear. There is excellent reason for believing that this order, whenever issued, did not reach Burnside till about nine. He immediately communicated it to Cox, and ordered him to carry it out. Cox immediately left him, took personal direction of the troops, and did not see him again till about 3 P.M., when he crossed the bridge to hasten the movements of Willcox's division under circumstances which will be mentioned hereafter. Crook's brigade was ordered to advance, covered by the Eleventh Connecticut deployed as skirmishers, and supported by the division of Sturgis, and attempt to carry the bridge by assault. The plan was to carry the bridge by a rush of two columns of fours, the one to move to the right and the other to the left so soon as they should get across. Rodman's division was to endeavor to cross by a ford a third of a mile below the bridge. The commands, once across, were to carry the heights above and there unite.

Crook, in some unexplained manner, missed his way to the bridge and reached the stream above it, and came under so heavy a fire, of both infantry and artillery, that he was obliged to halt and open fire. A new storming party had to be organized from Sturgis's division, which reached the bridge first. The Second Maryland and Sixth New Hampshire were told off for the work. They charged at the double-quick with fixed bayonets, but the concentrated fire on the bridge was too much for them, and after repeated brave efforts they were withdrawn. The Fifty-first New York and Fifty-first Pennsylvania were ordered up. They were followed and supported by the Thirty-fifth and Twenty-first Massachusetts, and at the same time Crook obtained a direct fire from two heavy guns upon the Confederates at the further end of the bridge. Aided by these guns, and charging brilliantly, the fresh troops carried the bridge, and the division of Sturgis and the brigade of Crook immediately followed them across. The loss before the bridge was carried exceeded five hundred men, including Colonel Kingsbury killed, and a number of very valuable officers. In the meanwhile, Ewing's brigade and Rodman's division, after losing some time in searching for a ford, under fire—guides proving worthless or worse—found the ford, crossed it, and took up the position assigned them, and thus at 1 P.M. or thereabouts, the three divisions of the corps across the Antietam occupied exactly their intended relative positions, except that Crook was behind Sturgis instead of in front of him. Unfortunately it *was* one o'clock, the fighting on the Federal right was practically over, and A. P. Hill was drawing very near. This was bad, but it was not the worst of it. Sturgis had expended his ammunition, and he now reported that his division was totally unfit for a forward movement. He was taken at his word, and Willcox's division was ordered to relieve him. It seems to have been assumed that there was no ford in the vicinity, and Willcox's men crossed the bridge. This proved slow work, though the command showed reasonable alacrity. The movement was completed at about three o'clock, General Burnside himself coming over to hasten it, and Sturgis's division was placed in reserve at the head of the bridge. All this time the Confederates kept up a severe and damaging artillery fire. Two rifled guns of Moody's battery, and a section of the Washington Artillery, with much aid from the batteries of Longstreet's command, were firing upon the Federals.

At about three o'clock, the whole of the Ninth Corps, except Sturgis's division, was put in motion. The general scheme of the advance was that Willcox, supported by Crook, should move on Sharpsburg, and that Rodman, supported by Scammon with Ewing's brigade, should follow the movement, first dislodging the enemy in their front, and then changing direction to the right, so as to bring the left wing in echelon on the left of Willcox. The artillery of the corps partly covered the advance. The right wing advanced rapidly, but the left met with more resistance. The appearance of the Confederate line, the number of their batteries and battle-flags, all indicated a force fully equal to that of the Federals. Toombs's men had been reinforced by the arrival of the Fifteenth and Seventeenth Georgia, and five companies of the Eleventh Georgia, but the Second and Twentieth Georgia were sent to the rear. With these troops and some of Kearse's regiment, and a part of the Twentieth Georgia, which had returned with a fresh supply of cartridges, Toombs formed on D. R. Jones's right.

The right wing of the Federal force was so successful as to drive in the Confederate skirmishers, capture McIntosh's battery of A. P. Hill's division (which had been sent forward by Hill), and press their advance to the southern suburbs of the town. The resistance on the other flank, however, delayed the Federal left wing, and thus there was an interval between the two wings which grew wider as the right advanced. This interval proved fatal to the enterprise on the Federal left. At half-past two, A. P. Hill's division, having made a march of seventeen miles in seven hours, arrived upon the field. McIntosh's battery had been sent forward to strengthen D. R. Jones's right, the brigades of Pender and Brockenbrough were placed on the extreme right, and Branch, Gregg, and Archer, to their left, connected and completed the line, joining hands with Toombs and D. R. Jones. Braxton's battery was placed on a commanding point on Gregg's right, and Crenshaw's and Pegram's on a hill to the left. Toombs and Archer charged, while the other troops held their ground and fired sharply. McIntosh's battery was retaken, and the Federal line repulsed. Hill lost one brigadier-general killed, and three hundred and forty-six officers and men killed and wounded. He says himself that he was not a moment too soon, and that the Federals had broken through D. R. Jones's division, and were in the full tide of success. He was himself most fortunate in the time and place of his arrival, as Sumner was on the 31st of May at Fair Oaks. He struck Rodman in flank, killed him, and caused his division to break. The nature and character of the attack made it necessary to change Scammon's front, bring up Sturgis, and withdraw the left of Willcox. That of twenty-two hundred and twenty-two casualties in the Ninth Corps only one hundred and twenty-three were missing, may be accepted as proof that the breaking of Rodman's division was not of a discreditable character, and that the disaster was promptly repaired.

Thus the battle of the Antietam, so far as it is really interesting, came to an end. To complete the story of the fighting on the south and southeast of the town, a few details may be added. It seems that when D. R. Jones's division was broken, Kemper gave way first, then Drayton and Jenkins, and that Pickett's Virginia brigade, commanded by Garnett, and Evans's South Carolina brigade, were then ordered back. The repulse must have been very complete, for Colonel Hunton of the Eighth Virginia, of Pickett's brigade, found near the town troops scattered in squads from various parts of the army, so that it was impossible to distinguish men of the different commands. It appears that even in the Southern army human frailty was not unknown, for the colonel commanding Jenkins's brigade of D. R. Jones's division reports that the First South Carolina went in with one hundred and six rank and file, had forty killed and wounded, and only one officer and fifteen men at evening roll-call, and adds that "such officers are a disgrace to the service, and unworthy to wear a sword," while Colonel McMaster, commanding Evans's brigade, says that some of the Holcombe Legion and Seventeenth South Carolina, of his brigade, "in spite of my efforts, broke and ran."

As one reads many of the Southern reports, he finds the doubt growing upon him whether they were made primarily for the information of the superior officers who were entitled to receive them, or for publication in local newspapers and the glorification of the writers. This is especially true of the commanders of batteries and artillery battalions. They all "check the Federal advance," "drive large bodies of infantry from view," "break their ranks," "drive them to cover," cause them to "recoil," "break them and throw them into great confusion," etc., etc., etc., till one is led to wonder at the folly of the Southern leaders in exposing their infantry at all. With artillery so efficient and sufficient, and such admirable cover as the ground afforded, it would seem that they might as well have kept their infantry out of sight, and spared themselves the ten thousand casualties which thinned their ranks at Sharpsburg. Thus it is stated that the batteries of Hood's division were used mainly in resisting the attack of the Ninth Corps. It would appear that Garden's guns and a section of Squires's rifles drive back the enemy advancing from the Burnside bridge; that this force, with Brown's battery and Squires's two howitzers added, break the Federals a second time, when they have got up to within one hundred yards; that only three Confederate guns are then left fit for action, but Ramsey's battery then comes up, with Reilly's two rifles, opens fire, and soon breaks the Federals again. Going a little further to the Confederate right, we find the batteries of Longstreet's corps, notably Miller's, checking the Federal advance. A. P. Hill and his chief of artillery are less blind to the doings of the infantry. A. P. Hill says that the three brigades of his division actively engaged, with the help of his "splendid batteries," drove back Burnside's corps of 15,000 men. The wonderful sight which D. H. Hill saw, when he caused three, or probably five guns to open on an "imposing force of Yankees" at twelve hundred yards distance, and routed them by artillery fire alone, unaided by musketry, has already been mentioned. It hardly need be added that the Confederate batteries seldom, if ever, retire till they are out of ammunition.

The truth is that the Confederate batteries were extremely well taken care of by their infantry, as a rule, and that they very seldom lost a gun. At Sharpsburg they were wise very generally in abstaining from costly and useless "artillery duels," and in directing their fire upon the Federal infantry, but they did not do all the fighting that was done there by the Confederates.

There are many questions presented by the action of the Ninth Corps at Sharpsburg, some of them affecting the conduct of Burnside and Cox principally, others which rather affect McClellan, but as this volume is intended more for a narrative than for a critical discussion, they will hardly be more than stated—the questions of the former class in this place, and those of the latter a little later. The question of Burnside's loyalty is too large a one for discussion here. Thus much is plain, he could not be disloyal to McClellan without being disloyal to his country. But between the utmost putting forth of the powers of an able and energetic man, and the lukewarm use of the powers of a commonplace and sluggish man, there is a vast difference, and the small results accomplished by Burnside on McClellan's left may readily be understood without any imputation of disloyalty by those who think that they see in his whole career that he had mistaken his vocation, and that it was a misfortune for the country that he was ever promoted beyond the rank of colonel. There are those who judge him very harshly, but wars are unfortunately apt to produce sharp jealousies and enmities among soldiers, and the explanation afforded by the theory of limited capacity may well be preferred to that based on the suggestion of bad faith.

The peculiar position of Burnside and Cox was probably a drawback to the efficiency of the corps. Burnside became a mere receiver and transmitter of orders to the commander of the Ninth Corps, and on the other hand it may easily be believed that so good a soldier as Cox would have shown more activity and accomplished more, if he had felt himself really the commander of the Ninth Corps. With Burnside close to him, he probably felt as if he were the mere tactical leader of the corps, not thinking for it, but simply seeing that it executed the orders which came to him from or through Burnside. It is possible on this theory to explain the puzzling facts that so little was known of the ground which Burnside had been ordered, before 2 P.M. of the 16th, to carefully reconnoitre, that Crook actually missed his way to the very bridge which he was to carry by assault, and that nothing or next to nothing seems to have been known about the fords till they were searched for under fire. Why, when the difficulties of the ground must have been so apparent, the bridge was not turned by the lower fords, the existence of which at least was known, instead of being carried with such loss of time and men, does not appear, and it is as hard to explain why, when Willcox was sent across, his troops were not sent partly by the ford which Burnside says[1] Crook found, and partly by the bridge, instead of all by the bridge. Why, in brief, did it take Burnside's four divisions, with their powerful artillery, from six to seven hours to get across the stream and form line upon the heights above? Finally, how did it happen that when the three divisions with their guns had crossed and formed and begun their advance, no such tactical precautions were taken as to enable them to present a front in a moment to a flank attack on the left? Probably it was not thought of; probably all attention was concentrated on the enemy in front and on the right. The scales were inclining rapidly in favor of the North. Sharpsburg was almost occupied, Lee's line of retreat gravely compromised. A Confederate battery had been taken, a Confederate brigade and division had been driven in. It must have been because all eyes were turned in this direction that the advance of A. P. Hill was not seen. If it had been, nothing would have been easier than to form up the first brigade of the Kanawha division to meet it, and with a fresh brigade so formed, and a battery or two to aid, Hill's five brigades, weary with their rapid march of seventeen miles, would have found a good deal of serious work laid out for them before they could join in the main battle against the victorious Ninth Corps.[2] But it was not to be, and for the second time that day a Federal division was broken for want of protection to its flank. It is hardly too

---

[1] C. C. W., i., 640.

[2] The instructed reader will not need to be reminded of the care of their flanks taken by great commanders. Napoleon's detaching Lobau to his right at Waterloo is a familiar instance. The whole Federal army knew of the capture of Harper's Ferry. It was most probable that some of the Confederates would hasten from there to Sharpsburg by the bridge at the iron works, and so come on the left of the Ninth Corps.

THE ANTIETAM. 119

much to say that for the second time that day a victory was lost for want of protection to the flank of a division.

Tactically, the battle of the Antietam was a drawn battle, with the advantage inclining slightly to the side of the Federals, who gained some ground and took more trophies than they lost. The Confederates, however, held most of the ground on which they fought, and held it not only to the close of the battle, but for more than twenty-four hours after, and then retired, unmolested and in good order. The steady tramp of their retreating columns, like the steady flowing of a river, was heard all through the still night of the 18th of September, as they streamed along the road to the Shepherdstown ford of the Potomac. But, for an invading army, a drawn battle is little less than a lost battle, and so it was in this case. Lee drew off successfully and defiantly, but the invasion of Maryland was at an end.

Of McClellan's conduct of this battle there is little to be said in the way of praise beyond the fact that he did fight it voluntarily, without having it forced upon him. After his interminable delays upon the Peninsula, his action at South Mountain and Sharpsburg shows progress. He formed a plan of battle which was respectable but rather vague, and could not have been called brilliant, even if it had been crowned with brilliant success. He fought his battle one day too late, if not two. His orders were not well adapted to the success of his plan, and he did very little in the way of compelling the execution of the orders which he did give. He passed the whole day, till toward the middle of the afternoon, when all the fighting was over, on the high ground near Fry's house, where he had some glasses strapped to the fence, so that he could look in different directions. He made absolutely no use of the magnificent enthusiasm which the army then felt for him. By the use which he made of the First Corps on the 16th, he told Lee where the blow was to fall. By his orders in regard to the Twelfth and Second Corps, he made it certain that the three corps would not act in unison the next morning. By giving the charge of his main attack to Sumner, he placed the lives of tens of thousands and the destiny of a great day of battle, with all its far-reaching issues, in the hands of an excellent elderly man who eighteen months before had had no wider experience than that of a colonel of cavalry, instead of in the hands of the man whom the President had made Commander of the Army of the Potomac. He let Burnside have his own way so completely on the left, that his divisions were not ready to advance upon the enemy till seven hours after the order was sent to him to carry the bridge and move on Sharpsburg. Finally, and what one is tempted to call worst of all, because it was the throwing away of an almost certainly winning card at the end of a game which he had so far lost by error after error, he made so little use of the Fifth and Sixth Corps that the total losses of their four divisions and of the artillery reserve was less than six hundred men. It has been seen that all his movements of troops were without connection and were successive. The First Corps finished its fighting before the Twelfth Corps became engaged. One of the best soldiers in the Twelfth Corps has recently asserted with emphasis that the Twelfth Corps received no assistance from the First, "none whatever," and his evidence must be accepted so far as the first division of the Twelfth Corps (in which he held a command), is concerned. The Second Corps went in when the Twelfth Corps had about finished; its leading division went forward entirely alone and received its punishment entirely alone. It might as well have been in another county for any direct aid it received from

THE ANTIETAM. 121

the rest of the Army of the Potomac. The other two divisions of the Second Corps became engaged later, and not quite simultaneously, and not with close connection. The Ninth Corps got actively to work some hours later still. The Fifth and Sixth Corps were not only not used, either of them, as a whole, but only used at all by breaking them up into pieces no one of which exceeded a division, if indeed it can with fairness be asserted that any whole division of these corps was used as a unit, or anything like it.

The time when Lee was probably in the greatest danger was when Franklin had come up in the rear of the centre. The loss of life in Jackson's two divisions and in the divisions of Hood and D. H. Hill had been awful. There was a good deal of fight left in the Second Corps, Franklin's corps was almost fresh, and all of Porter's was entirely so, while Pleasonton had a considerable force of cavalry and artillery ready to take a hand. There is a story—probably apocryphal, for it is not like Jackson—that he said, when his men finally entered the West Woods, "We will die here." There is no question that after the Federals had crossed the sunken road, the danger to Lee was extreme. D. H. Hill says that there were no troops left to hold the centre except a few hundred rallied from various brigades, that the Yankees had got within a few hundred yards of the hill which commanded Sharpsburg and the Confederate rear. "Affairs looked very critical."[1] Franklin wished to attack, and made his preliminary dispositions for doing so, but Sumner first and then McClellan forbade the resumption of offensive operations. It is probable, almost to the point of certainty, that if a good part of the Second and Fifth Corps and all the Sixth Corps, animated by the personal presence

---

[1] A. N. Va., ii., 117.

of McClellan, had attacked vigorously in the centre, and Burnside on the Federal left, leaving part of Porter's Corps and Pleasonton's command to hold the centre and cover the trains, the result would have been the practical annihilation of Lee's army. But Sumner, brave as he was personally, was demoralized by the hard fighting, loss of life, stubborn defence, and dashing offensive action which he had witnessed, and he displayed the same want in his nature which he had displayed before at Fair Oaks. McClellan, too, made the same mistake which he had made before at Gaines's Mill, and accepted the judgment of his lieutenant instead of deciding for himself. Both McClellan and Sumner exhibited their deficiency in those qualities which appear to be Grant's most valuable endowments—absolutely clear perception of the end to be attained, absolute insensibility to cost so long as the end appears attainable, and never forgetting and always acting upon the theory that when both sides are about exhausted, then is the time to push, and that he who pushes then will find the other side give way. In criticising McClellan, however, such weight as it deserves is to be given to his extraordinary estimate of his adversary's numbers, but it is true, as has already been suggested, that if he believed his own statements, prudence of the commonest kind would have forbidden any attack at all. Only one word more remains to be said about McClellan, and that is that the instant he decided not to resume offensive operations on the right centre and right, he should have used every man and gun he could possibly spare from Porter and Franklin to co-operate in the attack of the Ninth Corps, by moving out to the south of the Keedysville pike, where Pleasonton's horse artillery and Sykes's regulars had made an opening for an energetic movement to the left front of the Federal centre.

Porter has been blamed for his inaction at the Antietam, but absolutely without reason. The commander of one of several corps acting together cannot do as he likes, or according to his individual judgment. He must take his orders from the commander-in-chief, and this is precisely what Porter did. A considerable part of Sykes's division of his corps was used by Pleasonton, under orders from McClellan, to support the horse-artillery and cavalry immediately in front of Sharpsburg, and they not only performed this duty, but drove the Confederate skirmishers back to their reserves. Miller's battery and Warren's brigade were sent to Burnside on the left, and two brigades of Morell's division were sent to Sumner on the right. These detachments were not carried into action, but their absence reduced Porter's command to 4,000 men, and so, when later in the afternoon Pleasonton asked him for a division to press a success he fancied he had won, Porter not only could not, under his orders, comply with his request, but actually had not the division to send him. His duty was, with what troops were left him, to guard the artillery and trains and the line of retreat, supply, and communication of the army, and not to risk the safety of the centre and perhaps imperil the result of the day, by complying with the request of an officer who was not even a corps commander, who was his inferior in rank, and whose request had not received the approval of the general commanding. His duty at the Antietam must have been trying and mortifying, but he did it faithfully.

In painful contrast to the passive attitude of the principal Federal army on the afternoon of the 17th is the undoubted fact that the indomitable Lee and Jackson, unaffected by the terrible losses which their troops had suffered, actually the one ordered and the other attempted to execute that afternoon a turning movement on the Federal right. Stuart had the advance in this movement, and he was reinforced by the Forty-eighth North Carolina of Walker's division, and the light batteries of French and Branch, and perhaps by Semmes's brigade, though this is not clear. The Federal artillery was found so judiciously established in their front, and so near to the Potomac, that it was thought inexpedient to hazard the attempt. It should also be stated in this connection that the plan of a general Confederate advance in the afternoon was at least considered, but the idea was abandoned because the strength of McClellan's position, the field of fire offered to his artillery, the presence of his fresh troops, and the fact that a Confederate advance would enforce concentration upon his reserves, while the Confederates had no reserves and were much exhausted, both men and ammunition, all combined to make it appear injudicious.

As the sun sank to rest on the 17th of September, the last sounds of battle along Antietam Creek died away. The cannon could at last grow cool, and unwounded men and horses could enjoy rest and food, but there were thousands already sleeping the sleep that knows no waking, and many times as many thousands who were suffering all the agonies that attend on wounds. The corn and the trees, so fresh and green in the morning, were reddened with blood and torn by bullet and shell, and the very earth was furrowed by the incessant impact of lead and iron. The blessed night came, and brought with it sleep and forgetfulness and refreshment to many; but the murmur of the night wind, breathing over fields of wheat and clover, was mingled with the groans of the countless sufferers of both armies. Who can tell, who can even imagine, the horrors of such a night, while the unconscious stars shone above, and the unconscious river went rippling by? A very gallant officer, who had played out his part well, though drooping over his horse's neck with the weakness of oncoming typhoid fever, lost his senses as the shadows deepened, and groped about the battle-field all night, so far as his failing strength would let him, turning up to the stars the faces of the dead men, to try to find his missing brother. But death is merciful, and comes to the relief of many; and man is merciful, and the wounded had not very long to wait for care.

One question calls for some discussion, and it may as well receive attention here. The question is, Did the Southern men fight better than the Northern men, and if they did, why did they? These questions are interesting, but they are also difficult, and they should be answered with diffidence. What is said here is offered rather as a contribution to the discussion of the subject, than as an absolute solution of the problem. There can be no doubt about the proposition that greater results were habitually achieved by a certain number of thousands or tens of thousands of Lee's army than by an equal number of the Army of the Potomac. The reason for this is not to be found in any difference of patriotic zeal in the two armies. The first reason probably was that the different modes of life at the South and at the North made the Southern soldiers more fond of fighting than the Northern men. Not to mention the intenser and more passionate character of the Southerner as compared with that of the Northerner, the comparatively lawless (not to speak invidiously) life at the South, where the population was scattered, and the gun came ready to the hand, made the Southern man an apter soldier than the peaceful, prosperous, steady-going recruit from the North. The Southerners showed that they felt the *gaudium certaminis*. With the Northerners it was different. They were ready to obey orders, they were ready to do the work to which they had set their hands, they were ready to die in their tracks if need be, but they did not go to battle as to a feast. With officers and men it was the same. They did not like fighting. Sheridan, Hancock, Humphreys, Kearny, Custer, Barlow, and such as they, were exceptions, but the rule was otherwise.

Another reason may probably be found in the needy condition which was common among the Southerners. Their stomachs were not seldom empty, their backs and feet ill-clothed and ill-shod, while the Northern soldiers were abundantly provided with everything. "I can whip any army that is followed by a flock of cattle," said Jackson, and it was a pregnant saying. A sermon might be preached upon that text. It is known that the Southerners were eager to take everything of value from the persons of the corpses which came into their possession, even to boots, shoes, and clothing, and they were far from nice in their treatment of their prisoners. A field won meant to them not only a field won, but clothing for body and feet, food, money, watches, and arms and equipments as well. To the Northerners a field won meant simply a field won. In this difference it is almost certain there existed a powerful motive to stimulate the avidity with which the Southerners went into action. The Southerners were not only gallant soldiers, but they were keen plunderers as well. This is no fanciful statement. In this very battle of the Antietam, a medical officer of Sedgwick's division was shot dead as he was tending a wounded man of his regiment close to the front line, and his body was plundered almost before the breath left it, and thus a watch which he was carrying till an opportunity should present itself for returning it to the relatives of its dead owner, a field officer of a Georgia regiment who died in our hands, went back into the Confederacy in a way which was neither expected nor desired.

Enough has already been written to show that this was a bloody battle, with terrible losses to some of the commands engaged. General McClellan reported that he lost, on the 16th and 17th, 2,010 killed, 9,416 wounded, and 1,043 missing, a total of 12,469. Sedgwick's division of the Second Corps were the principal sufferers in his army. Their total loss was 2,255, of whom 355 were killed. The Confederate loss was not known with accuracy. McClellan reported that 2,700 of their dead were counted and buried by his officers, and that a portion had been previously buried by their comrades. From the losses they report, it is probable that their total loss must have at least equalled the Federal loss. But, as Swinton says, it is needless to sound deeper in this sea of blood. McClellan captured a good many prisoners and colors and a few guns.

General McClellan decided not to renew the attack on the 18th. It is hardly worth while to state his reasons. It has been already strongly urged that he ought to have fought out the battle on the 17th, and there do not appear to have existed any better reasons for energetic action on the following day, except that two divisions then joined him after a hard march. The fault was in the man. There was force enough at his command either day, had he seen fit to use it. The most important change in the position of troops which took place on the 18th was the movement of Morell's division of the Fifth Corps. In answer to some far from plucky representations of Burnside, McClellan directed that Morell's division should be placed on the east side of the Antietam, near Burnside's Bridge. "Late in the afternoon," he says, "I found that, although he had not been attacked, General Burnside had withdrawn his own corps to this side of the Antietam, and sent over Morell's division alone to hold the opposite side." General McClellan lets this extraordinary proceeding pass without comment. Humphreys's division of new troops, marching with commendable rapidity from Frederick, arrived on the 18th, and took Morell's place. Couch, also, having nearly reached Maryland Heights, was countermarched, pressed forward, and reached the field early the same day. Orders were given by McClellan for a renewal of the attack at daylight on the 19th, but at daylight on the 19th Lee was gone.

On the 19th, the Fifth Corps was ordered to support the cavalry. It was found that the Confederates beyond the river had artillery well posted to cover the fords. Porter determined to clear the fords and to try to capture some guns. He lined the eastern bank of the Potomac with skirmishers and sharpshooters, supported them by the divisions of Morell and Sykes, and by guns so posted as to command the opposite bank. Volunteers from the Fourth Michigan, One Hundred and Eighteenth Pennsylvania, and Eighteenth and Twenty-second Massachusetts, crossed the river under the charge of General Griffin. Sykes was ordered to advance a similar party, but by some misunderstanding the orders did not reach him seasonably. The attempt was made at dark, and resulted in the capture of five guns and some of their appurtenances. Among the guns taken was one of Battery D of the Fifth Artillery, which had been lost at the first Bull Run. A reconnoissance in force was sent across the river the following morning, at seven o'clock, under Morell and Sykes. The cavalry ordered to co-operate, failed to do so, and the enterprise was unsuccessful. The troops were attacked sharply, and driven back across the river with considerable loss, the loss falling principally upon the One Hundred and Eighteenth Pennsylvania.[1]

---

[1] It lost in all 282 out of 800, of whom 64 were killed. It had been in the service just three weeks. It was known as the "Corn Exchange Regiment."

Nine or ten Confederate brigades took part in this affair, and the Confederates seem to believe that it ended with "an appalling scene of the destruction of human life."[1] Jackson, whose words these are, must have been imposed upon by A. P. Hill, who had charge of the operation, and whose report contains these assertions: "Then commenced the most terrible slaughter that this war has yet witnessed. The broad surface of the Potomac was blue with the floating bodies of our foe. But few escaped to tell the tale. By their own account, they lost 3,000 men killed and drowned from one brigade alone."[2]

> Or art thou drunk with wine, Sir Knight,
> Or art thyself beside?

The reader with a taste for figures will observe that this tale of deaths in one brigade alone wants only ten of being a thousand more than all the men killed in the Army of the Potomac on the 16th and 17th of September.

The movements of the two armies in the seven weeks which followed the battle of the Antietam do not require minute description. Both armies needed rest. Lee gradually withdrew his troops to the vicinity of Bunker Hill and Winchester, and busied himself to some extent with the destruction of those railroads which would have been of assistance to the Federals in the occupation of the Valley. His army seems to have increased rapidly, so that it numbered on the 20th of October 67,805 officers and men of the three arms. McClellan devoted his attention to guarding the line of the Potomac, and to the equipment and reorganization of his command. There is truth in his statement that he succeeded to the command of a force a large part of which had been badly beaten, and was in all respects in a

---

[1] A. N. Va., ii., 105.   [2] Ib., 130.

poor condition. In the respect of hard marching and hard fighting, its experiences had been less hard than those of the Confederates. He said that the means of transportation at his disposal were inadequate to furnish a single day's supply of subsistence in advance, and that he thought it improper to place the Potomac, a stream liable to rise suddenly, between himself and his base of supplies. He wanted horses, shoes, clothing, and blankets, and he wanted all the "old troops that could possibly be dispensed with around Washington and other places," and he repeated his assertion that in the recent battles the enemy was greatly superior in number. Indeed, his tone leaves much to be desired. He was far more ready to seek excuses for doing nothing than to make what he had go as far as possible. It never seems to occur to him that the wants he felt were felt by Lee in a greater degree. Why he could not supply himself, though across the Potomac, so long as he held Harper's Ferry, he does not say. He even permitted himself, on September 23d, to make the pitiful assertion "General Sumner with his corps and Williams's occupies Harper's Ferry and the surrounding heights. I think he will be able to hold his position till reinforcements arrive." If there was a doubt about the ability of the Second and Twelfth Corps, with Maryland Heights in their possession, and all the rest of the Army of the Potomac to back them, to hold their position, it was time for McClellan to place his army in a fortified camp.

By the 6th of October the President had become impatient, so much so that Halleck, the General-in-Chief, was instructed to telegraph McClellan as follows: "The President directs that you cross the Potomac and give battle to the enemy or drive him south. . . ." This, however, did not move McClellan, and on the 10th of October Stuart crossed the Potomac, above Williamsport, with orders to "endeavor to ascertain the position and designs of the enemy." He penetrated as far as Chambersburg, which he occupied for a time, destroyed public property, made the entire circuit of the Federal army, and recrossed the Potomac, near the mouth of the Monocacy, without any material loss. Thus for the second time a force of Confederate cavalry rode all around McClellan's army. The latter exploit was the more noteworthy, and the more discreditable to McClellan, because the raid was made on Union territory.

There was undoubtedly great delay in the arrival of supplies, and as the story is told, it is difficult to resist the temptation to believe that the delays were unnecessary, and would not have existed had headquarters at Washington been, not to say friendly to McClellan, but loyal to the general commanding. At last, however, near the end of October, affairs were in such condition that McClellan began to put his troops in motion. He determined to select the line east of the Blue Ridge, and to guard the upper Potomac by leaving the Twelfth Corps at Harper's Ferry, with three brigades of infantry and some cavalry extending up the river to Cumberland and Hancock. The crossing commenced on the 26th of October, and was not completed till the 2d of November. Heavy rains and the distribution of supplies that arrived late, delayed the movement. The army advanced parallel to the Blue Ridge, taking Warrenton as the point of direction, and seizing the passes to the westward as it advanced, and guarding them as long as they would enable the Confederates to trouble its communications with the Potomac. It depended upon Harper's Ferry and Berlin for supplies until the Manassas Gap Railroad was reached. That reached, the passes in rear were to be abandoned, supplies were to be drawn from Washington by the Orange and Alexandria Railroad and the Manassas Gap

Railroad, and the army massed for action or for movement in any direction. It is as well to give McClellan's expectations in his own words, especially as his words are both surprising and somewhat hard to understand.

> It was my intention if, upon reaching Ashby's or any other pass, I found that the enemy were in force between it and the Potomac in the Valley of the Shenandoah, to move into the Valley and endeavor to gain their rear.
>
> I hardly hoped to accomplish this, but did expect that by striking in between Culpeper Court House and Little Washington, I could either separate their army and beat them in detail, or else force them to concentrate as far back as Gordonsville, and thus place the Army of the Potomac in position either to adopt the Fredericksburg line of advance upon Richmond, or to be removed to the Peninsula, if, as I apprehended, it were found impossible to supply it by the Orange and Alexandria Railroad beyond Culpeper.

These sentences are a tempting theme, but want of space makes it inconvenient to consider them, and McClellan did not have the opportunity to show whether his expectations were well founded. Late on the night of the 7th November, he received an order relieving him from the command of the Army of the Potomac, and directing him to turn it over to General Burnside. The position in which he left the army, and the position which Lee's army then occupied, may well be stated when the story of General Burnside's career as Commander of the Army of the Potomac is taken up.

To relieve McClellan of his command so soon after he had forced Lee out of Maryland, was hard measure. He had succeeded to the command when Pope had been very badly beaten, and when the sound of the enemy's guns had been plainly audible at Washington. He had rapidly raised the troops from a condition of much discouragement and demoralization, and made of them a compact and efficient force. Within ten days after he left Washington, he had led this army against Lee's rear guard in the South Mountain passes, and had driven it from them, and had fought a great battle against Lee's entire army, in which he had so far gotten the advantage that the Confederate invasion of Maryland had come to an immediate end. He had since those battles gradually advanced his army to a position in which it both interposed itself between Lee and the Capital, and was at least fairly well placed for offensive action. And yet it can hardly be wondered at that he lost his place. His interminable and inexcusable delays upon the Peninsula afforded just ground for dissatisfaction, and they seemed, to say no more, to be followed by similar delays upon the Potomac. He had done much to justify the charge that he was a political general. He had probably offended many influential men of the perfervid type of Charles Sumner and Governor Andrew. His correspondence with Washington had been often uncomfortable, sometimes acrimonious, and once at least unwarrantable. The mildest of Secretaries of War was not likely to forget the sentence, "You have done your best to sacrifice this army," which closed his despatch of June 28 to Secretary Stanton, and Secretary Stanton was far from being the mildest of Secretaries of War. The evil habit then prevailed among civilians in high places of encouraging communications from the Adullamites of the army, and detraction was probably unceasing among the *mauvaises langues* of the time. Hooker was open in his denunciations of McClellan as "a baby," and such things as Hooker said openly others probably said with more prudence. So the "young Napoleon," the popular idol of 1861, was removed from the command of the army for which he had done so much, and while it seems that hard measure was meted to him, there is more ground for sympathy than there is for wonder.

These pages contain many outspoken criticisms of his military career. They are the expression of conclusions arrived at with deliberation by one who began as a passionate enthusiast for him, who has made his campaigns the subject of much study and thought, and who has sought only to compare the facts of those campaigns with the established principles of the military art. There is no occasion to repeat those criticisms here, but it may be well to add to them what the writer has said in another place in print, that there was in McClellan a sort of incapacity of doing anything till an ideal completeness of preparation was reached, and that the prevalence of the *commander-in-chief idea* was always pernicious to him, so that, from first to last, he never made his personal presence felt on a battle-field. With the further remark that he seems to have been totally devoid of ability to form a just estimate of the numerical strength of his opponent, our adverse criticisms come to an end, and it is a relief to keep silence no longer from good words.

It is little to say that his character was reputable, but it is true. He was a courteous gentleman. Not a word was ever said against his way of life nor his personal integrity. No orgies disgraced headquarters while he was in command. His capacity and energy as an organizer are universally recognized. He was an excellent strategist and in many respects an excellent soldier. He did not use his own troops with sufficient promptness, thoroughness and vigor, to achieve great and decisive results, but he was oftener successful than unsuccessful with them, and he so conducted affairs that they never suffered heavily without inflicting heavy loss upon their adversaries. It may appear a strange statement to follow the other matter which this volume contains, but it is none the less true, that there are strong grounds for believing that he was the best commander the Army of the Potomac ever had. No one would think for a moment of comparing Pope or Burnside or Hooker with him. The great service which Meade rendered his country at Gettysburg, and the elevated character of the man, are adverse to too close a scrutiny of his military ability. As for Grant, with his grim tenacity, his hard sense, and his absolute insensibility to wounds and death, it may well be admitted that he was a good general for a rich and populous country in a contest with a poor and thinly peopled land, but let any educated soldier ask himself what the result would have been if Grant had had only Southern resources and Southern numbers to rely on and use, and what will the answer be? While the Confederacy was young and fresh and rich, and its armies were numerous, McClellan fought a good, wary, damaging, respectable fight against it. He was not so quick in learning to attack as Joe Johnston and Lee and Jackson were, but South Mountain and the Antietam showed that he had learned the lesson, and with longer possession of command, greater things might fairly have been expected of him. Not to mention such lamentable failures as Fredericksburg and Chancellorsville, it is easy to believe that with him in command, the Army of the Potomac would never have seen such dark days as those of the Wilderness and Cold Harbor. At the same time it must be admitted that, in such a war as the War of Secession, it would probably have been impossible to retain in command of the Army of the Potomac a man who was not only a Democrat, but the probable Democratic candidate for the Presidency at the next election, and that his removal was therefore only a question of time. A growing familiarity with his history as a soldier increases the disposition to regard him with respect and gratitude, and to believe, while recognizing the limitations of his nature, that his failure to accomplish more was partly his misfortune and not altogether his fault.

CHAPTER IV.

FREDERICKSBURG.

WHEN General McClellan was relieved, he had already given the orders for the movements of the 8th and 9th November. These orders were carried into effect without change, and when General Burnside assumed command, on the 9th, general headquarters and the bulk of the army were at Warrenton, with the Ninth Corps advanced to the line of the Rappahannock, in the neighborhood of Waterloo, and the cavalry farther in advance to the front and left. The Sixth Corps was at New Baltimore, about six miles in rear of Warrenton. The Eleventh Corps and Sickles's division of the Third Corps, which had by this time joined the army from Washington, were posted, the former in the triangle formed by New Baltimore, Thoroughfare Gap, and Gainesville, and the latter along the line of the railroad from Manassas Junction to Warrenton Junction. Longstreet's Corps of the Confederate army had been moved across the Blue Ridge as soon as McClellan's intentions were developed, and was by this time at Culpeper Court House. One of Jackson's divisions had also been moved to the east side of the Blue Ridge, but the others, those of Ewell and A. P. Hill, appear to have remained in the Valley, between Winchester and Strasburg. It was by mutual agreement between Burnside and McClellan that the latter remained in command of the army till the 9th, and that his orders for the concentration of the army near Warrenton were carried out without change.

Soon after Burnside assumed command, he submitted a plan of operations to Halleck, in obedience to orders from him. Halleck did not approve the plan, and came himself to Burnside's headquarters at Warrenton, where they had long consultations on the 12th and 13th. They failed to agree, and the matter was left to the decision of the President. On the 14th, Halleck telegraphed Burnside that the President assented to his (Burnside's) plan. This plan was, in brief, to impress upon the enemy the belief that he was to attack Culpeper or Gordonsville, and at the same time accumulate a four or five days' supply of food and forage; then to make a rapid move of the whole force to Fredericksburg, with a view to a movement upon Richmond from that point. This plan of Burnside's went into considerable detail; it was delivered to the chief of staff in Washington on the 11th. It contained the statement, not made very prominent, that pontoon trains enough to span the Rappahannock with two tracks should precede a train of wagons which he said it was necessary should start at once from Washington or from Alexandria, by way of Dumfries, with small rations, and a herd of beef cattle. General Burnside says that, in his personal interview with Halleck, he told him that he relied upon him to see that such parts of his plan as required action in Washington should be carried out, and that Halleck told him that everything required by him should receive his attention, and that he would at once order by telegraph the pontoon trains spoken of in his plan, and would, upon his return to Washington, see that they were promptly forwarded. Moreover, Halleck's telegraph, informing Burnside of the President's assent to his plan, contained these words: "He thinks it (*i.e.*, Burnside's plan) will

138   ANTIETAM AND FREDERICKSBURG.

succeed if you move rapidly, otherwise not." Burnside received the despatch of the 14th on the same day, at 11 A.M., and at once issued orders for the different commands to move. His army was now divided into three "grand divisions." The Right Grand Division, under Sumner, composed of the Second and Ninth Corps, started at daylight on the morning of the 15th, the Centre and Left Grand Divisions and the cavalry on the 16th. General Franklin commanded the Left Grand Division, composed of the First and Sixth Corps, and General Hooker the Centre Grand Division, composed of the Third and Fifth Corps. A numerous artillery accompanied each division in these grand divisions. The total present for duty of the army on the 10th of November is said to have been 127,574 officers and men.

General Sumner's command reached Falmouth, opposite Fredericksburg, on the 17th. General Franklin, on the 18th, concentrated his command at Stafford Court House, ten miles northeast of Fredericksburg, and near Acquia Creek, an affluent of the Potomac. General Hooker's command moved to Hartwood, ten miles or less northwest of Fredericksburg, arriving there on the 19th. The cavalry was in the rear, and covering the fords of the Rappahannock further up the stream.

General Burnside's whole plan was based upon the expectation of an immediate occupation of Fredericksburg. Once there, he proposed to organize his wagon trains and fill them with at least twelve days' provisions, and then make a rapid and direct movement upon Richmond. As events shaped themselves, it has become unnecessary to consider his chances of success in pursuing this plan. Grant's campaign of 1864 will readily supply abundant illustration to the instructed reader. The promised pontoons did not arrive till the 25th, eight days after Sumner reached the river. As this is a history of what was done and not of what might have been done, it is not worth while to endeavor to determine where the blame should be laid, but, in justice to Burnside, it should be said that the fault does not appear to have been his. General Sumner proposed, as soon as he arrived, to cross a portion of his force over the fords, with a view to taking Fredericksburg, but Burnside decided that it was impracticable to cross large bodies there, and he was afraid to cross small bodies. It is almost certain that in so deciding he made a serious mistake. There was a Confederate garrison at Fredericksburg, but its strength is unknown. On the 15th of November, Lee sent a regiment of infantry and one battery to reinforce it. It is not stated when they arrived, but as the Fifteenth Virginia Cavalry, four companies of Mississippi infantry, and Lewis's battery, were there when Sumner arrived, it is probable that the reinforcements arrived there before he did. Yet fifteen brigades and thirteen batteries are a powerful force, and as the Right Grand Division contained over twenty New England regiments, it is a fair presumption that Yankee craft was not wanting, and that if there had been an earnest will to cross the Rappahannock, the way would have been found, and that the landing once effected, there was force enough to make it certain that there would have been no letting go of the hold. It is both possible and probable that if Burnside had permitted Sumner to cross the Rappahannock on the 17th of November, the costly and useless sacrifices of the 11th and 13th December might have been spared. But Sumner was not allowed to cross, and the very day that he reached Falmouth, Lee, hearing of his movement, sent McLaws's and Ransom's divisions, accompanied by W. H. F. Lee's brigade of cavalry and Lane's battery, to the town. Further instructed by a forced reconnoissance made by

Stuart, he put the rest of Longstreet's corps, on the morning of the 19th, in motion for the same point. Thus it happened that before the pontoons arrived, the Confederates had concentrated a large force on the opposite side of the river, and Burnside thought that it had become "necessary to make arrangements to cross in the face of a vigilant and formidable foe." It does not seem to have occurred to him to inquire whether Lee's army was all in front of him, and, if not, where the rest of them were, and if it was not possible for him, with his large army, to turn the strong position in his front, and at the same time interpose himself between Longstreet and Jackson, between the First and Second Corps of the Army of Northern Virginia. As a matter of fact, Jackson was in the neighborhood of Orange Court House, nearly forty miles west of Fredericksburg, till about the 26th of November, when he was directed to advance toward Fredericksburg. D. H. Hill's division was sent to Port Royal, on the Rappahannock, a considerable distance below Fredericksburg, upon a report that Federal gunboats had appeared in the river, and the rest of Jackson's Corps was so disposed as to support Hill or Longstreet as occasion might require. Lee's cavalry, under Hampton and W. H. F. Lee, guarded the river above and below the town. Nothing of importance occurred on either side during the last days of November and the first days of December. Burnside busied himself in accumulating supplies and preparing for the movement which he had determined to make, and Lee in strengthening his lines, which extended along a range of hills in the rear of the town, from about a mile and a half above it to the Richmond Railroad below. As these hills were lower than the hills in possession of the Federals on the north side of the river, earthworks were constructed upon their crests, at the most eligible positions. The narrowness of the Rappahannock and its deep bed presented opportunities for laying down bridges at points secure from the fire of the Confederate artillery, while the plain of Fredericksburg is so completely commanded by the Stafford Heights, that no effectual opposition could be made to the construction of bridges or the passage of the river, without exposing the Confederate troops to the destructive fire of the numerous Federal batteries. For these reasons, Lee selected a position with a view to resist the Federal advance after they should have crossed, and guarded the river with a force sufficient only for impeding their movements enough to afford him time for concentration.

It is a familiar military maxim that a general should never do what his adversary wishes him to do. There probably never was an occasion since the first body of troops was arrayed, when a general did more precisely what his adversary wished him to do than Burnside did at Fredericksburg. When the Confederates began to fortify the heights in the rear of Fredericksburg is uncertain, as it is uncertain just when the last of Lee's army arrived there, but their advance was there nearly a month before the battle, and their last arrivals probably a fortnight before it. Lee's present for duty December 10, 1862, was 78,228. Seventy or eighty thousand men, working with a will, throw up perfectly sufficient earthworks in a very few days, not to mention the assistance which the Confederates probably had from working parties of blacks. There was probably nothing that the engineering talent of the Confederacy could supply, wanting to the completeness of their defence on the 13th of December, 1862.

A statement of Swinton[1] is directly to the effect that Burnside hoped to be able to fight no battle at Fredericks-

---

[1] A. P., p. 233.

burg in December, but to be permitted to pass the winter there comfortably, and in the spring to embark his army for the James River. If such were his wishes, they were to his credit, for little certainly could be expected from an offensive movement against Lee, posted as he was, in December of all seasons. The result of McClellan's enterprise two months before, when Lee occupied a much weaker position with a much weaker army, was an instructive lesson. But it is probable that the public temper and the wishes of the administration made a movement so imperative, that it would have required a leader of much sterner mould than Burnside to declare that the thing must not be done. Whatever the causes that impelled him, and whether willingly or unwillingly, Burnside determined to cross the river and attack Lee. The mere crossing presented no serious difficulties. The important questions were where he should cross, in what force, and what he should do when he was across.

The town of Falmouth, which was in front of the centre of the Federal positions, is on the north bank of the Rappahannock, a little above Fredericksburg. The Confederate army occupied Fredericksburg, and a ridge extending from above the Falmouth Ford to Massaponax River, five miles below the town. The ridge forms an angle with the river, passes behind the town, and is itself overlooked by another ridge behind it. Between the ridge and the river extends the plain on which the town stands. It is narrow in its upper portion, but grows wider as it approaches the Massaponax. The whole length of the ridge is about six miles. The Richmond, Fredericksburg, and Potomac Railroad passes through the town, follows the general course of the river for three miles or more, at an average distance of a mile to the westward, and then turns southward. The old Richmond stage road runs about half way between the railroad and the river

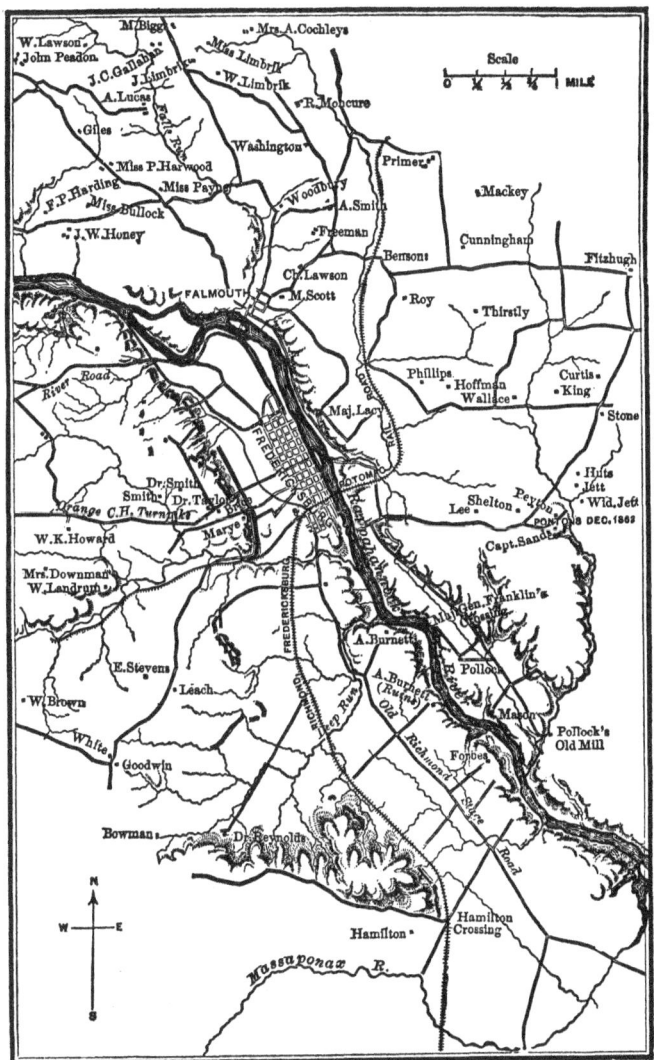

The Field of Fredericksburg.

for about three miles from the town, and then turns sharply to the south, and crosses the railroad at the southeastern extremity of the ridge. This point is called Hamilton's Crossing. The telegraph road runs from the southwestern part of the town, and pursues a circuitous, but generally southwesterly direction, which carries it across the ridge. The plank road is the old county road, which crosses the river, continues through the town under the name of Hanover Street, and thence proceeds in a generally westerly direction through Chancellorsville to Orange Court House. The plain between the river and the ridge slopes gently upward to the base of the latter, and it is broken slightly by low ridges, shallow ravines, and fences. Behind his first line of works, Lee had made or improved a communicating road from the old Richmond road to the telegraph road.

It is fortunate that the task proposed is to tell what Burnside did, and not what he might have done. To attack Lee and Jackson and Longstreet and 78,000 Confederates in a position of their own choosing and of their own fortifying, was an enterprise which would tax the powers of the ablest commander, and the possible plans of operation were reduced within very narrow limits by the fact that Burnside finally determined not to attempt to flank his opponent out of his position, but to cross at points which were only two miles apart, and to attack the enemy in his chosen position. He had abandoned strategy, and tied himself down to narrow tactical possibilities, and crossing as he did, it was simply a question whether his attack or attacks should be more or less directly in front.

Singular as the statement may appear, it seems to be true that Burnside formed no definite plan of battle at all. At the very last moment, after his orders had been given for the troops to be ready to move, with the requisite amount of ammunition and supplies, he abandoned the project, which he had entertained till then, of crossing at Skinker's Neck, ten miles or so below the town, and determined to throw his bridges two at a point opposite the upper part and one near the lower part of the town, and one or two a mile or so below the town. He ordered his Grand Division commanders to concentrate their troops near the proposed bridges, Sumner near the upper and middle bridges, with Hooker in his rear, and Franklin at the bridge or bridges below the town. The bridges were to be thrown on the morning of the 11th. How ill-defined and shadowy his plans were, may be gathered from his own language in his official report: "I hoped to be able to seize some point on the enemy's line near the Massaponax, and thereby separate his forces on the river below from those occupying the crest or ridge in rear of the town." If it had been sure, or probable, that the bridges would be thrown without opposition or delay, the army passed rapidly across, and the attack made at once, this would have been vague enough, but these are violent suppositions. That the throwing of the bridges would be opposed and delayed was reasonably certain, but suppose them laid without opposition. The laying of four or five bridges capable of bearing a great army is a work of some time, and the crossing of bridges is like passing a defile. To pass 100,000 men with a numerous artillery over four or five bridges is as far as possible from being a short or easy affair in a season of profound peace, and when there are scores of long-range rifled guns ready to fire upon every head of a column as it debouches from its bridge, a serious complication is brought into the affair, and it was as certain as anything future that as soon as it was announced that the engineers were at work on the bridges, the whole Confederate army would be on the alert, and that if the movement appeared to be serious, any troops that might be "on the river below" would be promptly called on to move to the scene of action as swiftly as their swift Southern legs could carry them, and it was altogether probable that they would not arrive too late. And when it is remembered that the bridges were not thrown early on the 11th, and that the attack was not made nor the army crossed that day, and that the attack was not made the following day, nor until more than forty-eight hours after work on the bridges was begun, it will be clear that all dreams of a surprise had vanished, and that the circumstances were well suited to filling the minds of Burnside's lieutenants with grave misgiving.

General Hunt was chief of artillery in Burnside's army. In that capacity he had charge of all the guns on the Federal side of the river. "In order," he says, "to control the enemy's movements on the plain, to reply to and silence his batteries along the crest of the ridge, to command the town, to cover and protect the throwing of the bridges and the crossing of the troops, and to protect the left flank of the army from attacks in the direction of the Massaponax River, it was necessary to cover the entire length with artillery, posted in such positions as were favorable to these purposes." To attain these ends, General Hunt placed forty rifled guns, of which six were 20-pounder Parrotts, on the right, from Falmouth down to a ravine about five hundred yards below Falmouth. From the ravine to the neighborhood of the middle bridge, he stationed twenty-four light rifles and fourteen light twelves. On the crest of the high ridge below the middle bridge, were twenty-seven rifled guns, of which seven were $4\frac{1}{2}$-inch siege guns, eight were 20-pounder Parrotts, and twelve were light rifles. On what was left of the high ridge, and on the low ridge below, as far as Pollock's Mill, were eight 20-pounder Parrotts and thirty-four 3-inch rifles; 147 guns in all.

Soon after three o'clock on the morning of the 11th, the work of throwing the bridges was begun. One of the lower bridges was laid without much opposition, and was finished by half-past ten. Another bridge was afterward constructed near it. One of the upper bridges, near the Lacy house, and the middle bridge, were about two-thirds built at six o'clock, but then the Confederate sharpshooters drove away the working parties. The morning was foggy, and the Federal artillery were unable to fire with sufficient accuracy to drive away the sharpshooters. About noon, the fog cleared away, and all the batteries that could be brought to bear were turned upon the town, and the fire of these guns soon checked the fire of the concealed riflemen. General Hunt suggested that advantage should be taken of this opportunity to send men over in pontoons. The suggestion was adopted, and the work was gallantly done by the Seventh Michigan, Nineteenth and Twentieth Massachusetts, and the Eighty-ninth New York. Under the cover which their presence on the opposite bank afforded, the throwing of the bridges was resumed, and they were soon finished.

A very sharp experience befel a part of Hall's (Third) brigade of the Second Division, immediately after the first of the upper bridges was completed. The Seventh Michigan and Nineteenth and Twentieth Massachusetts, which had crossed in boats, belonged to his command. As soon as the first of the upper bridges was completed, the three remaining regiments of his brigade crossed by it. It was growing dark, Howard's division, to which Hall's brigade belonged, was coming across, and the troops were crowding into an unmanageable mass near the bridge head. Hall sent back urgent requests to have the column halted the other side of the river, to give time (as he said) to fight the enemy in his own way, but was ordered to push ahead. He ordered Captain Macy, commanding the Twentieth Massachusetts, to clear the street leading from the bridge at all hazards. What follows is taken from his official report: "I cannot presume to express all that is due the officers and men of this regiment for the unflinching bravery and splendid discipline shown in the execution of the order. Platoon after platoon was swept away, but the head of the column did not falter. Ninety-seven officers and men were killed or wounded in the space of about fifty yards." Besides Howard's division of the Second Corps, one brigade of the Ninth Corps, also of Sumner's command, crossed the river above, and a brigade of Franklin's Grand Division did the same below, and the town was occupied before daylight on the 12th.

The 12th was a foggy day. Sumner's and Franklin's divisions crossed over and took position on the south bank. Nineteen batteries, of one hundred and four guns, passed the river with Sumner's command, but most of them could not be used, and were left in the streets of Fredericksburg or ordered back across the river. Of all the nineteen, seven were wholly or partially engaged the following day.

Twenty-three batteries, of one hundred and sixteen guns, crossed the river at the lower bridges; all but one of these batteries were engaged, and many of them were engaged very severely. The general position of the troops which crossed was as follows: the Second Corps at the town, on the right, the Ninth Corps next, then the Sixth Corps, and then the First. All these troops, excepting two divisions of the First Corps, were formed parallel to the river. Meade's division of the First Corps was formed at right angles to the rest of the army, facing southeast, his right touching the left of Gibbon of the same corps, and his left resting on the river near Smithfield. Doubleday's division of the same corps was in reserve, formed in column on the bank of the river in rear of Meade's left. It could be seen that the Confederates occupied with artillery and infantry the crests of the opposite heights, and the woods and railroad cuts opposite the Federal left with a line of skirmishers extending from the heights to a ravine and some houses on the river bank, opposite the extreme crest of hills on the Federal left. These dispositions of the Federal troops were made without material interruption. The fog was dense, and the Confederate artillery could only be used with effect when the occasional clearing of the mist rendered the Federal columns visible. Hooker's division was retained on the left bank of the river to support either the right or the left, or to press the enemy in case either command should succeed in moving him.

Lee's forces were arranged with Longstreet on the left, with Anderson's division resting upon the river, and the divisions of McLaws, Pickett, and Hood extending to the right, in the order named. Ransom's division supported the batteries on Marye's and Willis's hills, at the foot of which Cobb's brigade, of McLaws's division, and the Twenty-fourth North Carolina, of Ransom's brigade, were stationed, protected by a stone wall. The immediate care of this point was committed to General Ransom. The Washington artillery, under Colonel Walton, occupied the redoubts on the crests of Marye's Hill, and those on the heights to the right and left were held by part of the reserve artillery, Colonel E. P. Alexander's battalion, and the division batteries of Anderson, Ransom, and McLaws. A. P. Hill, of Jackson's corps, was posted between Hood's right and Hamilton's Crossing on the railroad. His front line, consisting of the brigades of Pender, Lane, and Archer, occupied the edge of a wood. Lieutenant-Colonel Walker, with fourteen pieces of artillery, was posted near the right, supported by the Thirty-fifth and Fortieth Virginia regiments, of Field's brigade, commanded by Colonel Brockenbrough. Lane's brigade, thrown forward in advance of the general line, held the woods which here projected into the open ground. Thomas's brigade was stationed behind the interval between Lane and Pender, and Gregg's in rear of that between Lane and Archer. These two brigades, with the Forty-seventh Virginia regiment and Twenty-second Virginia battalion of Field's brigade, constituted A. P. Hill's reserve. Early's and Taliaferro's divisions composed Jackson's second line, D. H. Hill's division his reserve. Jackson's artillery was distributed along his line in the most eligible positions, so as to command the open ground in front. General Stuart, with two brigades of cavalry and his horse artillery, occupied the plain on Jackson's right, extending to the Massaponax River.

According to Burnside's report, Sumner, Franklin, and Hooker showed by their morning reports of December 13th, about one hundred and thirteen thousand men present for duty. These were either across the river or able to cross it upon the receipt of orders. Lee's morning report showed his present for duty on December 10th to be upward of seventy-eight thousand men. Not to insist upon the considerations heretofore presented to show that the Federals habitually took into action a vastly less number of men in proportion to their morning reports than the Confederates, 113,000 against 78,000 was not a great disparity of forces for an army which proposed to attack troops of at least equal calibre in a position of their own choosing, strong by nature, and immensely strengthened by art.

As far as can be ascertained, Burnside's plan of attack, so

far as he had one, was formed on the night of December 12th. He says himself: "By the night of the 12th the troops were all in position, and I visited the different commands with a view to determining as to future movements." This in itself is sufficiently singular, but it may be urged with some slight show of plausibility that a general commanding a great army could not definitely determine his plan till he came into the immediate presence of the enemy. Unfortunately for Burnside's reputation, however, there is nowhere a word said about reconnoissances after crossing the river, not a word to indicate that he either sought or obtained a particle of information which he did not possess before crossing the river. General Franklin on the left had had placed under his command more than half of Burnside's army, comprising the First and Sixth Corps, two divisions of the Third Corps, Burns's division of the Ninth Corps, and Bayard's cavalry, and he asserts positively that at five o'clock in the afternoon of the 12th, General Burnside came to his headquarters, where he met, besides himself, General Smith, commanding the Sixth Corps, and General Reynolds, commanding the First Corps. He says: "The subject of conversation was a proposed attack upon the enemy on the following morning, when I strongly advised General Burnside to make an attack from my division upon the enemy's right, with a column of at least thirty thousand men, to be sent in at daylight in the morning." He also says that he told General Burnside that in order to make such an attack, two divisions of Hooker's command, then on the north side of the river, near Franklin's bridges, must be crossed during the night. He says that he reiterated his request that he should receive his orders as early as possible, that he might make the necessary dispositions of the troops before daylight. He also says that Burnside left him at about 6 P.M., and promised him that he should have his orders within two or three hours, or in any event before midnight, and that at midnight he sent an aide to ask for them, and received the reply that they were preparing and would be sent forthwith. It is admitted that he received no orders till half past seven on the morning of the 13th, and these orders came by the hand of General Hardie, of General Burnside's staff. They will be given presently. The night had passed without orders, and General Hooker's two divisions had remained on the farther (Northern) side of the river.

It is a pitiful picture, but is probably a true one, that Burnside passed the evening of the 12th riding about, not quite at his wits' end, but very near it. As far as can be made out, he finally came to the conclusion that he would attempt to do something, he did not quite know what, with his left, and if he succeeded, to do something with his right. He says: "Positive information had reached me that the enemy had built a new road in rear of the ridge or crest, from near Hamilton's to the telegraph road. . . . I decided to seize, if possible, a point on this road near Hamilton's, which would not divide the enemy's forces by breaking their line, but would place our forces in position to enable us to move in rear of the crest, and either force its evacuation or the capitulation of the forces occupying it. It was my intention, in case this point had been gained, to push Generals Sumner and Hooker against the left of the crest, and prevent, at least, the removal of the artillery of the enemy, in case they attempted a retreat." That is to say, operating with forces practically equal, used as they were to be against an enemy in an extremely strong position, he proposed to himself a difficult and doubtful enterprise, and intended, if that succeeded, to divide his forces in the immediate presence of a powerful enemy, concentrated and strengthened by the very success he hoped for. It is perfectly plain that if Franklin had planted himself solidly at the lower end of the ridge, near Hamilton's Crossing, Lee would still have had at least nine chances in ten of success. A lodgment there would have made Sumner's attack on the right no easier, and if Burnside had undertaken to pass his troops round the point of the ridge at Hamilton's Crossing, with a view either to attacking Lee in rear, or to a direct movement upon Richmond, he would in either case have exposed his flank at the outset, and still have had to attack difficult heights with a divided army if he had chosen the former course.

But bad and vague as the plan was, the orders issued were worse and more vague. The orders which reached Franklin at 7.30 A.M. of the 13th, after he had passed a night of "sleepless anxiety" in his tent, were as follows:

HEADQUARTERS ARMY OF POTOMAC,
December 13, 1862—5.55 A.M.

MAJOR-GENERAL FRANKLIN, *Commanding Left Grand Division Army of Potomac:*

General Hardie will carry this despatch to you, and remain with you during the day. The General Commanding directs that you keep your whole command in position for a rapid movement down the old Richmond road, and you will send out at once a division, at least, to pass below Smithfield, to seize, if possible, the heights near Captain Hamilton's, on this side of the Massaponax, taking care to keep it well supported and its line of retreat open. He has ordered another column of a division or more to be moved from General Sumner's command up the plank road, to its intersection with the telegraph road, where they will divide, with a view to seizing the heights on both of those roads. Holding those two heights, with the heights near Captain Hamilton's, will, he hopes, compel the enemy to evacuate the whole ridge between these points. I make these moves by columns distant from each other, with a view of avoiding the possibility of a collision of our own forces, which might occur in a general movement during the fog. Two of General Hooker's divisions are in your rear, at the bridges, and will remain there as supports.

Copies of instructions given to Generals Sumner and Hooker will be forwarded to you by an orderly very soon.

You will keep your whole command in readiness to move at once, as soon as the fog lifts. The watchword, which, if possible, should be given to every company, will be "Scott."

I have the honor to be, General, very respectfully, your obedient servant,

JNO. G. PARKE,
Chief of Staff.

This order is exceedingly hard to understand, even at this distance of time, and with all the light which has been thrown upon it. General Franklin says that in the state of facts existing when it was received, "General Burnside's order, though incongruous and contradictory on its face, admitted of but one interpretation, viz., that he intended to make an armed observation from the left to ascertain the strength of the enemy—an interpretation also given to it by both of my corps commanders." Without assenting unreservedly to this interpretation, two propositions seem to be safe, viz.: that the order meant

First.—That Franklin was to keep his whole command in readiness to move, and that the direction of the movement was to be down the old Richmond road.

Second.—That the seizure of the heights near Captain Hamilton's was hoped for, but not counted upon, as the language is "to seize, if possible," and the force told off for this task is to be kept well supported, with its line of retreat open.

Under this order it was not open to Franklin to engage his whole command. The minor enterprise, the seizure of the heights, might have required that, but the order showed that that enterprise was considered one of doubtful issue, as he was ordered to keep the line of retreat of the attacking force open. But the dominant feature of the order was the injunction, twice repeated, to keep his whole command in position and in readiness. It is idle to say that a general could obey this order and yet engage his whole command. When a general puts his troops in, it passes his and all human knowledge to know what the result will be, but it is absolutely and unqualifiedly true that he cannot both engage his whole command and at the same time hold his whole command in readiness to move anywhere or in position to do anything.

General Franklin was practically ruined as a soldier by the battle of Fredericksburg and his connection with it, but so far as the accessible evidence enables one to judge, he was most unjustly blamed. If there were a particle of evidence that any discretion was left to him, if we read anywhere that Burnside had said, "Now, Franklin, I have given you a large force, and I leave you to use your best discretion as to operations on my left," or anything nearly or remotely like it, he might justly be held liable to the grave charge of having lost the battle by his own inaction. But upon the evidence the charge is not sustained. More than that, the charge cannot be reconciled with the orders given. The fault was in the orders, and not in any failure on Franklin's part to understand them or obey them. This conclusion would be inevitable if the orders were the only evidence in the case, but, besides the orders, we have Franklin's statement of what he said to Burnside the night before, in the presence of Smith and Reynolds, which is very important, and also the series of despatches, twelve in number, sent to Burnside by his own staff officer who carried the orders to Franklin, and was instructed to remain with him during the day, at short intervals from 7.40 A.M. to 2.15 P.M. These despatches tell completely, and with very considerable detail, just what Franklin was doing, and there is absolutely not a suggestion in them that Hardie thought that Franklin had misapprehended his orders, or that his conduct was in any way or degree unsatisfactory. When we couple with this fact the other fact that not one word of disapproval or disappointment was sent back from Burnside to Franklin for six or seven hours, the conclusion is irresistible that Burnside, at the time, was satisfied with Franklin's construction and execution of his orders. The obscurity of Burnside's own language, both in the orders sent to Franklin and in his report of the battle, is such that it is difficult to determine what his expectations were, but it seems to be certain that he expected that Franklin's movement upon the heights near Hamilton's would be a movement upon the extreme right of the Confederates. If such was his expectation, he was all wrong, as will presently be made to appear.

The general position of Franklin's Grand Division has already been stated. Smith's Sixth Corps was formed on the right, with Brooks's division on the right and Howe's on the left, and Newton's in reserve. Brooks held the Richmond road and Deep Creek with one line in front of the creek, while Howe occupied the crest of a hill over which the Richmond road ran, his right at a sharp turn of Deep Creek. Gibbon's division of the First Corps formed on the left of Howe, and Meade's division, also of the First Corps, was formed facing to the left of the general position, his right joining nearly at right angles with the left of Gibbon, and his left resting on the river near Smithfield. The remaining division of the First Corps, Doubleday's, was formed on the bank of the river in rear of Meade's left. The position of Smithfield is not easy to identify. It is not marked upon the best maps. It was probably a Virginia estate, and situated on the Rappahannock, about a mile above the mouth of the Massaponax. These dispositions of the Left Grand Division were made, Franklin says, in compliance with the directions of the commanding general, and the very fact that they were made, is evidence that he was not confident, when he issued them, that such an attack as Franklin was ordered to make was to be an attack upon the extreme right of the Confederates. To form *en potence* so strong a force as two divisions, showed plainly that some solicitude was felt as to possible attacks from the direction of the Massaponax. The sequel showed that these apprehensions were well founded. It soon appeared that the Confederates had both artillery and infantry on Franklin's left as well as in his front. This fact is of very great importance. It is not to be lost sight of for a moment in considering either Burnside's plan or Franklin's action. It reduced Burnside's plan to two distant and isolated attempts to pierce the enemy's line, and it paralyzed, *pro tanto*, Franklin's action. It increased immensely the difficulty of the difficult, not to say impossible, task assigned him, to seize a strong point, keep the attacking force well supported and its line of retreat open, and to keep his whole command in readiness to do another and quite different thing.

Franklin informed Reynolds that his corps would make the attack indicated, and he ordered Meade's division to the point of attack, with Gibbon in support. He thought it impracticable to add Smith's Corps to the force detailed for the attack, and he also considered Reynolds's three divisions sufficient to carry out the spirit of the order, the words of which were "a division at least."

The point indicated for Meade's attack was near the (Federal) left of the ridge, where it terminated in the Massaponax Valley. The Confederates occupied the wooded heights, the railroad in front of them, and the woods in front of the railroad. On receiving its orders, the division moved down the river for nearly half a mile, then turned sharp to its own right, and crossed the old Richmond (or Bowling Green) road. The column of attack was formed between nine and ten o'clock, some time having been devoted to removing fences, and to bridging the drains on each side of the road, to admit of the passage of the artillery. As Meade's formation was completed, the Confederates opened on him from guns which reached his command from the left and rear, and there was so much strength developed by the Confederates still further to his left and rear in the neighborhood of the Massaponax, that Doubleday's division was advanced in that direction and did a good deal of fighting and gained some ground. As soon as the firing on the left and rear had been controlled, and the woods and heights in front had been smartly shelled, Meade attempted to advance again, but again a sharp artillery fire burst out from the heights on his extreme left, and it took rapid firing from three batteries for thirty minutes to silence it. The "incomparable Pelham" had charge of at least a section of the Confederate guns which checked Meade's progress by firing upon his left.

At last the Confederate guns were silenced, or silent, and Meade advanced. The first brigade succeeded in penetrating the woods, driving the enemy from the railroad beyond, and finally crossed the crest of the hill beyond, and reached open ground on the other side. With great gallantry and ardor, they had pressed back the troops in front of them, and made or found an interval between the brigades of Archer and Lane of A. P. Hill's division, and forced two regiments of the former and the whole of the latter to give way. The second brigade divided as it followed the first up the hill, to meet a sharp fire which assailed it on both flanks, but only a small portion of it reached the same point as the first brigade. One of its regiments took prisoners and a color. The Third Brigade was checked by a destructive fire from the battery on the left, its commander was killed, and it accomplished little. Meade's division fared as Pickett's division fared at Gettysburg. Having made a most brilliant advance, and penetrated the hostile line more deeply than Pickett's did, it was enveloped by fire closing in upon it from every direction, and compelled to withdraw. But it seems to have been better commanded and better supported than Pickett's division was, and instead of losing seventy-five per cent., as Pickett's division did, it lost only forty per cent., and it captured several standards and over three hundred prisoners. A brigade from Birney's division on the left and one from Gibbon's division on the right aided materially in the withdrawal of Meade's line. It is not quite clear why Gibbon, on the right of Meade, did not accomplish more. The wood was so dense that the connection between his line and Meade's could not be, or was not, kept up. At least that reason is assigned by Franklin, but as Gibbon himself says that the left of his leading brigade was thrown into confusion by the fire of the enemy posted behind the railroad embankment, and that all (except the Twelfth Massachusetts) of the brigade then ordered up in support and posted on the left "soon fell into confusion, and most of it retired in disorder," it is evident that a large part of his troops were poor, and that the failure of his attack was mainly owing to the inferiority of his men. After all of Lyle's brigade, and all of Taylor's except the Ninety-seventh New York and Eighty-eighth Pennsylvania, had given away, Root's brigade was ordered up. The Twelfth

Massachusetts and some remnants joined it, and the force advanced gallantly and took the embankment and some prisoners. But the embankment was a long way from the coveted point, and a brigade and a regiment cannot cover the ground or do the work of three brigades. Gibbon's division failed to give substantial support to Meade, and Meade's enterprise was too much for a single division. The Confederate troops engaged in this repulse were A. P. Hill's division, with the aid of a large part of Early's division (formerly Ewell's), and a small part of Taliaferro's (formerly Jackson's). The reported loss of Gregg's South Carolina brigade, of the second line, was 41 killed and 295 wounded, out of about fifteen hundred. Gregg himself received a wound of which he died the following day.

Meade and Gibbon were driven back by 2.15 P.M. After an unsuccessful attempt to reform Meade's division further to the front than the old Richmond (or Bowling Green) road, it was marched to the ground occupied the night before, and there held in reserve. Gibbon's division, under Taylor, Gibbon having been wounded near the wood, also fell back to its original position.

Reserving for the moment such comments as Franklin's action may seem to call for, it may be well to turn from the left to the right of the Army of the Potomac, and thus to observe, as nearly as may be, the order of time. It has been seen that, in compliance with Burnside's order to send out "a division at least," Franklin had sent out three entire divisions, and had had two of them pretty completely used up. He had also used the whole of Birney's division to resist the enemy when they showed a disposition to follow up the retreat of Meade, and Sickles's division to relieve Gibbon's division when the latter fell back. These two divisions belonged to Stoneman's corps, the Third.

Early on the morning of the 13th, Burnside sent to Sumner, commanding the Right Grand Division, the following orders:

> The General Commanding directs that you extend the left of your command to Deep Run, connecting with General Franklin, extending your right as far as your judgment may dictate. He also directs that you push a column of a division or more along the plank and telegraph roads, with a view to seizing the heights in the rear of the town. The latter movement should be well covered with skirmishers, and supported so as to keep its line of retreat well open. Copy of instructions given to General Franklin will be sent to you very soon. You will please await them at your present headquarters, where he (the General Commanding) will meet you. Great care should be taken to prevent a collision of our own forces during the fog. The watchword for the day will be "Scott." The column for a movement up the telegraph and plank roads will be got in readiness to move, but will not move till the General Commanding communicates with you.

These orders were dated at 6 A.M.

The orders to Hooker were dated at 7 A.M., and were as follows:

> The General Commanding directs that you place General Butterfield's Corps and Whipple's division in position to cross, at a moment's notice, at the three upper bridges, in support of the other troops, over the river, and the two remaining divisions of General Stoneman's Corps in readiness to cross at the lower ford, in support of General Franklin. The General Commanding will meet you at headquarters (Phillips's house) very soon. Copies of instructions to General Sumner and General Franklin will be sent to you.

It may be remarked upon the orders to Hooker, that the instruction as to placing two of Stoneman's divisions at the lower ford seems out of place, as Burnside states that on the evening of the 12th he ordered General Stoneman, with two divisions of his corps, to a point near the lower bridge, as a support to General Franklin. To find a general-in-chief ordering one of his three chief officers, on the morning of the 13th, to do what he himself had ordered done the evening before, does not give a high idea of the clearness of head and strength of memory of the superior, nor of the orderly and efficient management of staff business at general headquarters.

It is to be remembered that the plank road mentioned in the order to Sumner, is the county road, which crosses the Rappahannock about seven hundred yards above the railroad bridge, continues through the centre of the town under the name of Hanover Street,[1] and afterward becomes the plank road, extending through Chancellorsville to Orange Court House. West of the town, and at a distance of about half a mile from it, the ridge runs from northwest to southeast for about a mile, in a line very accurately parallel to the river and to the length of the town. Then it bends and runs southerly for nearly half a mile. On the high ground above the angle thus formed, stands the estate known as Marye's. The eastern boundary of this estate is a road which presently bends to the west and southwest and crosses the hills under the name of the telegraph road. The eastern front of the Marye estate has a retaining wall of stone, and another similar wall, shoulder high, makes the eastern boundary of this road in front. Earth was piled up against the eastern face of this eastern wall, and thus there was formed the most perfect infantry parapet conceivable. It was a better position for troops than the parapet of ordinary field works affords, for while it insured perfect protection against fire from the front, it placed the troops behind it perfectly at their ease, with plenty of room, and a good, hard, flat, broad road beneath their feet, while the elevation of the ground in their

---

[1] Or perhaps Commerce Street.

rear gave an admirable position for the sharpshooters in rifle-pits and the guns in earthworks. The sharpshooters and the cannoneers could fire over the heads of the men in the road with absolute safety to them. It can hardly be necessary to say more of the artificial strength of the whole position, whether at Marye's or above or below, than that the Confederates had constructed rifle-pits, breast-highs, earthworks, and redoubts, wherever they thought them likely to be of service.

It is to be remarked upon the morning orders to Sumner and Hooker that they gave no plan of battle at all. Hooker was not even ordered to cross the river, and Sumner was not ordered to attack, or even to move, but simply to get a column of "a division or more" in readiness to move in a direction indicated. The injunction to take great care to prevent a collision of the Federal forces, must be taken to mean a collision between Sumner's men advancing by the plank and telegraph roads, as Franklin's men were a long way from the nearest of these two roads, probably a mile and a half. The language of Burnside's orders to Sumner leads to the belief that when he spoke of a movement along the plank and telegraph roads, he meant a movement along the county road and the second road through the town to the south, which runs westward from the river parallel to the former and about a sixth of a mile from it, and then runs out straight to the Marye estate.

General Burnside says that he held Sumner's command in position until after eleven o'clock, in the hope that Franklin would make such an impression upon the enemy as would enable Sumner to carry the enemy's line near the telegraph and plank roads, and that, "feeling the importance of haste, I now (*i.e.*, at about 11 A.M.) directed General Sumner to commence his attack." He adds "I supposed when I ordered General Sumner to attack, that General Franklin's attack on the left would have been made before General Sumner's men would be engaged, and would have caused the enemy to weaken his forces in front of Sumner, and I therefore hoped to break through their lines at this point. It subsequently appeared that this attack had not been made at the time General Sumner moved. . . ." There is one short and painful criticism to be made upon this statement. It cannot be true. Burnside could not suppose, when he ordered Sumner to attack, that General Franklin's attack on the left would have been made before General Sumner's men would be engaged. His own report proves it. He gave his orders to Sumner to commence the attack very near 11 A.M., if not before. Sumner says that his advance division moved at 11 A.M., but he probably puts the hour too early, though Lee says,[1] that he moved forward about 11 A.M. The last despatch from Hardie, Burnside's own staff officer with Franklin, which was sent before 11, was dated 9.40 A.M. It told him that cannon on the left, playing upon Reynolds's advance, in rear of his first line, caused him to *desist the advance.* Hardie's next despatch is dated 11 A.M. It is not stated when Burnside received it, but unless Hardie was at one end of the wire, which is not likely, and Burnside at the other, which is still less likely, it did not reach Burnside for a good many minutes at least. Moreover, it has a postscript, simply dated "Later," which seems to have been sent at the same time. But if Burnside received the 11 A.M. despatch and the "Later" postscript before he ordered Sumner to advance, there was nothing in either to authorize him to believe or

---

[1] A. N. Va., i., 42. But see French's Report. He commanded the division which led, and he says he received his orders to attack at 12 A.M. He, again, almost certainly puts the hour too late. Longstreet and McLaws both state that the attack commenced at about 11 A.M.

even hope that Franklin's attack would have been made before Sumner's men would be engaged. The first paragraph of the 11 A.M. despatch contains these words: "Meade advanced half a mile and holds on." This language is not the language appropriate to a successful advance. It is language appropriate to a check. The language of the postscript is more ominous. It says: "Reynolds has been forced to develop his whole line. An attack of some force of enemy's troops on our left seems probable as far as can now be judged. . . ." This meant, not that the attacking force was in the way of carrying every thing before it, but that it was likely to be put on the defensive. The "division at least" had grown to a corps, and that not voluntarily, but Reynolds had been "forced to develop his whole line." The postscript added that Stoneman had been ordered to cross one division to support the left. Thus the "division at least" had grown, including its support, to four divisions. However the fact may be as to the time when the 11 A.M. despatch was received, Burnside himself establishes conclusively the fact that when he ordered Sumner forward he had received no encouraging information from the left, and nothing to lead him to suppose what he says he supposed, but the contrary.

Burnside says he ordered Sumner "to commence his attack." One would think from this language that a plan of attack proportioned to the strong force under his command, had been given to Sumner, but there is absolutely nothing to show that Sumner had received any other instructions than the "push a column of a division or more" sentence of the 6 A.M. order, except that Sumner says that he was to attack "with a division, supported closely by a second." All the evidence, Burnside's own testimony being most prominent, is to the effect that Burnside really had no comprehensive plan at all—that he proposed to tap the enemy's lines here and there, and see what would come of it. All his action on the further side of the Rappahannock was purely tentative, and it would have been vastly better for the Army of the Potomac if he had not been there at all. He contributed nothing—ideas and example were alike wanting. His superior rank was of no avail in combining and connecting the movements of the troops. With him away, Franklin might have made the grand attack he proposed, and driven in a large and sufficient wedge where under his orders he drove in a small and insufficient one. With him away, Sumner, probably, and Hooker, certainly, would not have made the disastrous attacks they did make. *Væ victis.* It was a dark day for the Army of the Potomac, and General Burnside's "generosity" and "magnanimity" after the battle, though they imposed upon many of his easily deluded fellow-countrymen, were slight comfort to the homes that were darkened and the lives that were crippled by his insane attempt upon the heights of Fredericksburg.

Into how much detail shall we go in telling the story of this attempt to carry wooded slopes and successive crests, this advance against a strong force of admirable troops, covered by breastworks and rifle-pits, with guns protected by earthworks, disposed in lines which gave both front and enfilading fires on their assailants as they moved up the gradual slope which swelled from the town to the hostile lines? We read with a certain equanimity of such events as the storming of Ciudad Rodrigo or Badajoz, or the assaults on the Redan and Malakoff, both because we feel that in these cases necessity determined the work to be attempted, and because we feel that the leaders of the assailants exerted their utmost powers to increase to the utmost their chances of success. But at Fredericksburg we see a gallant army engaged in an undertaking at once unnecessary and hopeless, and sent to destruction with no plan and no preparation.

Those who have been in battle know how much and how little they saw and heard. They remember how the smoke and the woods and the inequalities of ground limited their vision when they had leisure to look about them, and how every faculty was absorbed in their work when they were actively engaged; how the deafening noise made it almost impossible to hear orders; what ghastly sights they saw as men and horses near them were torn with shell; how peacefully the men sank to rest whom the more merciful rifle-bullet reached in a vital spot; how some wounded men shrieked and others lay quiet; how awful was the sound of the projectiles when they were near hostile batteries, how incessant was the singing and whistling of the balls from rifles and muskets; how little they commonly knew of what was going on a hundred yards to their right or left. Orderly advances of bodies of men may be easily described and easily imagined, but pictures of real fighting are and must be imperfect. Participants in real fighting know how limited and fragmentary and confused are their recollections of work after it became hot. The larger the force engaged, the more impossible it is to give an accurate presentation of its experiences. We can follow the charge of the six hundred at Balaclava, from which less than one in three came back unharmed, better than we can follow the advance of Hancock's five thousand at Fredericksburg, from which not quite three in five came back unharmed. And Hancock's advance was only one of many. "Six times," says Lee, "did the enemy, notwithstanding the havoc caused by our batteries, press on with great determination, to within one hundred yards of the foot of the hill, but here encountering the deadly fire of our infantry, his columns were broken, and fled in confusion to the town."

When Sumner received his orders, he selected French's division of the Second Corps as the leading column, and had Hancock's division formed in support. French's division, preceded by a strong body of skirmishers, moved out of the town by the two parallel streets above mentioned. About half way between the town and the ridge held by the Confederates, there was a canal, or mill race, which could not be crossed except at the bridges by which the two streets crossed it, on their way to become the telegraph and plank roads. A little beyond the canal the ground rises slightly, and this rise formed a cover behind which the troops were able to deploy. The skirmishers worked their way forward, followed by French's division, and Hancock pressed on and came up with French, and joined in the advance. Hancock estimated that the distance the troops had to march—first by the flank through the streets of the town and across the bridges, then still by the flank in a line parallel to the Confederate works, to effect a deployment, and, finally, in line to the hostile front—was probably seventeen hundred yards, all the way under a most murderous fire, the artillery fire reaching the Federals destructively even before they left the streets of the town. The troops were delayed also by the fact (which ought to have been known and provided for) that the planking of one of the bridges was partially taken up, which made it necessary for the men to cross on the stringers. By the time French and Hancock were within assaulting distance, their columns were too much reduced for their work. Their objective point was the strong position at Marye's, where Cobb's and Kershaw's brigades of McLaws's division, and Cook's and Ransom's brigades of

Ransom's division, were ready to receive them, with the important aid of the artillery, the fire of which, Longstreet says, "was very destructive and demoralizing in its effects, and frequently made gaps in the enemy's ranks that could be seen at the distance of a mile.[1]

At 1 P.M. Couch, commanding the Second Corps, ordered Hancock and French to carry the enemy's work by storm. Seeing shortly that this could not be done, the men falling by hundreds, he directed Howard, who commanded his remaining division, to move to the right and turn the enemy's left, but the order was immediately revoked by him, and Howard was ordered to support Hancock. The three divisions got well forward, Hall's brigade of Howard's division and some of Hancock's men apparently doing the best work that was done, but the difficulties to be overcome were too great, and the assault failed. The general line got up to a distance of some one hundred yards from the stone wall, and some men, probably of Kimball's brigade of Hancock's division, fell dead within twenty-five paces of it. The Twentieth Massachusetts of Hall's brigade was praised for "the matchless courage and discipline" it displayed, especially in standing firm and returning the fire of the enemy, when its comrades fell back, until the line was reformed. The hardest fighting was done by Hancock, who lost 2,000 men, and French, who lost 1,200. Howard was put into action later than Hancock and French, and lost 877 men.

The attack of the Second Corps had about spent its force by 2.30 P.M. Sturgis's division of the Ninth Corps had shared its efforts, and with a like result. Under orders received at about noon to support Couch, it was moved at once to the front. It had but two brigades. Ferrero's led,

---

[1] A. N. Va., ii., 429.

and did some good fighting, and was presently joined by Nagle's. The troops behaved to the satisfaction of their corps commander, and lost 1,028 of their number, but the stone wall was too much for them. They could not carry the position. To complete the story of the Ninth Corps, it may here be stated that Getty's division was sent forward much later in the day, at or after 4 P.M., and lower down in the general line. It was not very severely engaged, and lost only 284 men. The other division of the corps, that of Burns, was sent to the support of Franklin at 3 P.M., to cover his bridges. It had next to nothing to do, and sustained no losses of any consequence.

A strict observance of the order of time would perhaps dictate changing the scene at the point now reached to the Federal left, but when a battle is to be described in which large numbers of troops are engaged at different parts of a long line, there are objections to observing too closely the connections of either time or place. Upon the whole, the balance of convenience seems to incline in the direction of completing the story of the operations on the Federal right before returning to Franklin on the left.

Whipple's division of the Third Corps, composed of two brigades and a regiment, was ordered on the morning of the 13th to cross the river and send one brigade to report to General Willcox, and with the remainder to guard the approaches to the town from the west, and to protect the right flank of Howard's division while making an attack in front. The brigade and regiment assigned to the latter duty were not actively engaged, and suffered hardly any loss. The other brigade, under Carroll, was ordered at about 1.30 P.M. to move up to General Sturgis's support. Carroll moved up on the left of Sturgis, and took and held a crest on his front, and suffered a loss of 113 out of 850.

His conduct was highly praised by his division commander, but his action had no other influence upon the general result than perhaps to facilitate the withdrawal of Willcox's men. Griffin's division of the Fifth Corps was ordered also to move forward to the support of General Sturgis. Griffin's report does not agree nicely with Carroll's as to either time or position, but the discrepancy is of little consequence. One of his brigades relieved Ferrero's brigade of Sturgis's division, and this brigade, aided at first by one and then by both of the other brigades of the division, advanced gallantly. General Griffin says that his lines moved up to within a few yards of the enemy's infantry, but that then the fire became so galling that they were compelled to fall back behind the crest of a knoll. The loss of the division was 818 men killed and wounded. Sykes's division of the Fifth Corps was not actively engaged, but was exposed to the fire of both artillery and riflemen, and lost 228 men. It, or most of it, was in position near the southern edge of the town, except for a short time, while it was acting in connection with Humphreys's division, as will be seen hereafter.

Some of the very best fighting that was done at Fredericksburg was done by the Third Division of the Fifth Corps. The division was commanded by General Humphreys, who was probably the best officer in the Army of the Potomac that day. He was a thoroughly educated soldier, possessed of a quick eye and a clear head, and a man of fiery energy. That the fighting his division did was so good was due to him. He had but two brigades, and many of his regiments had never before been in battle. At 2.30 P.M. he was ordered to cross the river, and soon after received orders to support Couch on the left of the telegraph road. He hastily moved his Second Brigade, which was nearest, to the front, and sent orders to his other brigade to follow and form on the right. He led his Second Brigade, Allabach's, rapidly forward to the position occupied by Couch's men, whom he found in great numbers sheltering themselves by lying on the ground behind a slight rise about one hundred and fifty yards from the stone wall. The continued presence of these men proved a serious obstacle to his success. Allabach's men followed their example in lying down, and opened fire. As soon as Humphreys had ascertained the nature of the enemy's position, which the urgency of the case had put it out of his power to do before arriving with his men, he became satisfied that his fire could have little effect upon them, and he perceived that the only mode of attacking him successfully was with the bayonet. With great difficulty he stopped the firing of his men, and the charge was then made, but the deadly fire of artillery and musketry broke it after an advance of fifty yards. Allabach then reformed his brigade in the rear, part in the line from which the charge was made, and the remainder in the ravine from which it originally advanced. General Humphreys then rode to Tyler's brigade. It was already growing dusky. Riding along his lines, he directed his men not to fire; that it was useless; that the bayonet alone was the weapon to fight with here. Having learned from experience what a serious obstacle they would encounter from the presence of the masses of men lying behind the natural embankment in front, he directed them to disregard these men entirely, and to pass over them. He ordered the officers to the front, and "with a hurrah, the brigade, led by General Tyler and myself, advanced gallantly over the ground, under the heaviest fire yet opened, which poured upon it from the moment it rose from the ravine."

The scene which followed was most singular, and it is

well to describe it in General Humphreys's own words: "As the brigade reached the masses of men referred to, every effort was made by the latter to prevent our advance. They called to our men not to go forward, and some attempted to prevent by force their doing so. The effect upon my command was what I apprehended—the line was somewhat disordered, and in part forced to form into a column, but still advanced rapidly. The fire of the enemy's musketry and artillery, furious as it was before, now became still hotter. The stone wall was a sheet of flame that enveloped the head and flanks of the column. Officers and men were falling rapidly, and the head of the column was at length brought to a stand when close up to the wall. Up to this time, not a shot had been fired by the column, but now some firing began. It lasted but a minute, when, in spite of all our efforts, the column turned and began to retire slowly. I attempted to rally the brigade behind the natural embankment so often mentioned, but the united efforts of General Tyler, myself, our staffs, and the other officers, could not arrest the retiring mass."

General Humphreys had one horse disabled by wounds and another killed under him. He had but one staff officer remaining mounted, and his horse was wounded in three places. His force being now too small to try another charge, he was directed to bring in Allabach's men from the line of natural embankment. This was well done, two of his regiments in particular, the One Hundred and Twenty-third and One Hundred and Fifty-fifth Pennsylvania, "retiring slowly and in good order, singing and hurrahing." This jocund march of Allabach's men may have been what the Confederate General Ransom referred to when he said, "This last desperate and maddened attack met the same fate which had befallen those which preceded, and his hosts

FREDERICKSBURG. 173

were sent, actually howling, back to their beaten comrades in the town."[1] Humphreys had more than a thousand men killed and wounded in his two brigades.

With the repulse of Humphreys's division, the fighting on the Federal right came to an end, though it was not till well into the evening that the fire of the sharpshooters and the artillery entirely died out. The troops as a rule continued to hold the positions in which they found themselves when night fell, but some of them were relieved by commands which had been engaged less or not at all. Our story returns to Franklin and the Federal left.

It must be constantly borne in mind that, under Burnside's orders, four of his six corps had been arrayed on the south bank of the river, in what was substantially the parallel order of battle, with the Second Corps on the right, the Ninth Corps next, then the Sixth Corps, and then the First; that two divisions of the Third Corps, those of Birney and Sickles, had been also sent to Franklin; that Whipple's division of the Third Corps, and those of Griffin and Humphreys of the Fifth Corps, took part in the right attack, and that Sykes's division of the Fifth Corps, the only remaining division of Hooker's Centre Grand Division, was, for the most part, held in reserve near the town. The battle of Fredericksburg naturally divides itself into two parts: the left attack, conducted by Franklin with the Left Grand Division and reinforcements, and the right attack, conducted by Sumner with the Right Grand Division and reinforcements. Hooker's command, the Centre Grand Division, was so broken up that he can hardly be considered to have taken any part in the battle, and cannot at all be considered as responsible for the defeat. Especially must it not be forgotten that the

---

[1] A. N. Va., ii., 453.

Sixth Corps was formed, in compliance with Burnside's directions, parallel to the old Richmond road, with two divisions in front and one in reserve. The posting of the troops gives better indications of what was in Burnside's mind than his own language, and so far as a plan can be constructed from the indications so afforded, it would seem to have been his idea to arrange two of his Grand Divisions in line in front of the ridge held by the enemy, and to hold the third in reserve, and from his front so formed to make sallies wherever he fancied he might do so to advantage, and, with the rest of his line, be prepared to resist such sorties as the enemy might make from what was in reality their fortified camp. If Franklin believed that he entertained this idea, his conclusion was reasonable, and it is probable that he did, and in considering what he did or what he might have done, the general formation of the troops under Burnside's orders is an important matter, and one not to be lost sight of. Under these orders, Franklin's line extended from a point west of Deep Creek to at least as far down as Hamilton's Crossing, and must have been as much as three miles long.

Burnside's report contains the statement that between 12.30 and 1.30 of the 13th he sent three orders to Franklin —the first by Captain Cutts (probably written, though it is not so stated), directing him to advance his right and front; the next by telegraph, directing him to make an attack upon the heights immediately in his front; the third by Captain Goddard, given to him about 1.30, and delivered by him to Franklin, "in the presence of General Hardie, before 2.30 o'clock." This order was verbal. Burnside gives it as follows: "Tell General Franklin, with my compliments, that I wish him to make a vigorous attack with his whole force; our right is hard pressed." Franklin's official report, dated

January 2, 1863, makes no mention of any one of these orders. They are not referred to in Hardie's despatches to Burnside, except in a very brief one dated 2.25 P.M., which is as follows: "Despatch received. Franklin will do his best. New troops gone in. Will report soon again." In Franklin's printed Reply to the Joint Committee of Congress on the Conduct of the War on the First Battle of Fredericksburg, he says that the telegraph station connecting with General Burnside's headquarters was about one-third of a mile from his headquarters, and that General Burnside did not communicate with him *in any manner* from the time when he sent him the morning order by Hardie till about 2.25 P.M., when he sent him an order in writing, in which it was stated that his instructions of the morning were so far modified as to require an advance upon the heights immediately in his front. In his testimony before the committee, however, he admits that he received a message from General Burnside, and he *seems* to admit that it was to the effect that he should make a vigorous attack at once with his whole force, but he says that the message was not an order. "It was more in the light of a request to do it if I thought I could, and I sent back word that I could not do it." General Franklin's testimony is not absolutely clear, and, taking it in connection with Burnside's assertions in his report, it appears possible that he may have received messages from Burnside, by or before 2.30 P.M., by both Captain Cutts and Captain Goddard, besides the order by telegraph. If the fact be so, he knew that Burnside wished or ordered him to advance his right and front, and to make a vigorous attack with his whole force; that the right was hard pressed, and that Burnside ordered him to make an attack upon the heights immediately in his front. It is reasonably certain that the earliest of these orders did not reach him before 1.30, and that all that reached him were received by him by or before 2.25 P.M. It is therefore necessary to inquire what was the condition of his command at 1.30.

Smith's corps, the Sixth, was in position on both sides of Deep Creek, holding a line of considerable length. Its skirmish line was engaged pretty constantly, and the main body of the corps was exposed to artillery fire, but neither the corps nor any of its divisions or brigades had been engaged up to 2.30 or 3 P.M.

Of the First Corps, the divisions of Meade and Gibbon had been severely engaged, and had retired in no little confusion and disorder. "Regardless of threat and force, and deaf to all entreaties, they sullenly and persistently moved to the rear, and were reformed near the river by their officers."[1] Unacquainted as they were with Franklin's orders, they probably felt wronged and indignant that they had not been more efficiently supported. Doubleday's division of the same corps had done some fighting on the left, and was holding the extreme left of the general position. Of the Third Corps, two divisions, those of Birney and Sickles, and of the Ninth Corps the division of Burns, were with Franklin. Birney's division had reached the field at about 11.30 A.M., and when Meade's division was hard pressed, it had been used to support him, to help to cover his retreat, and to take his place in the general line. It had done some sharp and good fighting, and many of the regiments had lost a third of their effective force. The whole division had lost upward of a thousand men. The corps commander claimed for this division the credit of having first checked and then driven back the Confederate troops, "who, yelling,

---

[1] Stoneman's Report. See also Birney's Report.

were in hot pursuit of the two exhausted and retiring divisions of Meade and Gibbon;" of having "saved all their guns, which had been entirely abandoned by their supports; Doubleday's division from being cut off and taken in reverse; the left of Smith's corps, which had not been engaged, from being turned, and possibly, if not probably, the whole left wing of the army from disaster."[1] Sickles's division had taken or was about to take Gibbon's place in the general line, and Burns's division was in connection with Franklin's Grand Division, between Hazel Run and Deep Creek, and subject to his orders if called upon. These two divisions were fresh.

This was the position of Franklin's command when he received such orders as he did receive, and, for the sake of clearness, his formation may be briefly stated. From right to left, his line was formed of Burns's division, Smith's corps, Sickles's division, Birney's division, and Doubleday's division. His front, including the ground held by Burns, seems to have been over three miles long. Doubleday's division was bent back so that its left rested on the river. All these seven divisions were fresh, except those of Birney and Doubleday, and these two were not exhausted, though they had done a good deal of fighting. With such a force at his command, such a line to hold, two bridges to protect, and two hours of daylight left, Franklin was ordered "to advance his right and front," or "to make a vigorous attack with his whole force," or "to make an attack upon the heights immediately in his front." What did these orders mean? If the phrase his "right and front" were construed strictly, it meant all his line excepting the refused division of Doubleday, and this construction agreed with

---

[1] Stoneman's Report.

the order which directed an attack with his whole force. Again, what heights did Burnside refer to? There were "heights immediately in his front" along his whole line. This telegraphic order, about the language of which there could be no mistake, seemed also to mean an attack along his whole line. On this construction, all the orders or messages he received were harmonious, and this construction of the three agreed equally with any two, and was the only construction of which the telegraphic order admitted.

One of the nicest and most difficult questions which the operations of war present, is the question how far an officer may use his own judgment in acting under an order from a superior. Literal, unquestioning, immediate obedience is the first duty of a soldier, but it is universally admitted that a lieutenant exercising a large command and separated from his chief, is not necessarily and universally held to literal, immediate obedience. As a rule, he is, but there may be circumstances when he is not, as, for instance, when he is in possession of important information which he knows is not shared by his chief, and which he knows, if shared by him, would have altered the order, or prevented its being given. General Franklin had a very large command, he was separated from his chief, he knew the whole position of affairs on his own ground, and he received such extraordinary orders as gave him a right to believe that his knowledge could not be shared by his chief. Construing the orders which he received, whether one, two, or three, with the utmost possible liberality, they seem to be susceptible of but two interpretations:

First.—That he was to mass a strong force and make a vigorous attack with it; or,

Second.—That he was to make an attack in line upon the heights immediately in his front.

To adopt and act upon the second construction was, in our judgment, out of the question. He had attacked the heights in his front at one point, bringing at least as many troops to bear upon it as he could hope to bring to bear upon every point if he made a general assault in line, and the result had been not only a bloody repulse, but a repulse attended with such action on the part of the Confederates as showed that they were both able and willing to take the offensive wherever and whenever an opportunity for an offensive return might present itself. Strung out as his command was, and posted as the enemy were, a general attack upon the heights was altogether likely to be a mere sending of his men to useless slaughter, and a failure or weakness in any part of his line was altogether likely to be the signal for a downward rush of the Confederates, the consequences of which might have been disastrous in the extreme. For these reasons, he seems to us to have been fully justified in believing the second construction to be inadmissible, or in declining to obey it if he thought it the only construction the orders would bear.

It therefore remains to ascertain what he did, and to consider what he might have done, upon the theory that he understood his orders to mean that he was to mass a strong force and to make a vigorous attack with it. It has been shown that the Confederates had not far from three men for every four of the Federals, and three men behind breastworks and abattis are far more than a match for four advancing without cover. Jackson's men were better soldiers than the provincials at Bunker's Hill, and Franklin's men did not rate as high compared with Jackson's as did Howe's compared with Prescott's, but every one knows what hard times the British soldiers had before those slight defences. Franklin was prone to overestimating the force of the enemy, and he believed that at this time they greatly outnumbered him.[1] He knew that he could not look for assistance from the right, for Burnside had sent him word that his right was hard pressed. He knew that the enemy was in force on his left as well as in his front. With the lessons of the forenoon fighting fresh in his mind, he knew he could not safely attack without forming a strong column, that he could not form a strong column without stripping portions of his line, and that he could not strip portions of his line without putting what was left in position to perfectly cover the flanks of the column of attack and perfectly protect itself. The latter portion of this programme must be thoroughly attended to, because he had an unfordable river in his rear.

To do what was required to be done required time, and a great deal of time, and he decided that it was too late to do anything more that day. It is not easy to blame him. It is easy to defend him. He occupied a cruelly hard and difficult position. He was a good soldier and a man of character. He had a large command. He must have known that much was expected of him, though his chief was so incompetent that he did not know what he expected of him. His suggestions were not heeded, and he saw the light grow and fade with the painful consciousness that he was losing a great opportunity, and losing it because the general commanding neither gave him intelligent orders nor left his action to his own intelligence. He was right in saying, "Our failure was the natural consequence of the insufficient preparation and inadequate provision for an attack upon an army like that in front of us."

But while it is easy to defend Franklin, and impossible not to sympathize with him, it is not easy to feel entirely

---

[1] Franklin's Reply. Pamphlet, p. 4.

satisfied with him. To defeat Jackson with the men he had and the ground he held, would have been a desperately difficult enterprise for Franklin, even if the best possible plan had been made for him or made by him. It was a hopeless enterprise, absolutely hopeless, under the vague shadowings which Burnside issued under the name of orders. And yet one cannot help feeling that with his ability and training, Franklin might have done something more than he did, with the large force under his command, if he had been impelled by the energy of the strongest natures. What that something might have been, it is not worth while to attempt to say. The endeavor would lead into a region of speculation, not only military but metaphysical, for much would have depended upon his success in getting Burnside to comprehend and appreciate and sanction such plan as he might have formed. He tried the experiment the night before the battle, and failed. He may have been discouraged by the failure, as he certainly was disappointed. He was not a man of an active temperament, and he was certainly wanting in audacity, but perhaps it was just as well for the country and the army that, while Burnside commanded the army, Franklin commanded the left wing. The enterprise against Fredericksburg was so radically desperate that it might only have cost more lives, without any compensation, if a fiery fighter like Hood had been in Franklin's place. One remark must be added, and that is that it excites both surprise and regret to find such a total want of evidence that Franklin communicated to Burnside during the whole day of the battle anything in the way of suggestions, requests for instructions, or remonstrance. If it were shown that he let him know that he did not understand his orders, or that he had good reasons for disapproving of them, or that he desired to do something more or different, or that he wished he would come and see for himself, he would appear better in the history of the battle than he does now. He was cruelly wronged by the Committee on the Conduct of the War, but amiable and excellent as the members of that Committee may have been in private life, the worst spirit of the Inquisition characterized their doings as a committee. It is sufficient to say that their treatment of him was an act of gross injustice.

It could hardly be said that night ended the fighting of the 13th of December, for the fighting had mostly ceased when night came, though some more lives might have been lost had the day been longer. Most fortunately for the wounded, the deepening twilight did not bring with it the growing chill which is common to winter nights. The air was mild, and the wind came soft and almost balmy from the south. All the wounded who could be reached were brought in during the night, and some of the dead were buried. The losses of the Federal army had been very severe. Burnside reported them as follows:

	Killed.	Wounded.	Missing.
Right Grand Division	491	3,933	737
Left Grand Division	373	2,697	653
Centre Grand Division	316	2,398	755
	1,180	9,028	2,145

Hancock's division of the Second Corps suffered the most. Out of 5,006, he lost 2,013, of whom 156 were officers. He had seventeen regiments, of which two were consolidated under Miles, now a brigadier-general in the army. Of the officers who commanded these sixteen battalions during the engagement, 25 were killed or wounded and removed from the field. In eight of his regiments, numbering 2,548 officers and men, 1,324 officers and men were killed or wounded, an average of fifty-four per cent. No one of these regiments lost less than forty-five per cent.; one lost sixty per cent., and one lost sixty-seven per cent., or two more than two-thirds. Hancock was one of the very best soldiers in the immediate presence of the enemy that the Army of the Potomac ever had. He merited the epithet "superb" which McClellan applied to him early in the war. It is altogether probable that if more discretion had been left to him, he would have so used his troops as to achieve more and suffer less, but his formation for the attack was prescribed in the orders he received—brigade front, intervals between the brigades of two hundred paces. Left more to himself, he would have been likely to do more as Humphreys did and as Miles asked leave to do —attempt to carry the position in front by a spirited charge with the bayonet alone. But it must be confessed that it is a very singular fact in the history of this battle that this idea seems to have occurred to so few.

Longstreet's corps lost, in the five days during which the Federals were across the river, 1,894 men, of whom 339 were lost on the 11th. Thus it appears that all the heavy losses of the Army of the Potomac in its engagements in the rear of Fredericksburg, had only a loss of 1,555 to be set against them on the Confederate side. Jackson's corps, which was attacked by Franklin, lost 3,415. As well as can be made out from an analysis of the figures, Franklin, with a loss of only two men for Sumner's three, inflicted upon the enemy more than twice as much loss.

The Federal commanders were generally satisfied with the behavior of the troops. Hancock, in particular, says that the valor of his men was so marked, that had the enemy met them in the open field, the contest would have been decided in their favor in a very short time. Lee's acknowledgment of their "great determination" has already been cited. Ransom, who had immediate charge of the defence at Marye's, speaks of the Federals as moving to the attack heroically, and displaying "wonderful staunchness." Jackson's language is complimentary, but Longstreet's is less so, though the facts that he states show that he recognized merit in the troops which he repulsed. The gallantry displayed by the Federal army was the more to its credit, because of the feeling which prevailed in it. Swinton wrote to the *New York Times* that day, "It was with pain and alarm I found this morning a general want of confidence and gloomy forebodings among officers whose sound judgment I had learned to trust. The plan of attacking the rebel stronghold directly in front would, it was feared, prove a most hazardous enterprise." What the officers think, the men are apt to know, and soldiers of experience are sometimes more swift than their officers in coming to correct conclusions. The Army of the Potomac had been at Malvern Hill and at Sharpsburg. It knew how the Southern and Northern armies in turn had fared when either undertook to assail its opponent in a chosen position, and the difficulties of the position to be carried at Malvern Hill and at Sharpsburg were as nothing to the difficulties of the position at Fredericksburg.

Enough has already been said of the unwisdom of Burnside's determination to assault these heights, but something remains to be said of the true method of doing it, if the thing were decided on. To carry one or more points in the Confederate line was like storming a fort, except that it was not necessary that the artillery should first make a practicable breach. The character of the Confederate troops was perfectly well known, and it was necessary to recognize in them an even match, to say no more, all the conditions of the encounter, including numbers, being equal. But here the conditions were not equal. The Confederates occupied a position of great natural strength, and much of it was admirably strengthened by art. Intrenchments are sometimes said to quadruple the power of the defenders. To assault such a line as theirs, especially at the stone wall, columns of attack should have been so formed as to be as nearly as possible irresistible. Perfection of tactical arrangement should have been aimed at, and careful selection of material made. Every intelligent officer in the Army of the Potomac knew that there existed in it in 1862 enormous differences in the character of commands. Sometimes a brigade was all good, sometimes all bad. Sometimes in one brigade there were two or three excellent regiments, and one or two "scalawag" regiments, the presence of which was felt by their comrades to be an element of weakness and not of strength. The men did not differ so much. They were such soldiers as their officers made them, and the officers differed immensely. It was very commonly true that the efforts made to influence the press were in direct ratio to the worthlessness of the man or set of men who brought the influence to bear, but want of space forbids an adequate presentation of the degree to which the waters of history were thus poisoned at their source. In engagements of the ordinary character, troops must be used as they are organized, but in an exceptional case the very best regiments should be selected for the exceptional work. Second-class troops are useful for second-class work, and difficult as it would have been for any troops to force Longstreet's line behind Fredericksburg, it is just possible that a picked column of the very best Northern regiments might have done it, but failure was certain from the outset if the attack was to be in line and the weak were to advance with the strong. Nothing but the *optimum* of preparation, in every particular, was adequate to the solution of the problem.

The story of the battle of Fredericksburg should not end without some further mention of Hooker's part in it. His experience was a trying one, and he bore himself well. He had made a name for himself from the very beginning of the Peninsular campaign. He had his faults, and they were many, but he had a wholesome love of fighting, and much soldierly capacity. Up to the night of December 12th, his command consisted of two corps, each comprising three divisions. By two o'clock of the afternoon of the 13th, or at about that time, his Third Corps had been divided into seven different commands, distributed over a space of country many miles long, so that neither Hooker nor its direct commander, Stoneman, had any control of it. Of the Fifth Corps, Griffin's division had been sent to the support of Sturgis, and Hooker was left with the divisions of Humphreys and Sykes. When Hooker received orders to attack, these two divisions were all that were left to him. The Second Corps and part of the Fifth and Ninth had been at work all day on the ground assigned to him, and had failed to make any impression.

General Hooker makes a statement of such importance that it is given in his own words. He says: " A prisoner in the morning had given to General Burnside, General Sumner, and myself, full information of the position and defences of the enemy, stating that it was their desire that we should attack at that point, in rear of Fredericksburg on the telegraph road; that it was perfectly impossible for any troops to carry the position; that if the first line was carried, a second line of batteries commanded it." And Hooker adds: " The result of the operations of General Sumner's Corps, which had made a determined, spirited attack, without success, fully confirmed the statements of this prisoner." So impressed was Hooker with the hopelessness of the enterprise, that, after consulting with several of the general officers of his and Sumner's commands, he sent an aide to Burnside to say that he advised him not to attack. The reply came that the attack must be made. Not satisfied with this, and under a strong sense of his duty to his command, Hooker determined to give Burnside a fuller explanation, and to dissuade him, if possible. He did so, but Burnside insisted upon the attack being made. The attack was made, with the result to Humphreys's division which has been stated. This worthy action of Hooker should never be forgotten when his military history is under consideration. Sykes, he says, moved on Humphreys's right, to assault in *echelon* and support, but the loss and repulse of the attacking columns were so severe that Sykes had to be recalled, to cover the withdrawal of Humphreys. But for this precaution, Hooker feared that the Confederates might follow up their advantage, with results of the most disastrous character.

The short winter's day came to an end. Fifteen thousand men lay dead or wounded along the banks of the Rappahannock, and the Army of the Potomac was no nearer Richmond than it was when the sun rose. The Confederates were elated and the Federals were depressed. The Confederates had had a day of such savage pleasure as seldom falls to the lot of soldiers, a day on which they saw their opponents doing just what they wished them to do, but what they did not dare to hope they would do. The Federals had had a day of hard and hopeless effort, and they had nothing to cheer them but the consciousness of duty nobly done. It would be interesting to know with what feelings Burnside contemplated the day's work. Swinton, who was present, says that as he saw the failure of the assault of division after division, "there grew up in his mind something which those around him saw to be akin to desperation." Swinton also says that the chief commanders earnestly urged him, at the end of the day, to recross the Rappahannock, but he would not be persuaded. So far was he from assenting, that he proposed to recommence the action the following day, by storming the heights with a column of eighteen regiments of the Ninth Corps, and to direct the assault in person. There was nothing to be hoped for from this scheme, and the fact that Burnside determined upon it showed that his mind had lost its balance. There was nothing in the history of the Ninth Corps on which to base expectations of extraordinary efficiency. Besides some facile victories in North Carolina, some service of two of its divisions at the Second Bull Run, and its failure at the Antietam, it had had little military experience. It did not compare in sharp experience of war with many of the troops of the original Army of the Potomac, which had tried and failed. It is not strange that Burnside lost his head. He did not belong to the class of men of whom the poet said,

Impavidum ferient ruinæ.

The very fact that he proposed to assault in person on the 14th, shows that he was incapable of learning from the hard lessons of actual encounter, what persons of clearer perceptions knew before the first Federal troops moved out in rear of Fredericksburg. The cheerful prophet who wrote to the London *Times* from Lee's headquarters on the 13th of December that the day was memorable to the historian of the Decline and Fall of the American Republic, declared that Lee and his captains under him enjoyed a moment of proud gratification "when they realized beyond all question that the enemy was about to force an attack under circumstances which would have ensured defeat had the onslaught been made by the bravest disciplined troops of Europe," and what Lee and his captains knew before the assault was delivered, Burnside ought to have known then, and was mad not to recognize after the experience of the day. The same English authority declares "that any mortal men could have carried the position before which they were wantonly sacrificed, defended as it was, it seems to me idle for a moment to believe." The wiser counsels of Burnside's chief officers prevailed, and the attack was not made. Nothing of interest occurred on the Sunday or the Monday following the battle, and on Monday night, in a storm of wind and rain, the Army of the Potomac was quietly and skilfully withdrawn across the river, and returned to its camps.

The question whether Lee should have taken the offensive after the repulse of the Federal attacks on the 13th, has been much discussed, but it will only be touched lightly here. With his forces, and with the exhilaration incident to their success on the one hand, and the unfavorable position of the Federals on the other, it seems as if he might have attacked to advantage, but it is to be remembered that he must necessarily descend into the plain to attack, and there find not only a very powerful army, but expose his own troops to the fire of Hunt's almost countless guns across the river. He himself says that the Federal attack had been so easily repulsed, and by so small a part of his army, that it was not supposed the enemy would limit his efforts to one attempt, which, in view of the magnitude of his preparations and the extent of his force, seemed to be comparatively insignificant. In the belief that Burnside would attack again, he deemed it inexpedient to lose the advantages of his position, and expose his troops to the fire of the inaccessible batteries across the river. He probably decided wrongly, but the point may be left to his apologists.

It is not pleasant to say the things which the course of this story has made it necessary to say of Burnside, but the true aim of history is the pursuit of truth. War is a very dreadful thing. It should be so waged as to do the greatest possible injury to the enemy with the least possible injury to one's self. Then only it becomes merciful, and its tenderest mercies are hard. Modesty is an amiable quality, but it is not what is wanted in the commander of a hundred thousand men. No man should accept the command of an army who honestly feels himself unequal to it. No man should offer battle until he has satisfied himself that the battle must be fought, and how it should be fought. No such necessity compelled Burnside, and no adequate preparation was made by him. If he intrigued for the command of the Army of the Potomac, it is hard to understand how he ever could have slept soundly after the battle of Fredericksburg. If he did not, and his "*nolo episcopari*" was genuine, the recollection of the 13th of December must still have been bitter to him all his days.

It would be too much to say that there are no sadder stories in military history than that of the Army of the Potomac, but its story is sad enough. Always better than its commanders, always ready to "stand in the evil hour," and "having done all to stand," it marched and fought and hungered and thirsted for four long years, hardly ever animated by victory. It showed in all that it endured and achieved, that it was an admirable instrument for the hand that knew how to wield it, but it never had the good fortune to be commanded by a soldier who was worthy of it. It fought through to the end, it did its work, and gained its crown, but its path was long and rough and seldom cheered, and one of its saddest and sharpest experiences was its brave, hopeless effort at Fredericksburg.

APPENDIX A.

COMMANDERS IN THE ARMY OF THE POTOMAC UNDER MAJOR-GENERAL GEORGE B. McCLELLAN ON SEPTEMBER 14, 1862.[1]

RIGHT WING.
MAJOR-GENERAL A. E. BURNSIDE.

FIRST ARMY CORPS.
MAJOR-GENERAL JOSEPH HOOKER.

FIRST DIVISION.
(1) BRIGADIER-GENERAL RUFUS KING.
(2) BRIGADIER-GENERAL JOHN P. HATCH.
(3) BRIGADIER-GENERAL A. DOUBLEDAY.

First Brigade.
(1) Brig.-Gen. JOHN P. HATCH.
(2) Col. WALTER PHELPS, JR.

Second Brigade.
(1) Brig.-Gen. A. DOUBLEDAY.
(2) Col. WM. P. WAINWRIGHT.
(3) Lieut.-Col. J. W. HOFMANN.

Third Brigade.
Brig.-Gen. M. R. PATRICK.

Fourth Brigade.
Brig.-Gen. JOHN GIBBON.

SECOND DIVISION.
BRIGADIER-GENERAL JAMES B. RICKETTS.

First Brigade.   *Second Brigade.*   *Third Brigade.*
Brig.-Gen. A. DURYEA.   Col. WM. H. CHRISTIAN.   Brig.-Gen. GEO. L. HARTSUFF.

THIRD DIVISION.
BRIGADIER-GENERAL GEO. G. MEADE.

First Brigade.
Brig. Gen. T. SEYMOUR.

Second Brigade.
Col. A. L. MAGILTON.

Third Brigade.
(1) Col. THOMAS F. GALLAGHER.
(2) Lieut.-Col. ROB'T ANDERSON.

---

[1] As shown by the Records of the Adjutant-General's Office. Furnished General F. W. Palfrey, in compliance with his request dated July 4, 1881.

NINTH ARMY CORPS.
(1) Major-General JESSE L. RENO.
(2) Brigadier-General J. D. COX.

FIRST DIVISION.
Brigadier-General O. B. WILLCOX.

| *First Brigade.* | *Second Brigade.* |
| Col. B. C. Christ. | Col. Thomas Welsh. |

SECOND DIVISION.
Brigadier-General S. D. STURGIS.

| *First Brigade.* | *Second Brigade.* |
| Col. James Nagle. | Col. Edward Ferrero. |

THIRD DIVISION.
Brigadier General ISAAC P. RODMAN.

| *First Brigade.* | *Second Brigade.* |
| Col. H. S. Fairchild. | Col. Edward Harland. |

CENTRE.
Major-General E. V. SUMNER.

SECOND ARMY CORPS.
Major-General E. V. SUMNER.

FIRST DIVISION.
Brigadier-General ISRAEL B. RICHARDSON.

| *First Brigade.* | *Second Brigade.* |
| Brig.-Gen. Thomas F. Meagher. | Brig.-Gen. John C. Caldwell. |

Third Brigade.
Col. John R. Brooke.

SECOND DIVISION.
Major-General JOHN SEDGWICK.

| *First Brigade.* | *Second Brigade.* | *Third Brigade.* |
| Brig.-Gen. W. A. Gorman. | Brig.-Gen. O. O. Howard. | Brig.-Gen. N. J. T. Dana. |

THIRD DIVISION.
Brigadier-General W. H. FRENCH.

| *First Brigade.* | *Second Brigade.* | *Third Brigade.* |
| Brig.-Gen. Nathan Kimball. | Col. Dwight Morris. | Brig.-Gen. Max Weber. |

TWELFTH ARMY CORPS.
Brigadier-General A. S. WILLIAMS.

FIRST DIVISION.
Brigadier-General S. W. CRAWFORD.

| *First Brigade.* | *Third Brigade.* |
| Col. J. F. Knipe. | Brig.-Gen. Geo. H. Gordon. |

APPENDIX A. 193

SECOND DIVISION.
BRIGADIER-GENERAL GEO. S. GREENE.

First Brigade.   *Second Brigade.*   *Third Brigade.*
Lt.-Col. HECTOR TYNDALE.   Col. HENRY J. STAINROOK.   Col. WM. B. GOODRICH.

LEFT WING.
MAJOR-GENERAL WM. B. FRANKLIN.
SIXTH ARMY CORPS.
MAJOR-GENERAL WM. B. FRANKLIN.
FIRST DIVISION.
MAJOR-GENERAL H. W. SLOCUM.

First Brigade.   *Second Brigade.*   *Third Brigade.*
Col. A. T. A. TORBERT.   Col. J. J. BARTLETT.   Brig.-Gen. JOHN NEWTON.

SECOND DIVISION.
MAJOR-GENERAL WM. F. SMITH.

First Brigade.   *Second Brigade.*   *Third Brigade.*
Brig.-Gen. W. S. HANCOCK.   Brig.-Gen. W. T. H. BROOKS.   Col. W. H. IRWIN.

COUCH'S DIVISION (Fourth Corps).
MAJOR-GENERAL D. N. COUCH.

First Brigade.   *Second Brigade.*   *Third Brigade.*
Brig.-Gen. CHAS. DEVENS.   Brig.-Gen. A. P. HOWE.   Brig.-Gen. JOHN COCHRANE.

FIFTH ARMY CORPS.
MAJOR-GENERAL FITZ JOHN PORTER.
FIRST DIVISION.
BRIGADIER-GENERAL GEORGE MORELL.

First Brigade.   *Second Brigade.*   *Third Brigade.*
Col. JAMES BARNES.   Brig.-Gen. CHARLES GRIFFIN.   Col. T. B. W. STOCKTON.

SECOND DIVISION.
BRIGADIER-GENERAL GEORGE SYKES.

First Brigade.   *Second Brigade.*   *Third Brigade.*
Lieut.-Col. R. C. BUCHANAN.   Lieut.-Col. WM. CHAPMAN.   Col. G. K. WARREN.

ADJUTANT-GENERAL'S OFFICE,   C. McKEEVER,
   Washington, September 5, 1881.   *Assistant Adjutant-General.*

APPENDIX B.

ORGANIZATION[1] OF THE ARMY OF NORTHERN VIRGINIA, FROM AUGUST 13 TO NOVEMBER 15, 1862, FROM REPORTS OF MILITARY OPERATIONS DURING THE REBELLION, 1860–65, WASHINGTON, ADJUTANT-GENERAL'S PRINTING OFFICE.

LONGSTREET'S (FIRST) CORPS, OR RIGHT WING.

McLAWS'S DIVISION.[2]

Barksdale's Brigade.
13th Mississippi.
17th "
18th "
21st "

Kershaw's Brigade.
2d South Carolina.
3d " "
7th " "
8th " "

Semmes's Brigade.
10th Georgia.
53d "
15th Virginia.
32d "
Manly's Battery.

Cobb's Brigade.
Col. SANDERS Com'd'g at Sharpsburg.
Cobb's Georgia Legion.
16th Georgia.
24th "
15th North Carolina.
Read's Battery.

R. H. ANDERSON'S DIVISION.[2]
Commanded by GENERAL WILLCOX.[3]

Willcox's Brigade.
8th Alabama.
9th "
10th "
11th "

Pryor's Brigade.
14th Alabama.
3d Virginia.
5th Florida.[4]
8th "

Featherston's Brigade.
Gen. FEATHERSTON and
  Col. POSEY Com'd'g.
2d Mississippi Battalion.
12th Mississippi.
16th "
19th "

---

[1] Made up from reports, casualty sheets, organization table of July 23d, and return of September 30th. The arrangement of divisions accords with the latter, except in the case of D. H. Hill's division, which is there made to belong to Jackson's corps. Between these sources, and owing to changes made during this campaign, there are some discrepancies, and some organizations will be found to appear twice, and an absolutely accurate table has been impossible.

[2] These two divisions were under McLaws's command in Maryland campaign.

[3] General Willcox, in his report, states that his division was composed of three brigades (the first named), but the casualty sheet makes the division to consist of six.

[4] Fifth in report of Pryor, Second in Guild's report.

APPENDIX B.

Wright's Brigade.
3d Georgia.
22d "
48th "
44th Alabama.
44th Georgia.

Armistead's Brigade.
14th Virginia.
38th "
53d "
57th "
Dixie Battery (Chapman's).

Mahone's Brigade.
Col. PARHAM commanding at Sharpsburg.
6th Virginia.
12th "
16th "
41st "

JONES'S (D. R.) DIVISION.

Anderson's (G.T.) Brigade.[1]
Gen. EVANS Com'd'g.
1st Georgia Regulars.
7th Georgia.
8th "
9th "

Toombs's Brigade.[1]
Gen. TOOMBS, Com'd'g.
Col. BENNING Com'd'g in Maryland.
2d Georgia.
15th "
17th "
20th "

Drayton's Brigade.[1]
15th South Carolina.
50th [2] " "
51st [2] " "

Kemper's Brigade.[3]
Col. CORSE Com'd'g at battles of Groveton and Manassas.
1st Virginia.
7th "
11th "
17th "
24th "

Pickett's (or Garnett's) Brigade.[3]
8th Virginia.
18th "
19th "
28th "
56th "

Jenkins's Brigade.[4]
Col. WALKER Com'd'g.
1st South Carolina.
2d " "
5th " "
6th " "
Palmetto Sharpshooters.

WALKER'S DIVISION.

Ransom's Brigade.
24th North Carolina.
25th " "
35th " "
49th " "
J. R. Branch's Battery.

Walker's Brigade.
Col. MANNING Com'd'g.
30th Virginia.
46th North Carolina.
48th " "
27th " "
3d Arkansas.
French's Battery.

Whiting's Brigade.
(See Hood's or Whiting's Division.)

PICKETT'S DIVISION.[5]

Kemper's Brigade.[6]
1st Virginia.
7th "
11th "
17th "
24th "

Pickett's (or Garnett's) Brigade.[6]
8th Virginia.
18th "
19th "
28th "
56th "

---

[1] In Maryland campaign these three brigades formed a temporary division under General Toombs.
[2] Called Georgia in Guild's report.
[3] Attached to this division in the Maryland campaign, previous to which it was in Pickett's division.
[4] Attached to this division in the Maryland campaign; belonged to Pickett's division in Northeastern Virginia.
[5] Jenkins's brigade was in this division in Northeastern Virginia.
[6] Belonged to D. R. Jones's division in Maryland campaign.

HOOD'S (OR WHITING'S) DIVISION.

INFANTRY.

Hood's Brigade.
Col. WOFFORD Com'd'g.
18th Georgia.
1st Texas.
4th "
5th "
Hampton Legion.

Whiting's (Law's) Brigade.
4th Alabama.
6th North Carolina.
2d Mississippi.
11th "

Evans's Brigade.[1]
Gen. EVANS and Col. STEVENS Com'd'g.
17th South Carolina.
18th " "
22d " "
23d " "
Holcombe Legion.
Boyce's Battery, Macbeth's Artillery.

ARTILLERY.

Reilly's Battery.[2]
Garden's Battery.[2]
Bachman's Battery.[2]

Walton's Artillery Battalion, Washington Artillery, of Louisiana.
Lee's Artillery Battalion.

JACKSON'S (SECOND) CORPS.

JACKSON'S DIVISION.
TALIAFERRO, STARKE, and J. R. JONES, Commanding.

INFANTRY.

Winder's Brigade.
Cols. BAYLOR and GRIGSBY Com'd'g.
2d Virginia.
4th "
5th "
27th "
33d "

J. R. Jones's (or Campbell's) Brigade.
JONES, B. T. JOHNSON, and SEDDON, Com'd'g.
21st Virginia.
42d "
48th "
1st Virginia Battalion.

Taliaferro's Brigade.
Cols. TALIAFERRO and WARREN Com'd'g.
23d Virginia.
47th Alabama.
48th "
37th Virginia.
10th "

Starke's Brigade.
STARKE, STAFFORD, and PENDLETON, Com'd'g.
1st Louisiana.
2d "
9th "[3]
10th "
15th "
Coppen's Louisiana Battalion.

ARTILLERY.
Major L. M. SHUMAKER Commanding.

Brockenbrough's Battery.
Wooding's Battery, Danville Artillery.
Poague's Battery, Rockbridge Artillery.

Carpenter's Battery.
Caskie's Battery.
Raine's Battery.

---

[1] Not attached to any division.
[2] In battle of Sharpsburg.
[3] October 5th transferred to Hays's Brigade.

APPENDIX B.

EWELL'S DIVISION.
EWELL, LAWTON, and EARLY, Commanding.

INFANTRY.

Lawton's Brigade.[1]
LAWTON and DOUGLASS Com'd'g.
13th Georgia.
31st "
60th "
61st "

Early's Brigade.
13th Virginia.
25th "
31st "
44th "
49th "
52d "
58th [2] "

Hays's Brigade.
Gen. HAYS and Cols. FORNO and STRONG Com'd'g.
5th Louisiana.
6th "
7th "
8th "

Trimble's Brigade.
TRIMBLE, WALKER, and BROWN Com'd'g.
12th Georgia.
21st "
15th Alabama.
20th North Carolina.[3]
21st " "

ARTILLERY.
Major COURTNEY Commanding.

Brown's Battery.
Dement's Battery.
D'Aquin's Battery.

Latimer's Battery.
Balthis' Battery (Lieut. Garber).

A. P. HILL'S DIVISION.

INFANTRY.

Branch's (or Lane's) Brigade.
37th North Carolina.
7th " "
18th " "
28th " "
33d " "

Gregg's (or McGowan's) Brigade.
1st South Carolina Rifles (Orr's).
1st South Carolina.
12th " "
13th " "
14th " "

Field's Brigade.
Col. BROCKENBROUGH Com'd'g.
55th Virginia.
47th "
2d " Battalion.
40th "

Pender's Brigade.
16th North Carolina.
22d " "
34th " "
38th " "

Archer's Brigade.
1st Tennessee.
7th "
14th "
19th Georgia.
5th Alabama Battalion.

Thomas' Brigade.
14th Georgia.
19th [4] "
35th "
45th "
49th "

---

[1] On Guild's report, Twenty-sixth and Thirty-eighth Georgia added.
[2] According to Guild's report.
[3] See also Garland's Brigade, D. H. Hill's Division.
[4] See Guild's Report.

ARTILLERY.
Major R. L. WALKER Commanding.

Braxton's Battery.
Latham's "
Crenshaw's "

McIntosh's Battery.
Davidson's "
Pegram's "

D. H. HILL'S DIVISION.[1]
INFANTRY.

Garland's Brigade.
GARLAND and MCRAE Com'd'g.
20th North Carolina.[2]
3d[3] " "
1st[3] " "
5th " "

Anderson's (G. B.) Brigade.
2d North Carolina.
4th " "
13th " "
14th " "
23d " "
30th " "

Ripley's Brigade.[4]
4th Georgia.
6th "
21st "
44th "

Colquitt's Brigade.
19th Georgia.
23d "
27th "
28th "
13th Alabama.

Rodes's Brigade.
3d Alabama.
5th "
6th "
12th "
26th "

ARTILLERY.

Jones's Battery.
Lane's "
King William Artillery.

Bondurant's Battery.
Hardaway's "
(Carter's) Cutts's Battalion.[5]

J. E. B. STUART'S CAVALRY DIVISION.

Robertson's Brigade.
7th Virginia Cavalry.
2d " "
6th " "
12th " "
17th Virginia Cavalry Battalion.[6]

Hampton's Brigade.
Jeff. Davis Legion (10 companies).[7]
1st North Carolina Cavalry.
Cavalry of Cobb's Legion (9 companies).[7]
2d South Carolina Cavalry.
Phillips's Legion (5 companies).[7]

Fitzhugh Lee's Brigade.
1st Virginia Cavalry.
5th[8] " "
3d " "
4th " "
Stuart Horse Artillery.
White's Battalion Virginia Cavalry (independent).[9]

---

[1] Appears to have been independent of any corps, though in field return of September 30th it is included in Jackson's corps.

[2] In Guild's report of Manassas the Twentieth North Carolina appears in Trimble's brigade, Ewell's division, but in his Maryland campaign it appears here.

[3] From Ripley's report it would appear these were in his brigade.

[4] See Garland's Brigade.

[5] Not known whether Cutts's battalion embraced any of the above batteries, or was separate and distinct from them.

[6] Called Eleventh Virginia on return of October 24, 1862, and attached to another brigade with Fifth, Ninth, White's Cavalry, and Scott's Rangers.

[7] From return of October 24, 1862.

[8] Return of October 24, 1862, makes Tenth Virginia in place of this Fifth Regiment, which is assigned to another brigade with Ninth, Eleventh, White's Battalion, and Scott's Rangers.

[9] Assigned to a brigade on return of October 24, 1862.

APPENDIX C.

ORGANIZATION OF THE ARMY OF THE POTOMAC, DECEMBER, 1862, MAJOR-GENERAL A. E. BURNSIDE, COMMANDING.[1]

LEFT GRAND DIVISION.
MAJOR-GENERAL W. B. FRANKLIN COMMANDING.

SIXTH CORPS.
MAJOR-GENERAL W. F. SMITH COMMANDING.

FIRST DIVISION.
BRIGADIER-GENERAL W. T. H. BROOKS COMMANDING.

INFANTRY
First Brigade.

Colonel A. T. A. TORBERT, 1st New Jersey Volunteers, Commanding.

1st New Jersey Volunteers, Lieut.-Colonel M. W. Collet.
2d " " Colonel Samuel L. Buck.
3d " " Colonel Henry W. Brown.
4th " " Colonel William B. Hatch.
15th " " Lieut.-Colonel E. L. Campbell.
23d " " Lieut.-Colonel H. O. Ryerson.

Second Brigade.

Brigadier-General J. J. BARTLETT Commanding.

27th New York Volunteers, Colonel A. D. Adams.
121st " " Colonel Emory Upton.
5th Maine Volunteers, Colonel E. A. Scammon.
16th New York Volunteers, Lieut.-Colonel J. J. Seaver.
96th Pennsylvania Volunteers, Colonel H. L. Cake.

Third Brigade.

Colonel G. W. TOWN, 95th Pennsylvania Volunteers, Commanding.

18th New York Volunteers, Colonel George R. Myers.
31st " " Lieut.-Colonel L. C. Newmann.
32d " " Captain Charles Hubbs.
95th Pennsylvania Volunteers, Lieut.-Colonel E. Hall.

---

[1] From Reports of Military Operations During the Rebellion, 1860-65. Washington. War Department Printing Office, 1877.

ARTILLERY.

Battery D, 2d U. S. Artillery, First Lieutenant E. B. Williston.
" A, 1st New Jersey Artillery, Captain W. Hexamer.
" A, 1st Massachusetts Artillery, Captain W. H. McCartney.
" A, 1st Maryland Artillery, Captain J. W. Wolcott.

SECOND DIVISION.
BRIGADIER-GENERAL A. P. HOWE COMMANDING.
INFANTRY.
First Brigade.

Brigadier-General CALVIN E. PRATT Commanding.
5th Wisconsin Volunteers, Colonel Amasa Cobb.
49th Pennsylvania Volunteers, Colonel William H. Irwin.
6th Maine Volunteers, Colonel Hiram Burnham.
43d New York Volunteers, Colonel B. F. Baker.
119th Pennsylvania Volunteers, Colonel P. C. Ellmaker.

Second Brigade.

Colonel HENRY WHITING, 2d Vermont Volunteers, Commanding.
2d Vermont Volunteers, Colonel ———.
3d " " Colonel B. N. Hyde.
4th " " Colonel C. B. Stoughton.
5th " " Colonel Lewis A. Grant.
6th " " Colonel N. Lord, Jr.
26th New Jersey Volunteers, Colonel A. J. Morrison.

Third Brigade.

Brigadier-General FRANCIS L. VINTON Commanding.
77th New York Volunteers, Colonel James B. McKean.
49th " " Colonel D. D. Bidwell.
20th " " Colonel E. Von Vegesack.
33d " " Colonel Robert F. Taylor.
21st New Jersey " Colonel Gilliam Van Houten.

ARTILLERY.

Battery F, 5th U. S. Artillery, Captain R. B. Ayres.
Battery B, 1st Maryland Artillery, Captain Alonzo Snow.
1st Battery, New York Light Artillery, Captain Andrew Cowan.
3d " " " Captain William Stewart.

THIRD DIVISION.
BRIGADIER-GENERAL JOHN NEWTON COMMANDING.
INFANTRY.
First Brigade.

Brigadier-General JOHN COCHRANE Commanding.
82d Pennsylvania Volunteers, Colonel D. H. Williams.
23d " " Colonel T. H. Neill.
61st " " Colonel G. C. Spear.
65th New York Volunteers (1st U. S. Chasseurs), Colonel Alexander Shaler.
122d " " Colonel Silas Titus.
67th " " (1st Long Island), Lieut.-Colonel Nelson Cross.

APPENDIX C. 201

Second Brigade.

Brigadier-General CHARLES DEVENS Commanding.

2d Rhode Island Volunteers, Colonel Frank Wheaton.
7th Massachusetts Volunteers, Colonel D. A. Russell.
10th   "   "   Colonel H. L. Eustis.
36th New York Volunteers, Colonel W. H. Browne.
37th Massachusetts Volunteers, Colonel Oliver Edwards.

Third Brigade.

Colonel THOMAS A. ROWLEY Commanding.

62d New York Volunteers, Colonel David I. Nevin.
93d Pennsylvania Volunteers, Colonel J. M. McCarter.
98th   "   "   Colonel J. F. Ballier.
102d   "   "   Lieut.-Colonel J. M. Kinkead.
139th "   "   Colonel F. H. Collier.

ARTILLERY.

Battery C, 1st Pennsylvania Artillery, Captain J. McCarthy.
   "   G, 2d U. S. Artillery, Lieutenant J. H. Butler.

FIRST CORPS.

BRIGADIER-GENERAL J. F. REYNOLDS COMMANDING.

FIRST DIVISION.

BRIGADIER-GENERAL A. DOUBLEDAY COMMANDING.

INFANTRY.

First Brigade.

Colonel WALTER PHELPS, JR., Commanding.

2d U. S. Sharpshooters, Major H. B. Stoughton.
14th New York State Militia, Lieut.-Colonel W. H. De Bevoise.
22d New York Volunteers, Lieut.-Colonel J. McKee, Jr.
24th   "   "   Major R. Oliver, Jr.
30th   "   "   Lieut.-Colonel M. H. Chrysler.

Second Brigade.

Colonel JAMES GAVIN Commanding.

56th Pennsylvania Volunteers, Lieut.-Colonel J. W. Hofmann.
95th New York Volunteers, Lieut.-Colonel J. B. Post.
76th   "   "   Colonel W. P. Wainwright.
7th Indiana Volunteers, Lieut.-Colonel J. F. Cheek.

Third Brigade.

Brigadier-General G. R. PAUL Commanding.

20th New York State Militia. Lieut.-Colonel J. B. Hardenbergh.
21st   "   Volunteers, Captain G. N. Layton.
23d   "   "   Colonel H. C. Hoffmann.
35th   "   "   Colonel N. B. Lord.

Fourth Brigade.

Colonel L. CUTLER Commanding.

6th Wisconsin Volunteers, Lieut.-Colonel E. S. Bragg.
2d   "   "   Colonel L. Fairchild.
7th   "   "   Lieut.-Colonel C. A. Hamilton.
19th Indiana Volunteers, Lieut.-Colonel S. J. Williams.
24th Michigan Volunteers, Colonel H. A. Morrow.

ARTILLERY.
Captain G. A. GERRISH Commanding.
Battery B, 4th U. S. Artillery, Lieutenant James Stewart.
" D, 1st Rhode Island Artillery, Lieutenant G. C. Harkness.
" D, 1st New Hampshire Artillery, Lieutenant F. M. Edgell.
" L, 1st New York Artillery, Captain J. A. Reynolds.

SECOND DIVISION.
BRIGADIER-GENERAL JOHN GIBBON COMMANDING.
INFANTRY.
First Brigade.
Colonel ADRIAN R. ROOT Commanding.
94th New York Volunteers, Major John A. Kress.
104th " " Major G. G. Prey.
105th " " Major D. A. Sharp.
107th Pennsylvania Volunteers, Colonel T. F. McCoy.
16th Maine Volunteers, Lieut.-Colonel C. W. Tilden.

Second Brigade.
Colonel P. LYLE, 90th Pennsylvania Volunteers, Commanding.
26th New York Volunteers, Colonel R. H. Richardson.
12th Massachusetts Volunteers, Colonel J. L. Bates.
90th Pennsylvania Volunteers, Lieut.-Colonel W. A. Leech.
136th " " Colonel Thomas M. Bayne.

Third Brigade.
Brigadier-General NELSON TAYLOR Commanding.
83d New York Volunteers, Colonel John W. Stiles.
97th " " Colonel Charles Wheelock.
13th Massachusetts Volunteers, Colonel S. H. Leonard.
11th Pennsylvania Volunteers, Colonel Richard Coulter.
88th " " Colonel G. P. McLean.

ARTILLERY.
Captain GEORGE F. LEPPIEN Commanding.
Battery F, 1st Pennsylvania, Lieutenant R. B. Ricketts.
Independent Battery, Pennsylvania, Captain J. Thompson.
Battery E, Maine, Captain G. F. Leppien.
" B, Maine, Captain J. A. Hall.

THIRD DIVISION.
BRIGADIER-GENERAL GEORGE G. MEADE COMMANDING.
INFANTRY.
First Brigade.
Colonel WILLIAM SINCLAIR, 6th Pennsylvania Reserves, Commanding.
1st Rifles, Pennsylvania Reserve Corps, Captain D. McGee.
1st Infantry, " " " Captain W. C. Talley.
2d " " " " Colonel W. McCandless.
6th " " " " Major W. H. Ent.
121st Pennsylvania Volunteers, Colonel C. Biddle.

APPENDIX C.

Second Brigade.

Colonel A. L. MAGILTON, 4th Pennsylvania Reserves, Commanding.
3d Pennsylvania Reserve Corps, Colonel H. G. Sickle.
4th " " " Lieut.-Colonel R. H. Woolworth.
7th " " " Colonel H. C. Bolinger.
8th " " " Major S. M. Bailey.
142d " Volunteers, Colonel R. P. Cummins.

Third Brigade.

Brigadier-General C. FEGER JACKSON Commanding.
5th Pennsylvania Reserve Corps, Colonel J. W. Fisher.
9th " " " Lieut.-Colonel R. Anderson.
10th " " " Lieut.-Colonel A. J. Warner.
11th " " " Colonel T. F. Gallagher.
12th " " " Colonel M. D. Hardin.

ARTILLERY.

Battery A, 1st Pennsylvania, Lieutenant J. G. Simpson.
" B, " Captain J. H. Cooper.
" G, " Captain F. P. Amsdon.
" C, 5th U. S. Artillery, Captain D. R. Ransom.

Line of Extra Caissons.

Captain J. M. CLARK, Co. F, 2d Pennsylvania Reserve Corps, Commanding.

CAVALRY BRIGADE.

Brigadier-General GEORGE D. BAYARD Commanding.
1st Pennsylvania Cavalry, Colonel Owen Jones.
10th New York Cavalry, Lieut.-Colonel William Irvine.
2d " " Major H. E. Davies.
1st New Jersey " Lieut.-Colonel Joseph Karge.

Artillery.

Battery C, 3d U. S. Artillery, Captain H. G. Gibson.

CENTRE GRAND DIVISION.
MAJOR-GENERAL JOSEPH HOOKER COMMANDING.
THIRD CORPS.
BRIGADIER-GENERAL GEORGE STONEMAN COMMANDING.
FIRST DIVISION.
BRIGADIER-GENERAL D. B. BIRNEY COMMANDING.

INFANTRY.

First Brigade.

Brigadier-General JOHN C. ROBINSON Commanding.
20th Indiana Volunteers, Colonel John Van Valkenburg.
63d Pennsylvania Volunteers, Major J. A. Danks.
105th " " Colonel A. A. McKnight.
114th " " Colonel C. H. T. Collis.
141st " " Colonel H. J. Madill.
68th " " Colonel A. H. Tippin.

ANTIETAM AND FREDERICKSBURG.

Second Brigade.

Brigadier-General J. H. HOBART WARD Commanding.
57th Pennsylvania Volunteers, Colonel C. T. Campbell.
99th " " Colonel A. S. Leidy.
3d Maine Volunteers, Colonel M. B. Lakeman.
4th " " Colonel E. Walker.
55th New York Volunteers, Colonel R. De Trobriand.
38th " " Lieut.-Colonel William Birney.
40th " " Lieut.-Colonel N. A. Gesner.

Third Brigade.

Brigadier-General H. G. BERRY Commanding.
5th Michigan Volunteers, Lieut.-Colonel John Gilluly.
37th New York Volunteers, Colonel S. B. Hayman.
101st " " Colonel G. F. Chester.
17th Maine Volunteers, Colonel T. A. Roberts.
1st New York Volunteers, Colonel J. Frederick Pierson.
3d Michigan Volunteers, Lieut.-Colonel Byron R. Pierce.

ARTILLERY.

Captain G. E. RANDOLPH Commanding.
Batteries K and F, 3d U. S. Artillery, Captain L. L. Livingston.
Battery E, 1st Rhode Island Artillery, Lieutenant P. S. Jastram.

SECOND DIVISION.

BRIGADIER-GENERAL DANIEL E. SICKLES COMMANDING.

INFANTRY.
First Brigade.

Brigadier-General JOSEPH B. CARR Commanding.
11th Massachusetts Volunteers, Colonel W. Blaisdell.
16th " " Colonel T. R. Tannatt.
1st " " Lieut.-Colonel C. B. Baldwin.
26th Pennsylvania " Lieut.-Colonel B. C. Tilghman.
11th New Jersey " Colonel R. McAllister.
2d New Hampshire " Colonel G. Marston.

Second Brigade.

Colonel GEORGE B. HALL Commanding.
70th (1st Excelsior) New York Volunteers, Colonel J. Egbert Farnum.
71st (2d Excelsior) " " Major Thomas Rafferty.
72d (3d Excelsior) " " Colonel William O. Stevens.
73d (4th Excelsior) " " Colonel William R. Brewster.
74th (5th Excelsior) " " Lieut.-Colonel W. H. Lounsbury.
120th New York Volunteers, Colonel George H. Sharp.

Third Brigade.

Brigadier-General J. W. REVERE Commanding.
5th New Jersey Volunteers, Colonel William J. Sewell.
7th " " Colonel Louis R. Francine.

ARTILLERY.

Battery K, 4th U. S. Artillery, Lieutenant F. W. Seeley.
Battery H, 1st U. S. Artillery, Lieutenant J. E. Dimick.
Battery B, 1st New Jersey Artillery, Captain A. J. Clark.
4th Battery, New York Artillery, Captain James E. Smith.

APPENDIX C. 205

THIRD DIVISION.
BRIGADIER-GENERAL A. W. WHIPPLE COMMANDING.
INFANTRY.
First Brigade.
Brigadier-General A. SANDERS PIATT Commanding.
124th New York Volunteers, Colonel A. V. Ellis.
86th " " Lieut.-Colonel B. I. Chapin.
122d Pennsylvania " Colonel Emlen Franklin.

Second Brigade.
Colonel S. S. CARROLL Commanding.
84th Pennsylvania Volunteers, Colonel S. M. Bowman.
110th " " Lieut.-Colonel J. Crowther.
168d New York Volunteers, Major J. J. Byrne.

Independent Command.
Colonel J. H. POTTER Commanding.
Twelfth New Hampshire Volunteers.

ARTILLERY.
11th Battery, New York Artillery, Captain A. A. Von Pattkammer.
2d Battery (Excelsior), New York Artillery, Captain J. T. Bruen.
Battery H, 1st Ohio Artillery, Lieutenant G. W. Norton.

FIFTH CORPS.
BRIGADIER-GENERAL DANIEL BUTTERFIELD COMMANDING.
FIRST DIVISION.
BRIGADIER-GENERAL CHARLES GRIFFIN COMMANDING.
INFANTRY.
First Brigade.
Colonel JAMES BARNES, 18th Massachusetts Volunteers, Commanding.
18th Massachusetts Volunteers, Lieut.-Colonel J. Hayes.
25th New York Volunteers, Captain P. Connelly.
13th " " Colonel E. G. Marshall.
118th Pennsylvania Volunteers, Lieut.-Colonel J. Gwyn.
1st Michigan Volunteers, Lieut.-Colonel I. C. Abbott.
22d Massachusetts Volunteers, Lieut.-Colonel W. S. Tilton.
2d Maine Volunteers, Lieut.-Colonel G. Varney.

Second Brigade.
Colonel J. B. SWEITZER Commanding.
14th New York Volunteers, Lieut.-Colonel T. M. Davies.
4th Michigan Volunteers, Lieut.-Colonel G. W. Lumbard.
9th Massachusetts Volunteers, Colonel P. R. Guiney.
62d Pennsylvania " Lieut.-Colonel J. C. Hull.
32d Massachusetts " Lieut.-Colonel G. L. Prescott.

Third Brigade.
Colonel T. B. W. STOCKTON Commanding.
12th New York Volunteers, Lieut.-Colonel R. M. Richardson.
17th " " Captain John Vickers.
44th " " Lieut.-Colonel F. Conner.
16th Michigan " Lieut.-Colonel N. E. Welch.
20th Maine " Colonel Adelbert Ames.
83d Pennsylvania " Colonel Strong Vincent.

206   ANTIETAM AND FREDERICKSBURG.

ARTILLERY.

Captain A. P. MARTIN, Battery C, Massachusetts Artillery, Commanding.
Battery C (3d), Massachusetts Artillery, First Lieutenant V. M. Drum.
" E (5th), " " Captain C. A. Phillips.

SECOND DIVISION.
BRIGADIER-GENERAL GEORGE SYKES COMMANDING.

INFANTRY.
First Brigade.

Lieut.-Colonel R. C. BUCHANAN, 4th U. S. Infantry, Commanding.

3d U. S. Infantry, Captain John D. Wilkins.
4th " " Captain Hiram Dryer.
1st Battalion, 12th U. S. Infantry, Captain M. M. Blunt.
2d " 12th " " Captain T. M. Anderson.
1st " 14th " " Captain J. D. O'Connell.
2d " 14th " " Captain G. B. Overton.

Second Brigade.

Major GEORGE L. ANDREWS, 17th U. S. Infantry, Commanding.

11th U. S. Infantry, Captain C. S. Russell.
Battalion of 1st and 2d U. S. Infantry, Captain Salem S. Marsh.
" of 6th U. S. Infantry, Captain Levi C. Bootes.
" of 7th " " Captain D. P. Hancock.
" of 10th " " Captain H. E. Maynadier.
" of 17th and 19th U. S. Infantry, Captain J. P. Wales.

Third Brigade.

Brigadier-General G. K. WARREN Commanding.

5th New York Volunteers, Colonel C. Winslow.
140th " " Colonel P. H. O'Rorke.
146th " " Colonel K. Garrard.

ARTILLERY.

First Lieutenant M. F. WATSON, 5th U. S. Artillery, Commanding.

Battery I, 5th U. S. Artillery, Lieutenant M. F. Watson.
" L, 1st Ohio Artillery, First Lieutenant F. Dorries.

THIRD DIVISION.
BRIGADIER-GENERAL A. A. HUMPHREYS COMMANDING.

INFANTRY.
First Brigade.

Brigadier General E. B. TYLER Commanding.

91st Pennsylvania Volunteers, Colonel E. M. Gregory.
134th " " Lieut.-Colonel E. O'Brien.
126th " " Colonel James G. Elder.
129th " " Colonel J. G. Frick.

Second Brigade.

Colonel P. H. ALLABACH, 131st Pennsylvania Volunteers, Commanding.

131st Pennsylvania Volunteers, Lieut.-Colonel W. B. Shunt.
123d " " Colonel J. B. Clark.
133d " " Colonel B. F. Speakman.
155th " " Colonel E. J. Allen.

APPENDIX C. 207

ARTILLERY.

Captain A. M. RANDOL, 1st U. S. Artillery, Commanding.

Battery H, 1st U. S. Artillery, Captain A. M. Randol.
Section of Battery C, 1st New York Artillery, Lieutenant W. H. Phillips.

GRAND DIVISION CAVALRY.

Brigadier-General W. W. AVERELL Commanding.

RIGHT GRAND DIVISION.
MAJOR-GENERAL E. V. SUMNER, U.S.A., COMMANDING.
SECOND CORPS.
MAJOR-GENERAL D. N. COUCH COMMANDING.

FIRST DIVISION.
BRIGADIER-GENERAL W. S. HANCOCK COMMANDING.

INFANTRY.
First Brigade.

Brigadier-General J. C. CALDWELL Commanding.

61st New York Volunteers, Colonel N. A. Miles.
64th   "   "   Captain Harvey L. Jones.
145th Pennsylvania Volunteers, Colonel H. L. Brown.
5th New Hampshire   "   Colonel E. E. Cross.
81st Pennsylvania   "   Lieut.-Colonel H. B. McKeen.
7th New York Volunteers, Colonel George Von Schack.

Second Brigade.

Brigadier-General THOMAS F. MEAGHER Commanding.

69th New York Volunteers, Colonel R. Nugent.
88th   "   "   Colonel P. Kelly.
63d   "   "   Major J. O'Neill.
28th Massachusetts Volunteers, Colonel R. Byrnes.
116th Pennsylvania   "   Colonel D. Heenan.

Third Brigade.

Colonel S. K. ZOOK, 57th New York Volunteers, Commanding.

57th New York Volunteers, Major N. G. Throop.
53d Pennsylvania   "   Colonel John R. Brooke
3d Delaware Volunteers, Colonel W. P. Bailey.
52d New York   "   Colonel Paul Frank.
66th   "   "   Captain Julius Wehle.
27th Connecticut   "   Colonel R. S. Bostwick.

ARTILLERY.

Battery C, 4th U. S. Artillery, Lieutenant Evan Thomas.
   "   B, 1st New York Artillery, Captain R. D. Pettit.

SECOND DIVISION.
Brigadier-General O. O. HOWARD Commanding.

INFANTRY.

First Brigade.
Brigadier-General ALFRED SULLY Commanding.
34th New York Volunteers, Colonel J. A. Suiter.
15th Massachusetts Volunteers, Major C. Philbrick.
82d New York Volunteers, Colonel H. W. Hudson.
19th Maine Volunteers, Colonel F. D. Sewell.
1st Minnesota Volunteers, Colonel G. N. Morgan.

Second Brigade.
Colonel J. T. OWEN, 69th Pennsylvania Volunteers, Commanding.
69th Pennsylvania Volunteers, Lieut.-Colonel D. O'Kane.
71st " " Lieut.-Colonel J. Markoe.
72d " " Colonel D. W. C. Baxter.
106th " " Colonel T. G. Morehead.

Third Brigade.
Colonel NORMAN A. HALL Commanding.
20th Massachusetts Volunteers, Captain George N. Macy.
19th " " Captain J. F. Plimpton.
42d New York Volunteers, Lieut.-Colonel G. N. Bomford.
127th Pennsylvania Volunteers, Colonel W. W. Jennings.
7th Michigan Volunteers, Lieut.-Colonel Henry Baxter.
59th New York Volunteers, Lieut.-Colonel William Northedge.

ARTILLERY.
Battery A, 1st Rhode Island Artillery, Captain Tompkins.
" B, 1st " " " Captain J. G. Hazard.

THIRD DIVISION.
Brigadier-General W. H. FRENCH Commanding.

INFANTRY.

First Brigade.
Brigadier-General NATHAN KIMBALL Commanding.
4th Ohio Volunteers, Colonel John S. Mason.
14th Indiana Volunteers, Major E. H. C. Cavins.
7th Virginia Volunteers, Colonel James Snyder.
8th Ohio Volunteers, Lieut.-Colonel F. Sawyer.
24th New Jersey Volunteers, Colonel W. B. Robertson.
28th " " Colonel M. N. Wisewell.

Second Brigade.
Colonel O. H. PALMER, 108th New York Volunteers, Commanding.
14th Connecticut Volunteers, Lieut.-Colonel S. H. Perkins.
108th New York " ——— ———.
130th Pennsylvania " Colonel H. I. Zinn.

Third Brigade.
Lieutenant-Colonel JOHN W. MARSHALL Commanding.
132d Pennsylvania Volunteers, Lieut.-Colonel Charles Albright.
4th New York Volunteers, Colonel John D. McGregor.
1st Delaware " Colonel J. W. Andrews.
10th New York " Colonel John E. Bendix.

APPENDIX C.   209

ARTILLERY.
Battery G, 1st New York Artillery, Captain John D. Frank.
" G, 1st Rhode Island Artillery, Captain C. D. Owen.

SECOND CORPS RESERVE ARTILLERY.
Battery I, 1st U. S. Artillery, Lieutenant E. Kirby.
" A, 4th U. S. " Lieutenant R. King.

NINTH CORPS.
BRIGADIER-GENERAL O. B. WILLCOX COMMANDING.
FIRST DIVISION.
BRIGADIER-GENERAL W. W. BURNS COMMANDING.

INFANTRY.
First Brigade.
79th New York Volunteers, Lieut.-Colonel David Morrison.
2d Michigan Volunteers, Colonel Orlando M. Poe.
17th   "   "   Colonel W. H. Withington.
20th   "   "   Colonel A. W. Williams.

Third Brigade.
45th Pennsylvania Volunteers, Colonel Thomas Welsh.

ARTILLERY.
Battery D, 1st New York Artillery, Captain T. W. Osborn.

SECOND DIVISION.
BRIGADIER-GENERAL S. D. STURGIS COMMANDING.

INFANTRY.
First Brigade.
Brigadier-General JAMES NAGLE Commanding.
6th New Hampshire Volunteers, Colonel S. G. Griffin.
7th Rhode Island Volunteers, Colonel Z. R. Bliss.
2d Maryland Volunteers, Major H. Howard.
48th Pennsylvania Volunteers, Colonel J. K. Sigfried.
12th Rhode Island   "   Colonel George H. Browne.
9th New Hampshire   "   Colonel E. R. Fellows.

Second Brigade.
Brigadier-General EDWARD FERRERO Commanding.
51st Pennsylvania Volunteers, Colonel J. F. Hartranft.
21st Massachusetts   "   Lieut.-Colonel W. S. Clark.
51st New York Volunteers,   Colonel R. B. Potter.
35th Massachusetts Volunteers, Lieut.-Colonel S. Carruth.
11th New Hampshire   "   Colonel W. Harriman.

ARTILLERY.
Battery E, 4th U. S. Artillery, Lieutenant George Dickenson.
" D, 1st Rhode Island Artillery, Captain W. W. Buckley.

THIRD DIVISION.

BRIGADIER-GENERAL GEORGE W. GETTY COMMANDING.

INFANTRY.

First Brigade.

Colonel RUSH C. HAWKINS Commanding.

9th New York Volunteers, Major E. A. Kimball.
89th   "   "   Colonel H. S. Fairchild.
103d   "   "   Major B. Ringold.
10th New Hampshire Volunteers, Colonel M. T. Donohoe.
13th   "   "   Colonel A. F. Stevens.
25th New Jersey Volunteers, Colonel Andrew Derrom.

Second Brigade.

Colonel EDWARD HARLAND Commanding.

4th Rhode Island Volunteers, Major Martin P. Buffom.
21st Connecticut   "   Colonel Arthur H. Dutton.
8th   "   "   Major John E. Ward.
11th   "   "   Colonel Griffin A. Stedman, Jr.
15th   "   "   Lieut. Colonel Samuel Tolles.
16th   "   "   Colonel Frank Beach (Captain 4th U.S. Artillery).

ARTILLERY.

Battery E, 2d U. S. Artillery, Lieutenant S. N. Benjamin.
    "   A, 5th "   "   Lieutenant C. P. Muhlenberg.

CAVALRY DIVISION.

BRIGADIER-GENERAL ALFRED PLEASONTON COMMANDING.

First Brigade.

Brigadier-General J. H. FARNSWORTH Commanding.

8th New York Volunteers, Colonel B. F. Davis.
6th   "   "   Colonel T. C. Devin.
8th Illinois   "   Colonel W. Gamble.

Second Brigade.

Colonel D. McM. GREGG, 8th Pennsylvania Volunteers, Commanding.

8th Pennsylvania Volunteers, ———— ————.
6th U. S. Cavalry, Captain G. C. Cram.

ARTILLERY.

Battery M, 2d U. S. Artillery, Captain A. C. M. Pennington.

NOTE TO PAGE 72.—A suggestion made to me by Colonel Archer Anderson, of Richmond, since the first edition of this book was published, seems to me of sufficient weight to justify my reproducing it here. "I do not think you establish your Sharpsburg contention, because the stress upon 10,000 men at deadly grip with an equal number is enormously increased if the first plainly see 5,000 fresh men standing in reserve to the second."—F. W. P.

INDEX.

NOTE.—*Regiments, batteries, etc., are indexed under the names of their States, excepting batteries called by their captain's or by some other special name. These are indexed under* BATTERIES.

ACQUIA Creek, 138
Alabama regiments: Fifth, 104; Sixth, 103
Alexander's, Colonel E. P., artillery of the Army of Northern Virginia, 148
Allabach's brigade of the Army of the Potomac at Fredericksburg, 171
Anderson, Colonel G. B., commanding brigade of the Army of Northern Virginia at Turner's Gap, 35, 36; at Sharpsburg, 93, 102, 103; killed, 104
Anderson, Colonel G. T., commanding brigade of the Army of Northern Virginia at Turner's Gap, 36; at Sharpsburg, 80
Anderson, General R. H., assists in capture of Harper's Ferry, 24; arrives at Sharpsburg, 57, 63; engaged there, 96 et seq., 102, 105; at Fredericksburg, 148

Antietam, battle of the, 42; divisible into five parts, 72 (see First Corps, Twelfth Corps, Second Corps, etc., etc.); its result considered, 119
Antietam Creek, position at, 48; character of stream, 49
Archer's, General J. J., brigade of the Army of Northern Virginia at Sharpsburg, 113 et seq.; at Fredericksburg, 149, 157
Armistead's brigade of the Army of Northern Virginia at Sharpsburg, 86, 90
Army of Northern Virginia, 2; composition and strength of, in September, 1862, 7; movements of, 11, 15; condition of, 15, 16; quality of, 17; crosses Potomac, 18; concentrated at Frederick, 18; character of, 39; at Sharpsburg, 63; its strength there, 63 et seq.; its character, compared with that

of the Army of the Potomac, 125; its movements after the battle of Sharpsburg, 129 et seq.; strength of, October 20, 1862, 129; position of, November 7th-9th, 136; strength of, December 10, 1862, 141; position of, December 12, 1862, 148; strength of, December 13, 1862, 149

Army of the Potomac, under McClellan, how composed, 6; strength of, September 20th, 1862, 6; moves out in Maryland campaign, 10; position of on September 9th and 13th, 13, 14; its burdens, 17; position of, when the Army of Northern Virginia concentrated, 18; movements of, after South Mountain, 45; strength of, at the Antietam, 63 et seq.; its character, compared with that of A.... y of Northern Virginia, 125; its movements after the battle of the Antietam, 129 et seq.; position of, September 7th-9th, 136; divided into three grand divisions, 138; strength of, November 10, 1862, 138; formation of the army December 12, 1862, 147; strength of army, December 13, 1862, 149; gallantry of its action at Fredericksburg, 166; its formation under Burnside's orders, December 13, 1862, 173; its behavior in the battle, 183 et seq.; its sense of the hopelessness of its task, 184; its inequality of merit, 185; withdrawn across the Rappahannock, 189; tribute to it, 190

Army of Virginia, composition of, 2; ceases to exist, 5

Artillery in the Army of Northern Virginia, 57

Artillery of the Army of the Potomac at Fredericksburg, 145 et seq.

Artillery regiments: First, 101; Second, 101-109; Fourth, 74; Fifth, 128; First New Hampshire, 74; First New York, I, 74; First Pennsylvania, F. 74; Independent, 74; Rhode Island, D, 74

BALL's Bluff, 52, 88

Banks, General N. P., placed in command of defences of Washington, 5

Barksdale's, General Wm., brigade of the Army of Northern Virginia at Sharpsburg, 86, 90

Barlow, Colonel F. C., at Sharpsburg, 100, 103, 104; his love of fighting, 126

Barnesville, 13

Bartlett's brigade of the Army of the Potomac at Sharpsburg, 106

Batteries. *Confederate:* Branch's, 124; Braxton's, 114; Brown's, 115; Carleton's, 90; Crenshaw's, 114; Ewbank's, 109; French's, 124; Garden's, 115; Lane's, 139; Lewis's, 139; McIntosh's, 113, 114; Miller's, 102, 116; Moody's, 112; Pegram's, 114; Ramsey's, 116; Read's, 90; Reilly's, 116; Richardson's, 109; Squires's,

INDEX. 213

115; Washington artillery, 112, 148. *Federal Batteries:* Benjamin's, 109, 110; Clark's, 110; Cook's, 110; Cothran's, 78, 91; Cowan's, 91; Durell's, 109, 110; Frank's, 91; Gibson's, 106; Graham's, 101; Hains's, 106; Hampton's, 78; Hexamer's, 101; Knapp's, 78; Kuserow's, 106; McMullin's, 110; Miller's, 123; Muhlenburg's, 110; Randol's, 106; Robertson's, 101, 106; Simmons's, 110; Tidball's, 106

Bayard's cavalry, 150

Berlin, 131

Birney's division of the Army of the Potomac, at Fredericksburg, 158, 176

Blue Ridge, 11, 15

Bolivar, 33–45

Bolivar Heights, 23, 25, 26

Boonsboro', 21, 23, 28

Bowling Green road, 157

Branch's brigade of the Army of Northern Virginia at Sharpsburg, 113 et seq.

Bridges over the Antietam, 48, 49

Brockenbrough's brigade of Army Northern Virginia at Sharpsburg, 113; at Fredericksburg, 149

Brooke's, J. R., brigade of the Army of the Potomac at Sharpsburg, 81, 91, 92, 95, 99 et seq.

Brooks's division of the Army of the Potomac at Fredericksburg, 155

Brookville, 13

Brownsville Gap, 31, 42

Buckeystown, 13, 14, 29

Bull Run, 52

Bunker Hill (Va.), 129

Burke, Colonel, assumes command of Meagher's brigade at Sharpsburg, 101

Burkittsville, 22, 24, 27, 28

Burning buildings, 51, 93

Burns's division of the Army of the Potomac at Fredericksburg, 169

Burnside Bridge, 48, 57, 58, 109 et seq.

Burnside, General A. E., commanding right of the Army of the Potomac, 6, 45; his history and character, 54; his command divided at Sharpsburg, 58; his consequent position, 59; his slowness at Sharpsburg, 59; his loyalty to McClellan, 107; his part in the battle of the Antietam, 107 et seq.; his conduct there reviewed, 120; his apparent want of firmness the following day, 127; appointed to command of the Army of the Potomac, 132, 136; submits plan, and discusses it with Halleck, 137; it is approved by President, ib.; it contemplates supply of pontoons, and Burnside not responsible for their failure to arrive, 137 et seq.; orders army to move, 138; prevents Sumner from crossing Rappahannock, 139; decides to cross in force, 140; his error, 140, 141; his hopes, 141, 142; his vague plans, 143 et seq.; throws bridges, 146; occupies town, 147; his uncertainties on the

214   INDEX.

night of December 12th, 150, 151; issues vague orders to Franklin, 152 et seq.; remarks upon them, 153; formation ordered by him, 156, 173; sends orders to Sumner, 160; and to Hooker, ib.; remarks upon these orders, ib.; upon his management of office business, ib.; upon his statement as to his hopes and beliefs, 162 et seq.; orders Sumner to attack, 162; vagueness of his orders to him, 164; and of his plan generally, 165; his uselessness there, 165; fighting on right ends, 173; his plan as gathered from his posting of troops, 174; his later orders to Franklin, and the same considered, 174 et seq.; the full knowledge with which he attacked in front of Marye's, 186; his condition at the close of the day, 187; proposes to renew the assault on the 14th, but is dissuaded, 188; remarks on his failure and his character, 188

CALDWELL'S brigade of the Army of the Potomac at Sharpsburg, 81, 99 et seq., 104

Carroll's brigade of the Army of the Potomac at Fredericksburg, 169

Catoctin Valley, 28

Cavalry, Confederate, at Sharpsburg, 74

Chambersburg occupied by Stuart, 131

Chancellorsville, 143

Character of Federal and Confederate armies and Federal and Confederate commanders compared, 52

Cheek's Ford, 21

Clarksburg, 14

Christ's brigade of the Army of the Potomac, at Sharpsburg, 108

Cobb's brigade of the Army of Northern Virginia at Crampton's Gap, 31, 32; at Sharpsburg, 86, 90; at Fredericksburg, 148, 167

Colquitt's, Colonel A. H., brigade of the Army of Northern Virginia at Turner's Gap, 32, 35, 36, 40; at Sharpsburg, 93, 103, 104

Committee on the Conduct of the War unjust to Franklin, 182

Connecticut regiment: Eleventh, 111

Cook's brigade of the Army of Northern Virginia at Fredericksburg, 167

Cooksville, 14

Corn Exchange Regiment, 128

Couch, General D. N., commanding division of Fourth Corps, 6; ordered to join Franklin, 30; does so, 43, 63; commanding division of the Army of the Potomac, sent to Maryland Heights, 90; hastens to join McClellan, 129; at Fredericksburg, 168

Cox, General J. D., commanding Kanawha division of the Army of the Potomac at South Mountain, 34; his character, 55; commanding Ninth Corps,

INDEX. 215

58; at Sharpsburg, 108 et seq.; his conduct there reviewed, 117
Crampton's Gap, 22, 27, 29, 31, 42, 63
Crawford, General, commanding division of the Army of the Potomac, at Sharpsburg, 78, 81 et seq.
Crook, Colonel, commanding brigade of the Army of the Potomac at South Mountain, 34
Crook's brigade of the Army of the Potomac at Sharpsburg, 108 et seq.
Cross, Colonel, commanding Fifth New Hampshire at Sharpsburg, 100, 105
Culpeper, 136
Cumberland Valley, 20
Cutts's battalion of artillery in the Army of Northern Virginia, 58

DAMASCUS, 14
Dana's brigade of the Army of the Potomac at Sharpsburg 81, et seq.
Darnestown, 13
Dawsonville, 13
Deep Creek, 155, 174
Delaware regiments: Third, 78; Second, 99
Doubleday, General Abner, commanding division of the Army of the Potomac at Sharpsburg, 62, 73, 75, 78; at Fredericksburg, 155 et seq.
Douglas, Colonel, commanding Lawton's brigade of the Army of Northern Virginia, killed at Sharpsburg, 76

Drayton's brigade of the Army of Northern Virginia at Turner's Gap, 36, 37; at Sharpsburg, 114
Dryer, Captain Hiram, commanding some regular infantry at Sharpsburg, 106
Dunker Church, 50, 51, 57, 61, 79, 80, 81, 84, 85 et seq., 92, 95, 96, 97, 106

EARLY, General Jubal A., commanding brigade and division of the Army of Northern Virginia at Sharpsburg, 74, 85 et seq.
Early's brigade of the Army of Northern Virginia at Sharpsburg, 57, 76, 90
Early's division of the Army of Northern Virginia at Fredericksburg, 149, 159
East Woods, 51, 61, 74, 78, 79, 82 et seq., 93
Eleventh Corps, under Sigel, 6; near New Baltimore, 136
Elk Ridge, 11, 24
Evans's, General N. G., brigade of the Army of Northern Virginia, 7, 36, 37, 114, 115
Ewell's division of the Army of Northern Virginia at Sharpsburg, 57, 79, 80, 85
Ewing's brigade of the Army of the Potomac, at Sharpsburg, 108 et seq.

FAIRCHILD, Colonel H. S., commanding brigade of the Army of the Potomac at Turner's Gap, 35
Fairchild's brigade of Army of the Potomac at Sharpsburg, 108

216 INDEX.

Falmouth, 138, 142
Featherston's, General Wm. S., brigade of the Army of Northern Virginia, 104, 105
Ferrero's, Colonel Edward, brigade of the Army of the Potomac at Sharpsburg, 108; at Fredericksburg, 168
Field's brigade of the Army of Northern Virginia, 149
Fifth Corps, under Porter, 6; ordered to join McClellan, 6; at Sharpsburg, 63, 71; captures some guns and meets with some loss across the river, 128 et seq.; part of Centre Grand Division of the Army of the Potomac, 138 et seq.
First Corps, under Hooker, 6; part of Right of the Army of the Potomac, 6; at Turner's Gap, 39, 45; at Sharpsburg, 71, 72, 77, 78, 79, 80, 83 et seq., 96; part of Left Grand Division of the Army of the Potomac, 138
Forces of the two armies at the Antietam compared, 63 et seq., 89
Fords of the Antietam, 49
Fourth Corps, 6; Couch's division of, attached to Sixth Corps, 6; part of Left of the Army of the Potomac, 6; sent to Maryland Heights, 90
Fox's Gap, 34
Franklin, General W. B., commanding Sixth Corps, 6; Left of the Army of the Potomac, 6; ordered to move on Crampton's Gap, 28; carries it, and moves into Pleasant Valley, 32; inactive after South Mountain, 43; responsible for loss of Harper's Ferry, 44; his history and character, 54; remains near Crampton's Gap, 63; ordered to join McClellan, 90; paralyzed by Sumner and McClellan, 106; his desire to attack from centre, 121; in command of Left Grand Division of the Army of the Potomac, under Burnside, 138 et seq.; large command assigned to him, 150; urges attack from his front, ib.; mystified by Burnside's orders, 153; his action under them considered, 154; position of his troops, 155; arranges his attack, 156; and makes it, 157 et seq.; long line held by him, 174; the later orders received by him, and the same considered, 174 et seq.; condition of his command when these orders reached him, 176; disposed to overestimate force of enemy, 180; general view of his conduct, 180
Frederick City, 11, 14, 15, 18, 23, 33
Fredericksburg, 136 et seq., 161; end of fighting on Federal right, 173; battle of, divisible into two parts, 173; end of battle, 182
French's division of the Army of the Potomac at Sharpsburg, 81 et seq., 91 et seq., 99; at Fredericksburg, 167 et seq.
Fry's house, 50, 51, 61, 119

INDEX. 217

GALLAGHER, Colonel, commanding brigade of the Army of the Potomac at Turner's Gap, 36
Garland's brigade of the Army of Northern Virginia at Turner's Gap, 32, 35, 36, 37; at Sharpsburg, 93
Garnett, General R. B., commanding brigade of the Army of Northern Virginia at Turner's Gap, 36, 37; at Sharpsburg, 114
Georgia regiments: Second, 66, 109, 113; Eleventh, 113; Fifteenth, 113; Seventeenth, 113; Twentieth, 109, 113; Fiftieth, 109
Getty's division of the Army of the Potomac at Fredericksburg, 169
Gibbon, General John, commanding brigade of the Army of the Potomac at Turner's Gap, 35, 40; at Sharpsburg, 75, 76; commanding division at Fredericksburg, 155 et seq., 176
Goodrich's brigade of the Army of the Potomac at Sharpsburg, 78
Gordon, General George H., commanding brigade of the Army of the Potomac at Sharpsburg, 78
Gordon's brigade of the Army of the Potomac at Sharpsburg, 78, 79, 81 et seq.
Gorman's brigade of the Army of the Potomac at Sharpsburg, 81 et seq.
Grant, General, character of, 135
Greene, General, commanding division of the Army of the Potomac at Sharpsburg, 78, 79, 81 et seq., 96
Gregg's brigade of the Army of Northern Virginia at Sharpsburg, 113 et seq.; at Fredericksburg, 149, 159; General Gregg killed, ib.
Griffin, General Charles, after Sharpsburg, 128; at Fredericksburg, 170
Grigsby, Colonel, commanding Jackson's division of the Army of Northern Virginia at Sharpsburg, 86

HAGERSTOWN, 20, 21
Hagerstown Pike, 28, 49, 50, 51, 61, 78, 81 et seq., 93 et seq., 97
Hall, Colonel E. D., commanding brigade of the Army of Northern Virginia at Sharpsburg, 94
Hall's brigade of the Army of the Potomac at Fredericksburg, 146, 168
Halleck, General H. W., commander-in-chief, 3; his attitude to McClellan, 3; declines to order garrison away from Harper's Ferry, 19; effect of his so doing, 43; his dealings with Burnside, 137 et seq.
Halltown, 23, 45
Hamilton's Crossing, 143 et seq., 174
Hampton's cavalry of the Army of Northern Virginia, 140
Hancock, General W. S., at Sharpsburg, 91 et seq., 101; his love of fighting, 126; at

V.—10

218 INDEX.

Fredericksburg, 167 et seq.; heavy losses of his division, 182; his brilliant leadership, 183
Hanover street, 143
Hardie, General, with Franklin at Fredericksburg, 151 et seq., 163.
Harlan, Colonel Edward, commanding brigade of the Army of the Potomac at Turner's Gap, 35
Harland's brigade of the Army of the Potomac at Sharpsburg, 108
Harper's Ferry, 11, 14, 15, 18, 19, 20, 21, 22, 23, 24, 25; surrendered to Jackson, 26, 27, 42, 44; the cause, 44; effect of retaining Federal garrison there, 48; reoccupied by Federals, 130, 131
Hartwood, 138
Hatch, General John P., commanding division of the Army of the Potomac at Turner's Gap, 35
Hayes, Colonel R. B., commanding regiment of the Army of the Potomac at South Mountain, 34
Hays's brigade of the Army of Northern Virginia at Sharpsburg, 57, 74, 76
Heintzelman, General S. P., commanding Third Corps, 6
Hill, General A. P., commanding division of the Army of Northern Virginia, engaged in capture of Harper's Ferry, 25; and left to receive the surrender, 27; arrives at Sharpsburg, 57, 63, 112 et seq.; his singular report about affair on the Potomac, 129; at Fredericksburg, 148, 159
Hill, General D. H., commanding division of the Army of Northern Virginia; 7, 15; leads the advance, 18; his division unattached, 21; his responsibility for loss of special order No. 191, 22; ordered to Turner's Gap, 32; his report of action there, 37, 38, 40; reaches Sharpsburg, 42, 57; his forces there, 58; and his position, 63, 77, 79, 80, 92 et seq., 116, 121; sent to Fredericksburg, 140; in position there, 149
Hillsborough, 24
Holcombe Legion, 115
Hoffman, Lieutenant-Colonel T. W., commanding brigade of the Army of the Potomac at Sharpsburg, 74, 75
Hood, General John B., commanding division of the Army of Northern Virginia at Turner's Gap, 36, 37; at Sharpsburg, 57, 62, 76, 79, 80, 81, 85, 102, 115; at Fredericksburg, 148
Hooker, General Joseph, commanding First Corps, 6; orders to, 31; at Turner's Gap, 35-45; his history and character, 55; his corps sent to right of army at Sharpsburg, and perhaps through his agency, 58; ordered to cross the Antietam, 61; does so, 62; and attacks, on the 16th, and again on the 17th, 73, 74, 75;

INDEX. 219

his forces in the battle, 75;
his part in it, 77 et seq., 80;
wounded, and his corps routed,
83; his language about Mc-
Clellan, 133; in command of
Centre Grand Division of the
Army of the Potomac under
Burnside, 138 et seq.; receives
orders from Burnside, 160;
takes small part in the battle
of Fredericksburg, 173; praise
of his conduct there, 186 et seq.
Howard's brigade of the Army of
the Potomac at Sharpsburg,
81 et seq.
Howard's division of the Army of
the Potomac at Fredericksburg, 168 et seq.
Howe's division of the Army of the
Potomac at Fredericksburg,
155
Humphreys, General A. A., his
love of fighting. 126; hastens
to join McClellan, 128; his
soldierly character, 170; his
part in the battle of Fredericksburg, ib.
Hunt, General H. J., posts Federal artillery opposite Fredericksburg, 145
Hunton, Colonel Eppa, commanding Eighth Virginia regiment
of the Army of Northern Virginia at Sharpsburg, 114

INDIANA regiments: Nineteenth,
75; Twenty-seventh, 78, 79;
Fourteenth, 95
Irwin's brigade of the Army of
the Potomac. 91, 92, 95

JACKSON, General T. J., commanding wing of the Army of
Northern Virginia, 7; his
captures at Manassas Junction, 16; engaged in capture
of Harper's Ferry, 23; hastens to rejoin Lee, 27; does so,
57; at Sharpsburg, 73, 74, 76,
79, 80 et seq.; saying attributed to, 121; his readiness to
take the offensive, 124; saying
of, 126; position of his command, November 7th-9th,
136, 140 et seq.
Jackson's division of the Army of
Northern Virginia at Sharpsburg, 80
Jefferson, 27, 28
Jenkins's brigade of the Army of
Northern Virginia at Sharpsburg, 114, 115
Jones's, D. R., division of the
Army of Northern Virginia
at Sharpsburg, 80, 110, 113,
114, 115
Jones, General J. R., commanding
division of the Army of Northern Virginia, engaged in capture of Harper's Ferry, 26; at
Sharpsburg, 57; his brigade, 74

KANAWHA division, losses of, at
Turner's Gap, 39; at Sharps-
burg, 108 et seq.
Kearny, General Philip, killed,
3; his love of fighting, 126
Kearse's regiment of the Army of
Northern Virginia, 113
Keedysville road, 61, 97, 106
Kemper's brigade of the Army of
Northern Virginia at Turner's
Gap, 36, 37; at Sharpsburg,
114
Kershaw's, General J. B., brigade

of the Army of Northern Virginia at Sharpsburg, 86, 90; at Fredericksburg, 167

Keys's Ford, 21

Kimball's brigade of the Army of the Potomac at Sharpsburg, 81–92 et seq.; at Fredericksburg, 168

Kingsbury, Colonel, killed at Sharpsburg, 112

Knipe's brigade of the Army of the Potomac at Sharpsburg, 78, 79, 80, 81 et seq.

Knoxville, 27

LACY House, 146

Lane's, General Jas. H., brigade of the Army of Northern Virginia, 148, 149, 157

Law, Colonel E. M., commanding brigade of the Army of Northern Virginia at Turner's Gap, 36; at Sharpsburg, 85

Lawton, General, commanding division of the Army of Northern Virginia engaged in capture of Harper's Ferry, 26; at Sharpsburg, 57, 62; wounded, 76, 79

Lawton's brigade of the Army of Northern Virginia at Sharpsburg, 57, 63, 74, 76

Lee, General R. E., his views as to Maryland campaign, 14; his plan, 16; his hopes of aid from Maryland, 17; his probable estimate of McClellan, 17; expects evacuation of Harper's Ferry, etc., 18; his action on finding that it was not, 19; his Special Order No. 191 falls into hands of McClellan, 20; orders troops to Turner's Gap, 32; his promptness after South Mountain, 42; forms his troops in front of Sharpsburg, 49; his position considered, 49; evacuates Maryland, 119; period of battle when his danger probably greatest, 121; his readiness to take the offensive, 124; his movements after recrossing the Potomac, 129 et seq.; reinforces garrison of Fredericksburg, 139; strengthens his position there, 140 et seq.; his inaction after repulsing Burnside's attack, 189

Lee, Colonel S. D., commanding battalion of artillery of the Army of Northern Virginia at Sharpsburg, 73, 74

Lee's, W. H. F., brigade of cavalry of the Army of Northern Virginia, 139, 140

Leesboro', 10

Leesburg, 11, 15, 18

Lincoln, President, orders McClellan to cross the Potomac, etc., 130; approves Burnside's plan, 137

Longstreet, General James, commanding wing of the Army of Northern Virginia, 7; ordered to Turner's Gap, 32, 38; reaches Sharpsburg, 42, 62; in action there, 112, 116; position of his command, Nov. 7th–9th, 136; sent to Fredericksburg, 140, 148, 168

Losses at Turner's Gap, 39, 40; Sharpsburg, 76, 90, 95, 106, 114, 127, 128; Fredericksburg,

INDEX. 221

168, 169, 170, 173, 176, 182 et seq.
Loudoun Heights, 11, 19, 21, 24, 25, 26
Lovettsville, 21
Lyle's brigade of the Army of the Potomac at Fredericksburg, 158

MACY, Captain George N., 147
Magilton, Colonel A. L., commanding brigade of the Army of the Potomac at Turner's Gap, 36
Mahone, General, commanding brigade of the Army of Northern Virginia at Crampton's Gap, 32
Maine regiments: Sixth, 91; Seventh, 101
Manassas, captures at, 16
Manassas Gap Railroad, 131
Manassas Junction, captures at, 16
Manning's brigade of the Army of Northern Virginia at Sharpsburg, 86, 94
Mansfield, General J. K. F., commanding Twelfth Corps, 6, 45; ordered to cross the Antietam, 61; does so, 63, 77; killed, 78
Martinsburg, 15, 18, 20, 22, 23
Marye's Hill, 148 et seq., 161, 167 et seq.
Maryland, Lee's hopes of aid from, 17
Maryland Heights, 11, 20, 21, 22, 24, 25, 26, 27, 31, 42, 90, 130
Maryland regiments: Second, 111; Third, 78
Massachusetts regiments: Second, 79; Twelfth, 158; Fifteenth,

87, 88; Eighteenth, 128; Nineteenth, 87, 146; Twentieth, 87, 88, 91, 146, 147, 168; Twenty-first, 112; Twenty-second, 128; Thirty-fifth, 112
McClellan, General Geo. B., position of at end of August, 1862, 3; placed in command, 5; movements of, 10; his field of possible operations, 12; gains information of enemy's plans, 14; perceives uselessness of retaining garrison at Harper's Ferry, 19; his application for its withdrawal refused, 19; his duty with his then knowledge, 20; his previous slowness, and the excuses for it, 20; comes into possession of Lee's "lost order," 20, 22; his plans thereupon, 27, and his instructions to Franklin, 28; comments thereon, 29; orders to the army, 30; his estimate of numbers at Turner's Gap, 38; loses his opportunity at South Mountain, 41; his orders to Franklin after, 43; responsible for loss of Harper's Ferry, 44; his opportunity after South Mountain, 46; his disposable forces, 46; loses his opportunity, 47; his history and character, 53; welcomed by his army near Sharpsburg, 56; does little September 15th and 16th, 56, 59; his plan of battle, 59; reveals his intentions to Lee, 60; criticisms on his orders, 62; paralyzes action of Sixth Corps, 106, 121; his plan for using Ninth Corps,

107; whether or not satisfied with Burnside's conduct, 107; his orders and connection with his left attack, 110 et seq.; his conduct of the battle reviewed, 119; want of simultaneousness in use of his troops, 120; error in not judging for himself, 122; his extraordinary estimate of the strength of his opponent, 122; decides not to renew the attack on the 18th, 127; remarks thereon, ib.; orders renewal of the attack on the 19th, but learns then that Lee is gone, 128; his movements thereafter, 129 et seq.; his calls for supplies and reinforcements, 130; his want of tone, ib.; ordered by President to cross the Potomac, etc., 130; delayed by want of supplies, 131; crosses Potomac and moves towards Warrenton, ib.; his plan of campaign, 132; relieved of command, 132; comments on his removal, career, and character, 132 et seq.

McLaws, General Lafayette, aids in capture of Harper's Ferry, 24; in command near Crampton's Gap, 31; after South Mountain, 42, 44; joins Lee, 45, 57, 63, 77

McLaws's division of the Army of Northern Virginia sent to Fredericksburg, 139, 148

McMaster, Colonel, commanding Evans's brigade of the Army of Northern Virginia, 115

McRae, Colonel D. K., commanding Garland's brigade at Sharpsburg, 93

Meade, General George G., commanding division of the Army of the Potomac at Turner's Gap, 35; his military character, 55; at Sharpsburg, 62, 73, 75; at Fredericksburg, 155 et seq.; his gallant assault, 157 et seq.; his troops after, 176

Meagher's brigade of the Army of the Potomac, at Sharpsburg, 81, 99 et seq.

Mercersville, 48

Meredith, Colonel, at Turner's Gap, 40

Michigan regiments: Fourth, 128; Seventh, 146

Middleburg, 13, 14

Middletown, 14, 20, 21, 22, 23, 27, 28, 33, 45

Miles, Colonel Dixon S., commanding at Harper's Ferry, 18, 24; mortally wounded there, 26

Miles, Colonel Nelson A., at Fredericksburg, 182, 183

Miller's house, 51, 80, 88

Minnesota regiment: First, 87

Mississippi regiments: Fourth, 139; Sixteenth, 105

Monocacy River, 13, 14

Morell, General George, commanding division of the Army of the Potomac at Sharpsburg, 63, 82, 123, 127, 128

Morris's brigade of the Army of the Potomac at Sharpsburg, 81–92 et seq.

Mountain House, 33, 34

Mount Tabor Church, 35 45

Mume's house, 51

NAGLE'S brigade of the Army of the Potomac at Sharpsburg, 108; at Fredericksburg, 169
National Cemetery at Sharpsburg, 49
New Baltimore, 136
New Hampshire regiments: Fifth, 100, 105; Sixth, 111
New Jersey regiment: Thirteenth, 78
New Market, 14
Newton's brigade of the Army of the Potomac at Sharpsburg, 106
Newton's division of the Army of the Potomac at Fredericksburg, 155
New York regiments: Thirty-third, 95; Forty-third, 91; Fifty-first, 112; Fifty-second, 99; Fifth-seventh, 100; Sixtieth, 78; Sixty-first, 100; Sixty-fourth, 100; Sixty-sixth, 100; Seventy-seventh, 95; Seventy-eighth, 78; Eighty-ninth, 146; Ninety-seventh, 158; One Hundred and Seventh, 78
Nicodemus's house, 51
Ninth Corps, under Reno, 6; part of right of the Army of the Potomac, 6; at Turner's Gap, 34, 35, 39; after, 45; at Sharpsburg, under Cox, 58, 59, 63, 71, 73, 107 et seq., 136; part of Right Grand Division of the Army of the Potomac, 138; at Fredericksburg, 143; its experience and character, 188
North Carolina regiments: Fourth, 105; Twenty-fourth, 148; Forty-eighth, 124

OFFUT'S Cross Roads, 10
Ohio regiments: Eighth, 95; Sixty-sixth, 78
Old Hagerstown road, 33, 35, 45
Old Richmond road, 142 et seq, 155
Old Sharpsburg road, 33, 45
Orange and Alexandria Railroad, 131
Orange Court House, 140, 143

PATRICK, General, commanding brigade of the Army of the Potomac at Sharpsburg, 75, 77
Pelham, Major John, 157
Pender's, General W. D., brigade of the Army of Northern Virginia at Sharpsburg, 113 et seq.; at Fredericksburg, 148
Pennsylvania regiments: Forty-ninth, 91; Fifty-first, 112; Fifty-third, 99; Eighty-first, 100; Eighty-eighth, 158; One Hundred and Eleventh, 78; One Hundred and Eighteenth, 205; One Hundred and Twenty-third, 172; One Hundred and Twenty-fourth, 78; One Hundred and Twenty-fifth, 78; One Hundred and Twenty-eighth, 78; One Hundred and Thirty-second, 95, 99; One Hundred and Thirty-seventh, 91; One Hundred and Fifty-fifth, 172
Pennsylvania Reserves, 73
Phelps, Colonel Walter, jr., commanding brigade of the Army of the Potomac at Sharpsburg, 75, 76
Philadelphia brigade, 87
Pickett's brigade of the Army of

Northern Virginia at Sharpsburg, 114
Pickett's division of the Army of Northern Virginia at Fredericksburg, 148
Piper's house, 97, 98 et seq., 104, 105
Plank road, 143 et seq., 161
Pleasant Valley, 24, 28, 31, 42, 43, 91
Pleasonton, General Alfred, commanding cavalry of the Army of the Potomac at South Mountain and Sharpsburg, 32, 34, 45, 105, 106, 123
Poffenbergers, 51
Point of Rocks, 24
Pollock's mill, 146
Poolesville, 10, 13
Pope, General John, commanding Army of Virginia, 2, 132
Port Royal, 140
Porter, General F. J., commanding Fifth Corps, 6, 45; his vindication by the military commission, 55; at Sharpsburg, 106; his conduct there approved, 123; captures guns two days, and loses men three days, after the battle, 128
Potomac river, 11, 18, 25, 48
Pryor, General R. A., assumes command of R. H. Anderson's division of the Army of Northern Virginia at Sharpsburg, 97, 103, 104, 105

RANSOM'S brigade of the Army of Northern Virginia at Sharpsburg, 86, 90; at Fredericksburg, 167
Ransom's division of the Army of Northern Virginia sent to Fredericksburg, 139, 148
Rappahannock River, 136 et seq.
Reno, General J. L., commanding Ninth Corps, 6; at South Mountain, 34; killed, 40
Reynolds's division of the Army of the Potomac at Fredericksburg, 156, 163, 164
Richardson, General Israel B., commanding division of the Army of the Potomac, 45, 48; at Sharpsburg, 81 et seq., 99 et seq.; mortally wounded, 101
Richmond, Fredericksburg and Potomac Railroad, 142 et seq.
Ricketts, General James B., commanding division of the Army of the Potomac at Turner's Gap, 36, 38; at Sharpsburg, 62, 73, 75, 76, 81 et seq., 96
Ridgeville, 14
Ripley's, General R. S., brigade of the Army of Northern Virginia at Turner's Gap, 35, 36, 37; at Sharpsburg, 92, 93
Roads: Sharpsburg to Rohrersville, 49; Sharpsburg to Keedysville and Boonsboro', 49; Keedysville to Williamsport, 49; Sharpsburg to Shepherdstown, 49; Sharpsburg to Hagerstown, 49; near Dunker Church, 51, 85; Sunken road, 61; Old Richmond, 142 et seq.
Rockville, 10, 13
Rodes, General R. E., commanding brigade of the Army of Northern Virginia at Turner's Gap, 36, 37, 38, 40; at Sharpsburg, 93, 98, 102, 103, 104

INDEX. 225

Rodman, General, commanding division of the Army of the Potomac at Turner's Gap, 35; at Sharpsburg, 108 et seq., killed, 114

Rohrersville, 28

Root's brigade of the Army of the Potomac at Fredericksburg, 158

Rosser, Colonel T. L., commanding some cavalry, etc., of the Army of Northern Virginia at Turner's Gap, 35-37

Rullet's house, 85, 92, 94, 97, 98, 99 et seq.

SCAMMON, Colonel, commanding brigade of the Army of the Potomac at South Mountain, 34

Scammon, General, commanding division of the Army of the Potomac at Sharpsburg, 108 et seq.

Second Corps, under Sumner, 6; part of Centre of the Army of the Potomac, 6; after South Mountain, 45, 48; at Sharpsburg, 61, 63, 71, 72, 81 et seq., 91 et seq., 95, 99 et seq.; character of, 81; losses at Sharpsburg, 127; at Harper's Ferry, 130; part of Right Grand Division of the Army of the Potomac, 138 et seq.

Sedgwick, General John, commanding division in the Army of the Potomac, 9; his career, 55; at Sharpsburg, 81 et seq.; strength of his division there and his losses, 90, 127

Semmes, General Paul J., commanding brigade of the Army of Northern Virginia at Crampton's Gap, 32; at Sharpsburg, 86, 90

Seneca Creek, 13

Seymour, General T., commanding brigade of the Army of the Potomac at Turner's Gap, 36

Sharpsburg, 20, 27, 40; character of Confederate position at, 42; distance from Turner's Gap, 47; description of position at, 48, 61, 72, 85

Shenandoah River, 11, 25, 26

Shenandoah Valley, 16, 17, 18

Shepherdstown and Shepherdstown Ford, 48

Sickles's division of the Army of the Potomac at Fredericksburg, 159

Skinker's Neck, 144

Sigel, General Franz, commanding Eleventh Corps, 6

Sixth Corps, under Franklin, 6; part of Left of the Army of the Potomac, 6, 63; at Sharpsburg, 71, 73, 90 et seq., 106; moved, 136; part of Left Grand Division of the Army of the Potomac, 138 et seq., 155; formation of, at Fredericksburg, 174

Slocum, General H. W., commanding division of the Army of the Potomac at Sharpsburg, 91 et seq., 105, 106

Smith, General W. F., commanding division of the Army of the Potomac at Sharpsburg, 91 et seq.; complains of division of his command, 96

Smithfield, 148, 155

10*

226   INDEX.

South Carolina regiments : First, 115; Seventeenth, 115
South Mountain, 11, 22, 24, 27, 33 ; remarks on battles at, 40
Stafford Court House, 138
Stafford Heights, 141
Stainrook's brigade of the Army of the Potomac at Sharpsburg, 78
Stanton, Secretary, 133
Starke, General, commanding Stonewall division, killed at Sharpsburg, 76
Stoneman's command ordered to support Franklin, 160
Stonewall division of the Army of Northern Virginia at Sharpsburg, 74
Stuart, General J. E B., commanding cavalry of the Army of Northern Virginia at South Mountain, 32 ; at Sharpsburg, 57, 74, 76, 80, 84, 124 ; raids through Maryland, 130 ; reconnoitres in Virginia, 140 ; at Fredericksburg, 149 et seq.
Sturgis, General S. D., commanding division of the Army of the Potomac at Turner's Gap, 35; at Sharpsburg, 108 et seq.; at Fredericksburg, 168 et seq.
Sumner, General E. V., commanding Second Corps, 6; Centre of the Army of the Potomac, 6 ; after South Mountain, 45 ; his history and character. 54 ; at Sharpsburg, 81 et seq. ; remarks upon his use of Sedgwick's division, 88 ; orders French in, 94 ; paralyzes action of the Sixth Corps, 106,

121 ; his previous experience. 120; his character, 122 ; at Harper's Ferry, 130 ; in command of Right Grand Division of the Army of the Potomac under Burnside, 138 et seq. ; proposes to cross the Rappahannock, 139 ; receives orders from Burnside, 160 ; ordered to attack, 162 ; time when he moved out, 163 ; his attack, 167 et seq.
Sunken road, 93 et seq., 97 et seq.
Swinton, William, statements as to feeling of the Army of the Potomac before the attack at Fredericksburg, 184 ; as to Burnside's condition at the close of the day, 187
Sykes, General George, commanding division of the Army of the Potomac, 45, 48, 122, 128, 170, 187

TALIAFERRO'S, General W.B., brigade of the Army of Northern Virginia. at Sharpsburg, 57
Taliaferro's division of the Army of Northern Virginia at Fredericksburg, 149, 159.
Taylor, Colonel Walter H., author of " Four Years with General Lee," accounts for loss of Special Order No. 191, 21 ; estimates forces at Sharpsburg, 64 et seq.
Taylor's brigade of the Army of the Potomac at Fredericksburg, 158
Telegraph road, 143 et seq.
Tenallytown, 10, 13
Third Corps, part of Centre Grand

INDEX. 227

Division of the Army of the Potomac, 138 et seq.
Thomas's, Colonel E. L., brigade of the Army of Northern Virginia, 149
Third Corps, under Heintzelman, 6; part of army under Burnside, 136
Torbert's brigade of the Army of the Potomac, at Sharpsburg, 106
Toombs, General R., commanding brigade of the Army of Northern Virginia at Sharpsburg, 57, 109 et seq.
Trimble's brigade of the Army of Northern Virginia at Sharpsburg, 57, 62, 74, 76
Turner's Gap, 22, 27, 31; action at, 32; distance from Sharpsburg, 47
Twelfth Corps, under Mansfield, 6; part of Centre of the Army of the Potomac, 6; after South Mountain, 45; at Sharpsburg, 61, 63, 71, 72, 77; under Williams (and its strength there), 78, 79, 80, 81 et seq.; losses at Sharpsburg, 90; retires, 96; at Harper's Ferry, 130 et seq.
Tyler's brigade of the Army of the Potomac at Fredericksburg, 171
Tyndale's brigade of the Army of the Potomac at Sharpsburg, 78

URBANNA, 13, 14

VALLEY of Virginia, 18, 25
Virginia (Confederate) regiments: Fifteenth Cavalry, 139; Twenty-second, 149; Thirty-fifth, 149; Fortieth, 149; Forty-seventh, 149
Virginia (Federal) regiment: Seventh, 99

WALKER, Colonel James A., commanding Trimble's brigade of the Army of Northern Virginia, 94; perhaps wounded at Sharpsburg, 76 (sed qu. and see p. 94)
Walker, Colonel Joseph, commanding brigade of the Army of Northern Virginia at Turner's Gap, 36; wounded at Sharpsburg, 76 (sed qu., see p. 94)
Walker, Colonel R. L., commanding artillery in the Army of Northern Virginia, 149
Walker, General J. G., aids in capture of Harper's Ferry, 24; rejoins Lee at Sharpsburg, 27; at Sharpsburg, 57, 94, 102
Walton, Colonel J. B., 148
Warren's brigade of the Army of the Potomac at Sharpsburg, 123
Warrenton, 131, 136; the Army of the Potomac concentrated near, 137
Waterloo, 136
Weber's brigade of the Army of the Potomac at Sharpsburg, 81, 92 et seq.
Welch's brigade of the Army of the Potomac at Sharpsburg, 108
West Woods, 51, 61, 74, 76, 84 et seq.

Weverton Pass, 42
Whipple's division of the Army of the Potomac, at Fredericksburg, 169
White, General Julius, at Martinsburg, 18, 23; surrenders Harper's Ferry, 26
Wilcox's, General C. M., brigade of the Army of Northern Virginia at Sharpsburg, 105
Willcox, General O. B., commanding division of the Army of the Potomac at Turner's Gap, 35; losses there, 39; at Sharpsburg, 108 et seq.
Williams, General A. S., succeeds to command of Twelfth Corps at Sharpsburg, 78 et seq.
Williamsport, 23
Willis's Hill, 148

Winchester, 15, 129
Winder, General, commanding division of the Army of Northern Virginia at Sharpsburg, 57, 74
Wisconsin regiments: Second, 75; Third, 79, 90; Fifth, 91; Sixth, 75; Seventh, 75
Wofford, Colonel W. T., commanding brigade of the Army of Northern Virginia at Turner's Gap, 36, 73, 80, 85
Woodruff, Lieutenant George A., commanding Battery I, First artillery, at Sharpsburg, 74, 101
Wright, General, commanding brigade of the Army of Northern Virginia, wounded at Sharpsburg, 102

www.ingramcontent.com/pod-product-compliance
Lightning Source LLC
Chambersburg PA
CBHW032107090426
42743CB00007B/264